The Subject in Question

C. CHRISTOPHER SOUFAS

The Subject in Question

EARLY CONTEMPORARY SPANISH

LITERATURE AND MODERNISM

The Catholic University of America Press
Washington, D.C.

LIBRARY OF CONGRESS CATALOGING-IN-PUBLICATION DATA
Soufas, C. Christopher.
    The subject in question: early contemporary Spanish literature and
Modernism / by C. Christopher Soufas.— 1st ed.
    p. cm.
    Includes bibliographical references and index.
    ISBN-13: 978-0-8132-1467-2 (cloth : alk. paper)
    ISBN-10: 0-8132-1467-x (cloth : alk. paper)   1. Spanish literature—
20th century—History and criticism.   2. Modernism (Literature)—Spain.
I. Title.
    PQ6073.M6s68 2007
    860.9'006—dc22

                                                            2006004939

FOR TERESA

Contents

Acknowledgments

I should like to thank the John Simon Guggenheim Memorial Foundation, whose generous fellowship greatly assisted in the timely completion of this project.

Part of chapter 1 was earlier published as "Julius Petersen and the Construction of the Spanish Literary Generation" in *Bulletin of Spanish Studies* (2002), used by permission (http://www.tandf.co.uk). The translations, entirely my own, are intended to help non-readers of Spanish to follow the text.

I want especially to thank my dogs ("gods" spelled backwards) who have helped me so much through the years: Alice (beautiful girl), Maddie (kind, loyal, smart), Truffle (who loved life so much), and Rudy (baby bear). Also, my new pals Dix(on) and Tux(edo).

Last but not least, I want to acknowledge my grandchildren, Taylor, Cassie, and Payton, who are simply marvelous.

The Subject in Question

Introduction

This study presents an alternative to the standard organization of Spanish literary history of the early decades of the twentieth century by abandoning the nation-centered generational model that has long dominated critical orientation in Spain in favor of a framework associated with a more far-reaching, international literary movement specified by the period concept "modernism." To do so requires an examination and succinct critique of the literary generation approach to early contemporary Spanish literary history, which has stressed Spanish uniqueness and separateness from Europe and which has fostered an overly narrow view of the aesthetic agenda of this period. This inquiry recognizes, however, that the elaboration of a more comprehensive literary critical framework also requires consideration of the role of other artistic phenomena of this historical moment that often continue to be discussed apart from modernism, specifically, avant-garde literary groups that are also largely nation-based ("Italian" Futurism, "French" Surrealism, etc.) and that evince other similarities with the Spanish "generación literaria." That prominent critics continue to advance the view of the historical avant-garde as separate from, or even opposed to, the intentions of literary modernism[1] may, in the present day, actually serve to buttress entrenched positions in Spanish criticism[2] that have in-

1. Peter Bürger, *Theory of the Avant-Garde*, trans. Michael Shaw (Minneapolis: University of Minnesota Press, 1984); Frank Kermode, *The Sense of an Ending: Studies in the Theory of Fiction* (London: Oxford University Press, 1966).
2. See Andrew P. Debicki, *Spanish Poetry of the Twentieth Century: Modernity and Beyond* (Lexington: University Press of Kentucky, 1994), 30–39; Derek Harris, ed., *The*

sisted on a sharp division between what are termed traditional, "Spanish" modes of expression and less conventional literary practices (often lumped together under the vague designation *las vanguardias*) also consistently tagged as "foreign." Spanish criticism's fragmentation of the literary history of this period has impeded the formation of more compelling criteria to discuss early contemporary Spanish literature.

Although there are continuing objections in the wider profession to the view of modernism as the principal literary critical instrument from which early contemporary European literature is profitably studied and there is ongoing debate as to what meaning the concept should have to various constituencies,[3] the authority of modernism has continued to advance even in the face of a variety of critiques, attacks, and refinements upon its agenda over the last two decades. As criticism has turned from formalist strategies in favor of broader cultural-ideological analysis, a segment of which has dedicated substantial effort to exploring the implications of modernism's often radical political affiliations,[4] the concept of modernism nevertheless continues to thrive and, at present, has come to refer to a much greater circumstance that encompasses most of European and American writing and much of world literature as well. The concept of "modernism" had been used primarily to designate a rather specific form of British (and some American) writing, principally "high" modernist masters (T. S. Eliot, James Joyce, Ezra Pound), that hardly satisfied rigorous criteria for a full-blown literary period.[5] Indeed,

---

Spanish Avant-Garde (Manchester: Manchester University Press, 1995), 1–14; C. Brian Morris, *Son of Andalusia: The Lyrical Landscapes of Federico García Lorca* (Nashville, Tenn.: Vanderbilt University Press, 1997); more recently Harald Wentzlaff-Eggebert and Doris Wansch, eds., *Las vanguardias literarias en España. Bibliografía y antología crítica* (Frankfurt: Verveurt, 1999), and Manuel Bonet, *Diccionario de las vanguardias en España* (Madrid: Alianza Editorial, 1995).

3. Astradur Eysteinsson, *The Concept of Modernism* (Ithaca, N.Y.: Cornell University Press, 1990), 143–78.

4. Among others, see Peter Bürger, *The Decline of Modernism*, trans. Nicholas Walker (Cambridge: Polity Press, 1992); Erin G. Carlston, *Thinking Fascism: Sapphic Modernism and Fascist Modernity* (Stanford: Stanford University Press, 1998); Andrew Hewitt, *Political Inversions: Homosexuality, Fascism, and the Modernist Imaginary* (Stanford: Stanford University Press, 1996); Paul A. Morrison, *The Poetics of Fascism: Ezra Pound, T. S. Eliot, Paul de Man* (New York: Oxford University Press, 1996); Alan Young, *Dada and After: Extremist Modernism and English Literature* (Manchester: Manchester University Press, 1981).

5. See Michael Levenson, ed., *The Cambridge Companion to Modernism* (Cambridge: Cambridge University Press, 1999).

and recalling the Spanish literary generation model, alternative labels for approaches to literary modernism have, in fact, been cast in generational terms, conspicuous among them being Robert Wohl's notion of a trans-European "Generation of 1914" (see also pioneering contributions to the concept of modernism by Lukács, Levin, Bradbury and McFarlane, Habermas, among others).

While there has been significant movement toward establishing the authority of modernism as a transnational literary concept and of minimizing differences with nationally identified historical avant-garde movements, there has also been a thoroughgoing reevaluation in recent years of the earlier modernist canon—again, largely the consequence of the repudiation of formalism—in order to embrace subsequently what may be called historicist paradigms (the New Historicism, the "cultural studies movement," etc.). The work of previously unassailable figures such as T. S. Eliot (regularly acknowledged, according to the standards of an earlier paradigm, as the "greatest poet of the twentieth century") and others has been reexamined and criticized for harboring allegedly anti-Semitic and/or fascistic attitudes,[6] while other previously marginal authors are now also acknowledged as meaningful contributors to an international, multi-dimensional agenda.

Even though contemporary discourse continues to uncover an abundance of unflattering adjectives ("radical," "fascist," "deviant," "extremist," etc.) that now characterize many current discussions of "high" modernism (the historical moment between the two world wars), the time frame of modernism has nevertheless expanded considerably. Many point to modernism's beginnings as early as the mid-nineteenth century in Baudelaire, Flaubert, Rimbaud, Nietzsche, and even lectures by Matthew Arnold ("On the Modern Element in Literature");[7] others see the begin-

6. See Terry Eagleton, *Criticism and Ideology: A Study in Marxist Literary Theory* (London: Verso, 1978); Anthony Julius, *T. S. Eliot: Anti-Semitism and Literary Form* (Cambridge: Cambridge University Press, 1995); Morris, *Son of Andalusia*; Christopher Ricks, *T. S. Eliot and Prejudice* (London: Faber and Faber, 1988); among others.
7. See, e.g., Vassiliki Kolocotroni, Jane Goldman, and Olga Taxidou, eds., *Modernism: An Anthology of Sources and Documents* (Chicago: University of Chicago Press, 1998); Richard Sheppard, "The Problematics of European Modernism," in *Theorizing Modernism: Essays in Critical Theory*, ed. Steve Giles (New York: Routledge, 1993), 1–52.

nings as somewhat later, after 1890 and the decline of poetic symbolism, in Mallarmé, Proust, James, Conrad, and Yeats.[8] One of the most prominent authorities on modernism, Marjorie Perloff, maintains that modernism does not abruptly conclude after 1945 but actually continued well into the second half of the twentieth century or even later.[9] While certainly a welcome corrective in many respects to the formalist approaches of an earlier critical moment, none of these more generous judgments of a fuller modernist program have been embraced by Spanish criticism,[10] which historically has been inhospitable to attempts to situate early contemporary Peninsular literature in a transnational context. Although any usefulness of the literary generation model has long since past, Spanish criticism, whether from a misguided sense of devotion to the "national critical tradition" or simply from a lingering sense of comfort with entrenched critical tenets, continues to adhere substantially to this ultranationalistic critical paradigm premised on extremist criteria (discussed in chapter 1). Indeed, the last decade has witnessed significant revisionist efforts either to reinvigorate the generational model[11] or to propose dubious alternatives.[12]

8. See, e.g., Eysteinsson, *Concept of Modernism.*

9. Marjorie Perloff, *21st Century Modernism: The "New" Poetics* (Malden, Mass.: Blackwell, 2002).

10. Susan Kirkpatrick, *Mujer, modernismo y vanguardia en España (1898–1931)* (Madrid: Cátedra, 2003), is the most notable recent exception; also in this vein, Mary Lee Bretz, *Encounters across Borders: The Changing Visions of Spanish Modernism* (Lewisburg, Pa.: Bucknell University Press, 2001), and, peripherally, Roberta Johnson, *Gender and Nation in the Spanish Modernist Novel* (Nashville: Vanderbilt University Press, 2003).

11. Debicki, *Spanish Poetry;* Sumner Greenfield, *La generación de 1898 ante España,* 2nd ed., rev. and ed. Luis González-del-Valle (Boulder, Colo.: Society of Spanish and Spanish-American Studies, 1997).

12. Philip Silver, *Ruin and Restitution: Reinterpreting Romanticism in Spain* (Nashville: Vanderbilt University Press, 1997); also José-Carlos Mainer and Jordi Gracia, *En el 98 (Los nuevos escritores)* (Madrid: Visor, 1997); Richard Cardwell, "Los componentes del fin de siglo," in *En el 98 (Los nuevos escritores),* ed. José-Carlos Mainer and Jordi Gracia (Madrid: Visor, 1997), 172–75; Ricardo Gullón, "La invención del 98," in *La invención del 98 y otros ensayos* (Madrid: Gredos, 1969), 7–19; John Butt, "The 'Generation of 98': A Critical Fallacy?" *Forum for Modern Language Studies* 16 (1980): 136–53; D. Fernández-Mora, "The Term 'Modernism' in Literary History," in *Proceedings of the Xth Congress of the International Comparative Literature Association* (New York: Garland, 1985), 271–79; Nil Santiáñez-Tió, "Temporalidad y discurso histórico. Propuesta de una renovación metodológica de la historia literaria española moderna," *Hispanic Review* 65 (1997): 267–90.

Although a handful of Spanish critics have portrayed specific Spanish writers as sharing points of commonality with a variety of historical avant-garde groups or literary stylistic tendencies outside of Spain,[13] this has been for the most part a fragmentary and, indeed, conservative enterprise since these sporadic forays have not produced much support for a broader view of Spain's relationship to Europe or for an early contemporary period concept.

Until recently, however, even this type of piecemeal association of Spanish talents with Europe had been used with the opposite intention, to draw sharply negative contrasts between the Spanish writer and individuals or groups to whom he/she may have been compared, a favorite tactic of conservative Spanish critics to reaffirm the "national identity" of given authors.[14] Echoing literary debates in Spain as far back as the Golden Age (e.g., Quevedo, Góngora, and Lope's polemics over *conceptista* vs. *culterano* poetry), the standard critical line throughout most of the twentieth century has been that a given writer is either "truly Spanish" or else an imitator of "foreign" models. This attitude remains prominent, if slightly less strident, today.

The absence of advocates of a modernist paradigm for early contemporary Spanish literature has reinforced the isolation of Spain from other early contemporary European literary traditions as it has also diminished the possibilities for more universal recognition and higher valuation of early contemporary Spanish writing. Although the official critical disavowal of modernist/avant-garde Spanish literature begins before the Spanish Civil War and intensifies in the strident conservatism of the first post–world war decade, these critical attitudes become fully established by the early days of the Franco dictatorship. Outdated generational paradigms of the 1940s and '50s, however, have not been decisively challenged. The initial critical line advanced primarily by Pedro Salinas, Pedro Laín Entralgo, and Dámaso Alonso continues to uphold the idea of a fundamental separation between early contemporary Spanish litera-

---

13. Most frequently Ramón Gómez de la Serna; Luis Cernuda; Juan Larrea; José María Hinojosa; Rosa Chacel, *Estación. Ida y vuelta*, ed. Shirley Mangini (Madrid: Cátedra: 1989); Derek Harris, ed., *The Spanish Avant-Garde* (Manchester: Manchester University Press, 1995).
14. See Bretz, 13–69.

ture and modernist literary traditions elsewhere. Instead of identifying a more inclusive model lasting longer than the short time span accorded the Spanish literary generation (typically, fifteen years), an elitist, exclusionist, ultranationalist, sexist, historically atomizing generational concept becomes the sole basis for literary history and valuation. The paucity of meaningful critical discussion regarding the appropriateness of the generational model has been unfortunate. The literary generations of "1898," "1914," and "1927" become more rigorous critical categories, however, only as Spanish criticism engages in revisionist efforts to make pre–civil war literature compatible with the ultranationalist agenda of Francoism. The resultant fragmentation of literary historiography has left a legacy of unsatisfying developments that strongly discourage discussions of early contemporary Spanish literature in transnational contexts. With the rest of the world open to the idea of an international modernism, however, the time is certainly ripe to move in such a direction.

Period concepts throughout modern literary history have typically been delineated with greater clarity and precision after the fact of their historical prominence even though the specific critical term that may eventually describe that period may have gained wide currency with critics and the public. The extension of the concept of modernism to Spanish literature is postulate on the identification of major formal-ideological patterns in early contemporary Peninsular literature shared with modernist Europe and other parts of the world.[15] In bringing such motifs into critical focus, it is necessary to acknowledge the difficulty in separating multifaceted aspects that extend beyond aesthetic categories. This is why my arguments have been developed around a flexible yet intellectually cogent amalgam of aesthetic/ideological potentialities rather than to be tied to overly specific definitions. Modernism is both "revolutionary" (it features a "high" period of some twenty years when most of the modernist "masterpieces" are produced) yet also "evolutionary" (it has a much longer gestation period, which lays the groundwork for its crowning achieve-

15. See Richard Sheppard, "The Problematics of European Modernism," in *Theorizing Modernism: Essays in Critical Theory*, ed. Steve Giles (New York: Routledge, 1993), 1–12.

ments). Modernism's two aspects thus present parallels with earlier literary periods, the "evolutionary" movement from sixteenth-century renaissance to the seventeenth-century baroque and the much more abrupt and seemingly "revolutionary" emergence of romanticism.

Yet even the accepted period concepts that have long guided European literary historiography have themselves presented difficulties because they have evoked a multitude of diverse and seemingly contradictory sentiments. It must be remembered that the desirability of the term "romanticism" to describe even a minimally unified phenomenon was the subject of an important critical debate between prominent critics of an earlier generation, Arthur O. Lovejoy and René Wellek.[16] For Lovejoy, the concept of romanticism was so multilayered and variously defined that it evoked too much to be useful as a critical designation, whereas Wellek attempted to identify specific if rather aseptic universal formal features applicable to all national expressions of the wider program. While it is important to acknowledge that period concepts often feature what seem to be unreconcilable contradictions as they endeavor to narrate complex historical developments, it is also necessary to affirm that such apparent contradictions only further confirm the need to identify intellectually available concepts for phenomena that run a course across nations and generations.

As mentioned above, there remains no universal consensus concerning a specific historical moment by which literary modernism acquires sufficient prominence to be recognized as an autonomous literary phenomenon. The general awareness of fresh and challenging forms of literary expression had become apparent in intellectual circles by the turn of the twentieth century. Yet it is obvious that the "generational" interwar moment of "high" modernism would not have been possible without the extensive underpinning that preceded it. Erratic economic and political cycles, the challenge to the hegemony of middle-class val-

16. Arthur O. Lovejoy, "On the Discrimination of Romanticisms," *PMLA* 39 (1924): 229–53; René Wellek, "The Concept of 'Romanticism' in Literary History," *Comparative Literature* 1 (1949): 1–23; 147–62.

ues and political systems, and new scientific and technological advances are fully reflected in the early-century development of a literary style that reflects a culture, a modernist culture, spawned during a period of unprecedented turmoil. Notwithstanding Perloff's well-spoken argument for the continuity of modernism, there is, however, substantial critical agreement that literary modernism comes to a rather abrupt conclusion by the end of World War II. In Spain, this span of years coincides well with the emergence, at the end of the nineteenth century, of a "medio Siglo de Oro" that thrives and enhances itself over the ensuing decades, yet that is also quickly dispersed as a consequence of the Spanish Civil War.

The primary challenge today to modernism's growing authority to speak for a much expanded historical and geographical sphere comes from a cadre of left-leaning critics whose primary interest in modernism has been as the foil for a new field of inquiry, postmodernism, that as it continues to address textual studies has, in fact, shifted the focus of inquiry to areas outside literature. A disciple of this attitude, Martin Donougho, has suggested that the stakes for contemporary criticism are high since for him and others "[e]ither we view ourselves as trapped within the now rather pointless rites of modernism, or else postmodernism may be seen as offering a new beginning."[17] Indeed, many critics believe that for postmodernism to thrive it must somehow discredit a modernism that it has outgrown. This attitude goes far to explain, for example, why critics such as Bürger insist so strongly on a sharp division between the historical avant-garde and modernism.[18] According to these critics, the political positions of avant-garde groups are more "progressive," that is, leftist, since they attack the institution of bourgeois art, while modernists, as individuals, tend to experience a greater sense of cultural-political alienation and thus are more likely to harbor reactionary, rightist sentiments. In very broad terms, there is some truth to this argument. However, such a position is not exclusively leftist or revolu-

17. "Postmodern Jameson," in *Postmodernism-Jameson-Critique,* ed. Douglas Kellner (Washington, D.C.: Maisonneuve Press, 1989), 88.
18. *Theory of the Avant-Garde.*

tionary since others who openly attack the institution of art are just as likely to be fascists, as exemplified in the rightist sympathies of Marinetti and the futurists, the English vorticists and imagists, and many others.[19] The variety of positions that have been premised on an antagonism between modernism/postmodernism or modernism and the historical avant-garde, in fact, are more the logical consequences of the contemporary politics of many of these critics rather than anything specifically unique to modernism. Undoubtedly, a great many modernists were fascists. As many, in fact, were leftists (anarchists, radical socialists, communists), whose political positions have also been discredited, if belatedly so in comparison to fascism, everywhere except the academy, where many of its adherents continue to extol the dubious virtues of Marxism and related doctrines as literary critical methods. In short, this amounts to an all-or-nothing strategy. The most prominent of such critics is Fredric Jameson, who, with a new postmodern paradigm largely of his making, considers that "this remarkable aesthetic [of modernism] is today meaningless."[20] Modernism thus becomes synonymous with fascism and reactionary politics.[21] It is quite ironic, therefore, that the zealous exposure of modernism's extremist "dark side," which remained almost completely hidden during the formalist postwar decades, has coincided with the much expanded scope and authority of modernism. The postformalist emphasis on modernist excess has thus actually led to invigorated examinations of the radical positions of modernism, especially its political relationships and sympathies, which, indeed, include extreme political affiliations of all varieties.[22]

Unlike other period concepts that have been generally approached

19. For a strong critique of Bürger's Theory, see Richard Murphy, Theorizing the Avant-Garde (Cambridge: Cambridge University Press, 1998), 1–12.
20. Postmodernism, or, the Cultural Logic of Late Capitalism (Durham: Duke University Press, 1991), 121,
21. Fredric Jameson, Fables of Aggression: Wyndham Lewis, the Modernist as Fascist (Berkeley: University of California Press, 1979), 1–23.
22. See Vincent Sherry, Ezra Pound, Wyndham Lewis, and Radical Modernism (Oxford: Oxford University Press, 1993); Colleen Lamos, Deviant Modernism: Sexual and Textual Errancy in

in terms of a common ideology or aesthetic intention, modernism in its more expansive characterizations continues to vie for critical attention with primarily metropolis-centered avant-garde groups, even though the concepts "modernism" and "avant-garde" are often interchangeable.[23] Spanish criticism has decisively rejected the broader notion of a European modernism in favor of an approach that has splintered the avant-garde into its individual fragments rather than to associate its positions with a mainstream consensus that understands the historical avant-garde as a vital, autonomous, yet nevertheless integral part of modernism. Traditional Spanish criticism has long seized upon lingering questions of territoriality in the wider profession to reaffirm its own outdated paradigms, frequently overlooking possibly more moderate positions in favor of making simplistic, often extreme, and invariably unfavorable comparisons with more eccentric manifestations of avant-garde expression. Such a strategy both asserts the dissimilarity of Spanish writers to their European avant-garde/modernist counterparts and reaffirms the uniqueness of Spanish literary values and traditions.[24] Even when more favorable comparisons with avant-garde writing are made, the analogies tend to be strongly qualified and often considered peculiar and even infelicitous.[25] This, at the conservative end of the critical spectrum, is another instance of all-or-nothing criticism.

Although such ungenerous approaches to literary history have also had the effect of denying a number of writers, especially female writers, a place in the Spanish literary canon, the goal of this study is not the rehabilitation of marginalized talents (Kirkpatrick provides a notable step in this direction). Although it is certainly hoped that a stronger foundation to discuss writers and texts excluded from canonical generational groupings will emerge as a consequence of the arguments offered here,

---

T. S. Eliot, James Joyce, and Marcel Proust (Cambridge: Cambridge University Press, 1998); Young, Dada and After; Louis Arnorsson Sass, Madness and Modernism: Insanity in the Light of Modern Art (New York: Basic Books, 1992); Bürger, Decline of Modernism.

23. See Kolocotroni Goldman, and Taxidou's organizational scheme in Modernism, v–xv.
24. See Debicki, Spanish Poetry of the Twentieth Century; Silver, Ruin and Restitution.
25. Harris, The Spanish Avant-Garde, 1–14.

the more immediate task, nevertheless, is the incorporation into a succinct modernist paradigm of a milieu of early contemporary canonical Spanish texts and writers whose wider appeal has also been diminished as the consequence of the infelicities of Spanish literary historiography. An important aspect of this study, therefore, must be to provide a more compelling yet uncomplicated reading framework, a theory and a practice by which early contemporary Spanish literature may integrate into a wider critical mainstream. In my opinion, to advocate "Spanish modernism" does not mean to examine historical Spanish positions on "Spanish modernity." Although often insightful and useful in the advocacy of a greater awareness of common literary/cultural issues for the Spanish-speaking world (see recent forays by Bretz and also Mainer/Gracia, Cardwell),[26] this approach does not directly address the specific issue of the isolation of Spanish modernist literature from international mainstream traditions. The "Spanish modernism" that I propose is as a literary critical concept in relation to the European modernist canon.

My principal strategy for the advocacy of a prominent Spanish participation in the fuller agenda of modernism is to identify a spectrum of formal features that, in turn, suggest an ideological itinerary. In an examination of the multiple meanings associated with the concept of modernism, Astradur Eysteinsson characterizes modernism's fundamental aesthetic in simple terms: modernist texts interrupt the conventions of late nineteenth-century realism.[27] Such formal disruptions range from the relatively moderate to the more aggressive, indeed, even to the overturning of conventional representational models. Eysteinsson, nevertheless, stresses modernism's dependence upon realism, a necessary coexistence and interdependence of the "conventional" with the "modern." Modernist disruptions of mimetic models, which begin as varieties of meta-literary expressiveness, eventually lead to a stronger and more af-

---

26. See recent forays by Bretz, *Encounters across Borders*, and also José-Carlos Mainer and Jordi Gracia, *En el 98 (Los nuevos escritores)* (Madrid: Visor, 1997); Richard Cardwell, "Los componentes del fin de siglo," in *En el 98 (Los nuevos escritores)*.
27. *The Concept of Modernism*, 179–241.

firmative position: the intuition of a more significant and valuable space/ place, an alternate, "second reality." It is in the elaboration of this "second reality," fully dependent upon the "first," where the ideological dimensions of modernism become more apparent. Indeed, it might be said that the great difference between the literary realist and the modernist is that the realist believes in one, and only one, empirical, sensually communicated reality, while the modernist believes in a second reality invariably considered superior to ordinary, conventional reality.

Concomitant with the affirmation of alternative aesthetic spaces typically portrayed as private, hidden, "inner" locales, in sharp contrast to conventional, sensually available public settings, is the facilitating mode of force(s): personal, aggressive, conscious agents or, at the other extreme, impersonal, supra-personal, unconscious. Modernists typically consider realism a shallow means to portray more complex notions of what it means to be. More than simply a style, the modernist aesthetic is also a means to interrogate the dominant middle-class subjectivity that guides realist representation. The implied ideological dimension, fresh subjective formulations, hints at an alternative social arrangement at the source of their fuller articulation.

If meta-literary moments, brief or extended, tend to characterize the more modest forays into a new aesthetic, more intense modernist departures from realist norms may be characterized in terms of a "hieroglyphic" mode of expression, in which symbolic-verbal signs are imbued with greater iconicity as the boundaries between domains of the verbal and the visual and the temporal and the spatial become blurred. In practical terms, this more extended form of interruption expresses itself in terms of a displacement of conventional meanings whereby verbal signs come to represent something entirely different, requiring the reader to "decipher" private referents. Typically encountered in poetic expression, this more emphatic mode is often overwhelming to the uninitiated reader conditioned to expect that verbal signs refer exclusively to the empirical world. Readers are thus faced with the practical task of discovering their own "Rosetta stone," a key to the code through which such words actually make sense.

At its most forceful, the desire may actually become to surpass mimetic representation altogether. Particularly intense, sometimes ecstatic moments or states of being often described in terms akin to an existential "mysticism," epiphanies of "the full presence of being," "oceanic" fullness, secular "eternity" contrast sharply with its counterpart, the loss, typically traumatic or catastrophic, of "presence." In these more intense modes, realist ends, the mimetic representation of reality (and psychology), become instead a means to redirect art to the goal of affirming a "better" reality, as Jorge Guillén has expressed it, a "realidad no [. . .] reduplicada en copias sino recreada de manera libérrima" ("reality not [. . .] duplicated in copies but created in the freest manner").[28] Not a product or a "copy," such a reality is often portrayed as an alternate "geography" or "tierra" (recall Aleixandre's *Pasión de la tierra*, Neruda's *Residencia en la tierra*), a superior domain where the values of being may be actualized over and above the flux of temporal-historical existence. It is in these more fervent aesthetic manifestations that the idea of "force(s)" becomes particularly important in an ideological sense.

The prominence of the role of force in the exploration of "better" realities is integrally related to modernist attitudes to history, historical consciousness, and tradition. The desirability of journeying into the private spaces of a "second reality" frequently clashes with the public demands of ordinary contemporary life conditioned by convention and an often narrow idea of "tradition." Although many modernists are more interested in the antidotes to the mundane and the narrowly historical, thus the stereotypical reputation for "anti-historical" postures (recall Joyce's Stephen Dedaelus, for whom history is a "nightmare" from which he is "trying to awake"), the fuller record demonstrates that many modernists and avant-garde groups were also keenly interested in affirming their modernity in relation to traditions of which they typically understood themselves as the present standard-bearers. This seems to be the attitude of many of the most notable individual talents such as Eliot and Pound, for example, for whom historical consciousness mani-

28. El *argumento de la obra* (Barcelona: Sinera, 1969), 20.

fests itself as a comprehensible phenomenon in nonobjective, personal terms. Indeed, they, and others, evince striking similarities to the attitudes toward history of the writers of "1898" (Unamuno, Azorín, Baroja, and Machado) that underscore the greater value of enduring human attitudes in history irrespective of specific circumstances (recall Unamuno's idea of *intrahistoria*).

The issue of tradition has been especially burdensome as regards Spanish participation in continental literary movements. The "Spanish tradition"—separate, narrow, unique—is the standard recourse for critics for whom Spain's participation in any European literary agenda since the renaissance is minimal or nonexistent. Advocates of Spanish "uniqueness" during the Golden Age (Parker, Reichenberger, among a host of others) continue to dominate early modern critical opinions as well. It is more productive, however, to understand Spanish writing as engaging, *dialectically*, a European agenda with which it is recurrently at odds across the modern era, especially regarding the important issue of subjectivity. One of the major themes of European literature of the modern era is the construction of the Western subject: autonomous, freethinking, materialistic, willful, a true believer in the superiority of European civilization and values, chief among which are the contradictory phenomena of liberal democracy and imperialism. Spanish literature is suspicious of and resistant to this model and engages it consistently from its inception in the Renaissance to its triumph in the nineteenth century, as the culture of the European middle class establishes its hegemony in most aspects of modern life. The critique of this ideology in Europe manifests itself in the "modernist style," whose principal "content" is the rejection of such "modern values." Beginning in earnest around the turn of the twentieth century, perhaps the most important aspect of such an agenda is the creation of newer models of subjectivity, a "new man" (and a "new woman") whose outlook and values clash with bourgeois cultural, literary, and political norms. The great irony of this development is that Europe is at this time certainly not initiating a discourse, but rather joining a centuries-long discourse in Spain that never fully acquiesced in middle-class definitions of subjectivity. In effect, the advent of "high" literary modernism in the early decades of the twentieth century marks a moment of rapprochement between European and Spanish writers as regards this major, indeed principal, theme of the modernist ideological agenda. My thesis in this regard is that Spain comes to modernism not in imitation of European trends but rather as a full participant in relation to the issue of postbourgeois subjectivity that dominates all of modernist literature. The crisis of the European bourgeois "thinking subject" forms the bedrock of modernist form/content and ideology and provides a strong bridge between Spanish mainstream writing and the full array of European responses to this central issue.

Modernist dissatisfaction with middle-class subjectivity is expressed in irreverent, even nihilist, parody (see, for example, Vallejo's *Trilce*, Cernuda's *Un río, un amor*), yet also in more affirmative expressions, in the desire to bring forth this so-called new man, a new mode of superior consciousness in relation to then-current "modern" standards (Aleixandre's *La destrucción o el amor*; Huidobro's *Altazor*; in a different format, Guillén's *Cántico*). Both of these broad avenues of modernist articulation are prominent in Spanish writing from the Renaissance onward. Firstly, it expresses itself in the form of "monstrous" parodies and critiques of the dominant subjective model. Such an attitude continues a tradition in Spanish literature that I am calling the discourse on the "monster subject." The other trend expresses itself in more affirmative expressions that align themselves against personality-centered subjectivity, which I have chosen to characterize as "structural" subjectivity. Structural models of subjectivity that become prominent in Europe via Freudian, Jungian, and Lacanian psychology are embraced by a variety of modernist writers and avant-garde groups as superior expressions of a new understanding of human subjectivity. They correspond to a surprising degree to a long-standing Spanish premodern Christian tradition that also sanctions a view of the structurality of being. In both modes, "being" is never "full" in ordinary existence, but rather must attain its fulfillment in a "second," superior reality. It is my contention that modernist critiques

of bourgeois subjectivity from other parts of Europe actually move closer to traditional Spanish positions that never fully embrace the Cartesian
paradigm of the autonomous thinking subject (and its historical successors). It is here where early contemporary Spanish writing fully inter-
sects with continental modernist positions.

Spanish contemporary criticism has yet to confront a critical model
that advances the idea of a fundamental similarity of Spanish literature
to itself as it also accentuates differences with the rest of Europe. The
lingering effects of such a line have served to isolate Spanish literature
from a wider logical context and to devalue the standing of even its canonical writers, remaining largely intact, especially in Spain itself, thirty
years after the passing of the authoritarian governmental structure that
helped spawn it. "The Spanish tradition," however, demands an analysis
that stresses, as a defining feature across all the major literary periods, a
view of Spain's fuller participation in European discourse characterized
by a dialectical relationship with fundamental European positions. The
critique of the middle-class subjective model does not become prominent in the rest of Europe for three centuries, until the modernist period.
The most significant difference between Spanish and modernists elsewhere in Europe is not the beliefs espoused but rather the routes taken
to affirm them. European modernist writers are reacting to the latest developments of "modern" culture, now understood to be less than fulfill-
ing in an aesthetic, political, and personal sense. Similar disavowals by
Spanish writers are actually continuing a much longer tradition of dialectical resistance to European conceptions of modernity and subjectivity. Integral to the notion of Spanish participation in modernism, especially in the important context of evolving attitudes toward modernity, is
the acknowledgment of an intellectual underpinning in the "Spanish national tradition" that allows it to become much more than an infelicitous
imitation of imported foreign models.

The integration of early contemporary Spanish literature into a
"modernist tradition" requires the development of an affirmative yet read-
ily accessible interpretive model, the indispensable preliminary to which

begins with a strong critique of the Spanish "generación literaria." This is the intent of chapter 1, which begins by examining the scene of Spanish literary criticism at about the time of the Spanish Civil War and the isolationist positions of primarily three prestigious critics—Pedro Salinas, Dámaso Alonso, and Pedro Laín Entralgo—that transform the more generous ideas about literary generations of Ortega y Gasset into strict conformity with the extreme positions that become prominent in German literary criticism, specifically the generational model of Julius Petersen during the early 1930s. The chapter also examines the proto-Nazi ideology underlying Petersen's system of literary historiography, which is adopted in Spain in its entirety and quickly imposed upon the profession without discussion by the mid-1940s. Reformist attempts during the 1960s and '70s to loosen generational criteria (Gaos, Gónzalez) however, have encountered, during the last ten years, renewed interest in reaffirming the most conservative generational models (Debicki, Greenfield) as well as Spain-centered alternatives (Silver, Morris, Harris).[29] Chapter 2 establishes the context for a strong Spanish participation in literary modernism, objections to which are answered not by contemporary critical theory but rather by the "Spanish national tradition" itself, whose longstanding resistance to the middle-class subjective model affords Spanish writers equal footing with their modernist contemporaries to make important contributions to the discourse about the constitution of the "new European man." Spanish thinking about the "autonomous thinking subject" understands that at its very heart it is something monstrous.

Chapter 3 introduces Spanish modernism in relation to the growing discourse on new configurations of subjectivity in the modernist novel, where the dilemma of "monstrous" and "structural" approaches to subjectivity become prominent in representative canonical texts: Pío Baroja's El árbol de la ciencia, Miguel de Unamuno's Niebla, Ramón del Valle-Inclán's Tirano Banderas, Ramón Gómez de la Serna's El novelista, and

29. Vicente Gaos, Antología del grupo poético del 1927 (Madrid: Anaya, 1965); Angel González, El grupo poético de 1927 (Madrid: Taurus, 1979); Debicki, Spanish Poetry of the Twentieth Century; Greenfield, La generación de 1898 ante España; Silver, Ruin and Restitution; Morris, Son of Andalusia; Harris, Spanish Avant-Garde.

Rosa Chacel's belatedly acknowledged masterpiece, *Estación. Ida y vuelta*. Chapter 4 focuses on the poetry of Jorge Guillén and Vicente Aleixandre during the 1920s and '30s, where the affirmation of the ethic of monstrous subjectivity finds its most sublime expression. These poets affirm the possibility of "full being" summoned by an aggressive, solipsistic, monstrous subjectivity to whose will this poetry responds. Chapter 5 discusses the poetry of Luis Cernuda and Rafael Alberti to affirm a diametrically opposite position with regard to subjectivity, that "full being" is a mirage and that the sustaining values of existence can be encountered only in a wider and public context. Chapter 6 examines the mature vision of Federico García Lorca's theater in both his experimental plays and his commercial successes in which he articulates the ultimate creative-destructive possibilities of the discourse on modernist subjectivity, the tragic fragmentation of the structural model. Finally, I have chosen less obvious writers, avoiding for the most part experimental writing, in order to make my case with canonical writers identified with "Spanish uniqueness" as well as with those who are considered aesthetically "conservative." Thus by design this study is not as fully comprehensive as it might be. My aim is not to produce a compendium but to establish solid criteria in all the major genres for the view of a substantial Spanish participation in literary modernism, as it has been understood outside of Spain in the mainstream of the profession, to communicate succinct and relevant positions that are offered as an invitation for further discussion.

CHAPTER 1

The Spanish Literary Generation and Early Contemporary Literary History

An examination of some of the consequences of adopting the literary generation model in Spain instead of a period approach to its early contemporary literature requires a brief acknowledgment of parallel and opposing phenomena elsewhere in Europe. Resistance to the idea of a European modernism remains in large part because of the competing interests of avant-garde groups. More recently as well, for the first time prominent modernist writers have come under intense scrutiny of their political beliefs, which has overturned many long-held critical assumptions. The rapid canonization of modernist masters during the post–World War II era that ignored modernism's "dark side" has been superseded by views that aligned aspects of modernist production with elitism, anti-Semitism, and fascism.[1] Additionally, the impetus to solidify a strong concept of postmodernism often comes at modernism's expense, seeming at times to require the denigration of modernist aesthetics typically considered more interested in ingenious literary gamesmanship than in developing a "positive" human agenda. Recall Donougho's "pointless rites" argument; also Ortega's position, as early as *La des-*

1. Besides earlier efforts by Kermode (*The Sense of an Ending*) and Jameson (*Fables of Aggression*), see Morrison, *The Poetics of Fascism;* Carlston, *Thinking Fascism;* Julius, *T. S. Eliot;* among many others.

humanización del arte, of an "arte como juego y nada más [. . .] una cosa sin trascendencia alguna" ("art as a game and nothing more [. . .] something without any transcendence").[2] By contrast, nation-centered avant-garde groups have been treated much kinder, often portrayed as aligned with "progressive" affiliations.[3] Yet in spite of these attacks and revisions, modernism has acquired great authority in critical opinion as a period concept, even though its ultimate scope may still be in the process of clarification.

Spanish criticism has excluded itself from such debate in the wider profession, stressing alleged Spanish nonparticipation in a vaguely defined *vanguardismo* and largely leaving it at that. To speak about Spanish literature of the early twentieth century, it is necessary to do so in the fragmented context of the literary generation. Nevertheless, the similarities between the strongly nationalistic Spanish literary generation and nation-centered European avant-garde groups offer an opportunity to address the inadequacies in the literary generation model as well as to point to problems in opposing the historical avant-garde against modernism. In spite of longstanding dissatisfaction among Hispanists and notwithstanding some hopeful recent attempts to move in a positive direction (see discussion below of Mainer/Gracia, Cardwell, Kirkpatrick, Bretz), the "generación literaria" nevertheless remains the primary model for early contemporary Spanish literary history, through inertia if nothing else. Although the focus of this study is the early twentieth century designated by the generations of "1898," "1914," and "1927," the naming of subsequent literary generations at regular intervals has continued, albeit with less rigor, during the remainder of the century.

The most disturbing historical fact about the development of the concept of the literary generation in Spain is the paucity of critical discussion over the past century regarding its legitimacy. The theoretical underpinning for the generational model is grounded in tenets that come from German criticism of the early 1930s during the intense na-

---

2. Donougho, "Postmodern Jameson"; José Ortega y Gasset, *La deshumanización del arte y otros ensayos estéticos* (Madrid: Revosta de Occidente, 1970), 27.
3. Bürger, *Theory of the Avant-Garde*.

tionalistic upheavals in that nation, most prominently by the literary historian Julius Petersen. The concept of the literary generation in Spain in its more rigorous constitution, as an objective national literary phenomenon, is simply imposed at mid-century, during the height of Francoism, without discussion or debate. Nevertheless, more than three decades after its passing, the negative legacy of the literary generation continues. The fact that there has been very little examination of its continued desirability as a concept suggests the need for a fuller account of its history. The historical record demonstrates that, even as regards the handful of discussions that consolidated this concept, their themes remarkably overlap and thus have fitted well with the undemocratic nature of the literary generation's entry into Spanish criticism.

It has not been appreciated that the historical arguments of the Spanish literary critics most responsible for developing the literary generation as a more critically rigorous yet narrow and elitist model—Pedro Salinas, Pedro Laín Entralgo, and Dámaso Alonso—are part of a conservative effort that serves, whether specifically intended to or not, to repudiate the more generous and reasonable notion of a generation as outlined by Ortega before the Spanish Civil War. Indeed, the repeated invocations of the contributions of ultranationalistic German criticism aligns this view with extreme positions that have no place in enlightened critical discourse. The all too brief history of this discussion begins and ends with subjective accounts—Azorín's 1913 meditation on the generation of "1898" and Alonso's sentimental and emotional 1948 invocation of the generation of "1927"—accompanied with more rigorous "theoretical" commentaries immediately preceding and following the Spanish Civil War by Salinas and Laín Entralgo regarding the concept's specific applicability in both conceptual and practical terms to Spanish literary history.[4] The principal basis for these more precise judgments is

4. Azorín, "La generación del 1898," in *Clásicos y modernos*, vol. 12 of *Obras completas* (Madrid: Caro Raggio, 1919), 233–55; Dámaso Alonso, "Una generación poética (1920–36)," in *Obras completas*, vol. 4 (Madrid: Gredos, 1975), 653–76; Pedro Salinas, "El concepto de 'generación literaria' aplicado a la del 98," in *Literatura Española. Siglo XX* (Mexico City: Séneca, 1941), 43–58; Pedro Laín Entralgo, *Las generaciones en la historia* (Madrid: Instituto de Estudios Políticos, 1945).

their adherence to the tenets developed by Petersen in "Las generaciones literarias,"[5] which, significantly, feature specific disavowals of Ortega's important views about the generational phenomenon in El tema de nuestro tiempo (1923).[6] The consequence of these judgments is a continuing adherence to the idea that contemporary Spanish literature remains fundamentally different from contemporary literature of the rest of Europe.

The need to stress a similarity of national literary purpose is evident from the outset in Azorín's "La generación de 1898" in Clásicos y modernos (1913),[7] the only substantial literary critical statement to emerge regarding the literary generation or its place in a more universal historical context before Ortega's contributions in El tema de nuestro tiempo and En torno a Galileo (1933).[8] Salinas's 1935 essay "El concepto de generación literaria aplicado a la del 98"[9] specifically criticizes Azorín for his lack of critical rigor in offering "una opinión puramente personal" ("a purely personal opinion," 47) and invokes instead the "objective" authority of "la historiagrafía literaria alemana" ("German literary historiography," 47) of the seminal 1930 Petersen essay as a superior avenue of inquiry and thus the guarantor of rigorous critical conclusions, dismissing Azorín's influential essay as a stroke of "buena ventura" ("good luck," 47). Similar to Salinas's chiding of Azorín for his amateurism is Petersen's disparagement in his own treatise of Ortega, whom he strongly criticizes as simplistic for his views in El tema de nuestro tiempo. Ortega's description there of the generation as a fundamentally pluralistic "variedad humana" ("human variety," 742) internally susceptible to the most ex-

5. Julius Petersen, "Die literarischen Generationen," in Philosophie der Literaturwissenschaft (Berlin: Junker and Dünnhaupt, 1930), 130–87. References are to the Spanish translation: "Las generaciones literarias," in Filosofía de la ciencia literaria, ed. Emil Ermatinger, trans. Carlos Silva (Mexico City: Fondo de Cultura Económica, 1946), 137–93.

6. José Ortega y Gasset, El tema de nuestro tiempo, vol. 3 of Obras completas (Madrid: Revista de Occidente, 1955).

7. "La generación del 1898," in Clásicos y modernos, vol. 12 of Obras completas (Madrid: Caro Raggio, 1919), 233–55.

8. José Ortega y Gasset, En torno a Galileo, vol. 5 of Obras completas (Madrid: Revista de Occidente, 1951).

9. Pedro Salinas, "El concepto de 'generación literaria' aplicado a la del 98," in Literatura Española. Siglo XX (Mexico City: Séneca, 1941), 43–58.

treme antagonisms if indeed minimally associated by a similarity of age and physical circumstance (an argument refined in *Galileo*) is unacceptable to Petersen, who emphasizes, against Ortega alone in his essay, that "[l]a cosa no es tan fácil como pretende el 'generacionista' español José Ortega y Gasset" ("the issue is not as easy as the 'generationalist' José Ortega y Gasset suggests," 157). Salinas' critique of Azorín's amateurish "personal opinions" is also more poignantly a silent reproach to Ortega, whom he fully ignores in his 1935 essay as he upholds Petersen's agenda point by point. It will thus be instructive to consider Azorín, Ortega, Petersen, and Salinas as intimately interrelated for the purposes of this discussion.

Azorín quickly disabuses his readers of the notion that the generation of "1898" is something original or new, stressing instead the ideological continuity between those whom he identifies as belonging to the generation of "1898" and the preceding group, which he calls the generation of "1870," whose notables include José Echegaray, Ramón de Campoamor, Benito Pérez Galdós, and others. If the generation of "1898" is initially embraced in the press and in the popular imagination by its willingness to engage in "crítica social," no less so, according to Azorín, is the generation of "1870." In fact, "[l]a generación de 1898, en suma, no ha hecho sino continuir el movimiento ideológico de la generación anterior" ("the generation of 1898, in sum, has only continued the ideological movement of the previous generation," 255). Without such a tradition, the generation of "1898" would not have become viable:

> La gran corriente ideológica de 1870 a 1898 . . . concluye lógicamente—avivada por el Desastre—a la crítica social que florece desde 1898 hasta algunos años después. . . . Cuando hayáis considerado tal hecho histórico comprenderéis de qué manera ha podido moldearse la mentalidad de la generación de 1898, y cómo ese vasto y acre espíritu de crítica social . . . ha llegado a encarnarse hoy sólido, fuerte, profundamente en la muchedumbre. (247–48)

> The great ideological current from 1870 to 1898 . . . logically concludes—given new life because of the Disaster—in the social criticism that flowers in 1898 and persists a few years after . . . When you have

considered such a historical fact you will understand the way that the
mentality of the generation of 1898 has been able to form itself, and how
this vast and acrid spirit of social criticism . . . has become incarnate today solidly, strongly, profoundly in the population.

Contrary to popular myth, Azorín maintains that the generation of "1898"
does not rise in opposition to the immediately preceding historical moment but rather continues an earlier ideological position in a coopera-
tive and even conformist spirit. There is no sharp break with the past,
but rather a strongly felt sense of common purpose inherited from the
previous generation. At the very moment that Azorín identifies the generation of "1898," therefore, he is also undermining the popular myth of
its existence. The generation of "1898" upholds rather than opposes an
ideological line to give greater direction to preexisting ideas and themes
in the aftermath of the national "disaster," the humiliating war with the
United States. Such a posture coincides well with a realization common
to members of this group who, after initially flirting with radicalism,
conclude that a political solution to Spain's problems will not be possible in terms acceptable to them.[10] One of the goals of Azorín's essay
is thus to situate himself in a more conservative ideological mainstream
rather than to suggest that his generation continues to look to activist
solutions. Clearly presented in a context of politics and not as an autonomous literary phenomenon, Azorín's generation of "1898" emerges
more as a concept intended to establish and consolidate a position that
does not differ in essence from a larger "tradition" that has already been
validated by others who have already achieved a high valuation in critical
and public opinion.

Ironically, Azorín's expansion of the chronological context for discussion of the generation of "1898" and his specific and detailed references to European influences on Spanish writing from the nineteenth
century onward (250–52) further distances his "primitive" idea of the literary generation from what emerges later in Salinas, Laín Entralgo, and

10. See Carlos Blanco Aguinaga, *Juventud del 98*, 2nd ed. (Barcelona: Editorial Crítico,
1978).

Alonso. Indeed, Azorín's position corresponds well in analogy to a literary period—perhaps better than to a generation. As Richard Sheppard has noted on the varied range of dates suggested for the initiation of modernism—"some critics set as its starting-date as early as 1870 (so as to include Nietzsche and Rimbaud)"[11]—Azorín's suggestion of a preceding generation of "1870" to which the generation of "1898" is intimately related is not as arbitrary as it may initially seem. By the 1913 publication date of Azorín's essay, his loose conception of a generation of "1898," a group whose work he presents as far from concluded, aligns it—in everything except name—with other expressions of national literary flowering, the emergent "-isms" in other parts of Europe whose fuller history is more definitively constituted and consolidated in/as modernism. Embedded in the account of the one writer of this "generation" most willing to identify himself with the concept (in contrast, for example, to Pío Baroja's strong and enduring refusals),[12] therefore, is a reticence to create a strong generational model. Azorín's unwillingness to ground his discussion in the national ferment and crisis of 1898, and thus to make it clear that "crítica social" is not a defining characteristic of his generation, evinces a position that disavows sharp political differences with the immediate and extended past. It nevertheless also suggests his consciousness of an emergent literary context that has also become evident by 1913 that makes the generation of "1898" more relevant as part of a larger "tradition" or historical "period" in which the most recent writing has a more decisive role to play as a literary phenomenon. Azorín's initial list of writers belonging to the generation—which includes Juan Ramón Jiménez, Manuel Bueno, Jacinto Benavente, Ruben Darío, and Ramiro de Maeztu, all of whom have been subsequently eliminated or sharply marginalized—remains the most generous, in part because of his willingness to include a greater variety of literary expression and thus to keep the concept from becoming overly prescriptive. This view,

11. "The Problematics of European Modernism," in *Theorizing Modernism: Essays in Critical Theory*, ed. Steve Giles, 1–52 (New York: Routledge, 1993), 1.

12. See Greenfield, *La generación de 1898*, 400.

of course, does not prevail as the criteria for membership become more rigorous as a consequence of judgments offered in the name of greater objectivity with the appearance of Salinas's essay and subsequent solidification of the concept in Laín Entralgo's criticism during the 1940s. The ambiguities of Azorín's account are clearly unappealing to Salinas, whose exclusive reliance on the Petersen model moves the discussion, nearly a quarter century later, in a much different direction. Although Salinas's claim is to offer "objective" criteria demonstrably superior to Azorín's amateurish, impressionistic version, the implied target is Ortega, the specific recipient of harsh criticism by Petersen for similar offenses. Salinas's essay that via Laín Entralgo and Alonso eventually provides the principal conceptual model for the literary generation in Spanish criticism in the immediate aftermath of the Civil War is more fully understood in the wider context of Petersen's critique of Ortega's simpler and much more generous position than as a reply to Azorín, the nominal object of his inquiry. It will be important, therefore, to present Petersen's critical model, which is decisive in Salinas's thinking, in greater detail. More important to Petersen than what he claims are Ortega's naive criteria for the constitution of generations, however, is their serious difference in regard to the generation's relationship to history. While he concedes that Ortega's minimum requirements of a similarity of age and circumstance are not incompatible with his views, the real question for Petersen becomes the issue of the specific mechanisms by which generations come into existence: "En una palabra, se trata de la cuestión de si la unidad 'generación' nace o se hace" ("In a word, it all boils down to whether the concept 'generation' is born or is made," 146). While this ostensibly may not seem to be such a great difference, it lays bare a profound ideological breech between their positions.

Ortega clearly believes that one is born into a generation, that the concept itself is a seminal historical tool by which to mediate the conflicting demands of the individual and the mass, the historical tug and pull between the majority and minorities:

> Una generación no es un puñado de hombres egregios, ni simplemente una masa: es como un nuevo cuerpo social íntegro, con su minoría se-

lecta y su muchedumbre, que ha sido lanzado sobre el ámbito de la existencia con una trayectoria vital determinada. La generación, compromi-
so dinámico entre masa e individuo, es el concepto más importante de la
Historia, y, por decirlo así, el gozne sobre que ésta ejecuta sus movimientos. (Tema 742)

A generation is not a handful of exemplary men or simply a mass: it is
an integral new social body, with its select minority and its mass, that
has been launched into existence with a vital and determined trajectory.
The generation, dynamic compromise between mass and individual, is
the most important concept of History, and, so to speak, the hinge upon
which it executes its movements.

As he makes even more explicit later in En torno a Galileo, part of the individual's task is to understand his entry into history in relation to a moment
within an ongoing generational agenda: "desde la perspectiva individual el hombre no puede estar seguro de si en su fecha de edad comien-
za una generación o si acaba, o bien, si es ella el centro de la generación.
[. . .] Esto demuestra indirectamente el carácter objectivo, histórico y no
privado del concepto de generación" ("from the individual perspective a
person cannot be sure if his coming of age begins or concludes with a
generation, or perhaps, if it is in the middle of the generation. [. . .] This
demonstrates indirectly the objective, historical and not private character of the concept of the generation," 50). Considerations of the appropriateness of such a position in relation to other models of historical understanding notwithstanding, at the historical moment in which Ortega
presents his system of historiography the choices are evidently between
his view of a historical mediation of competing forces and those in which
the appeal is precisely to the power and authority of the masses on the
one hand and the will of strong leaders on the other, that is, the totalitar-
ian doctrines of communism/Stalinism and fascism/Nazism. In this context, Ortega's concept can be considered in an ideological sense to be a
moderate one, within a liberal-democratic ethic. Indeed, his description
of the generation is clearly pluralistic and democratic in character: "una
generación es una variedad humana. [. . .] Dentro de ese marco de iden-
tidad pueden ser los individuos del más diverso temple, hasta el punto
de que, habiendo de vivir los unos junto a los otros, a fuer de contem-

poráneos, se sienten a veces como antoganistas" ("a generation is a human cross-section. [. . .] Within this designation one can find individuals of the most diverse character, to the point that, having to live in close
proximity with each other, owing to their contemporaneity, they feel at
times that they are antagonists," *Tema* 742). His position thus elicits diversity, variety, and antagonisms appropriate for debate, and resolution,
in a democratic context.

Petersen's views are fully opposed to this since in his model the
generation becomes the vehicle by which history is made subject to the
will of a select minority and, even within that elite group, even stronger individuals who mold and lead their generation. Although he does
not discount the idea of historical evolution, Petersen is much more interested in developing a model to "cimentar teóricamente una práctica
[. . .] de explicar las causas de un desarrollo que procede por saltos" ("to
cement theoretically a practice [. . .] of explaining the causes of a development that proceeds by leaps," 139). After presenting a long survey of
widely differing chronologies for the duration of generations, Petersen
insists on a rather short span of time: "no ha alcanzado entre nosotros
[en Alemanía] una duración mayor de quince años" ("among us [in Ger-
many] it has not achieved a duration longer than fifteen years," 143). Indeed, if anything the rhythm of generations is becoming shorter still—
ten years rather than fifteen—as the twentieth century begins, since
"hacia 1900 está decidida la victoria de los neorrománticos, de los neo-
clásicos y de los simbolistas idealistas, victoria que en su mayor parte
trae consigo una crítica, un cambio o un desarrollo de los viejos naturalistas" ("around 1900 is decided the victory of the neo-romantics,
the neo-classicists and the symbolist idealists, victory that by and large
brings with it a criticism, a change or a movement beyond the old nat-
uralists," 143–44). The period concept Realism-Naturalism, especially
in relation to Germany, does not rightly apply. Instead, Petersen strongly emphasizes "diferencias nacionales que nos muestran que el natu-
ralismo constituye en Francia un elemento del espíritu nacional más
original, más genuino, más arraigado, así como en Alemania ocurre lo

mismo con el romanticismo simbólico" ("national differences that dem-
onstrate that naturalism constitutes in France a most original, genuine,
and deeply rooted element of the national spirit, as in Germany the same
thing happens with symbolic romanticism," 144). These strictly national
groupings are strong evidence that "concurren infinitas series de generaciones físicas sin confluir en modo alguno" ("there concur infinite series of physical generations without mingling together in any way," 145).
The role of the phenomenon of history is clearly negative; the only respite from such chaotic and competing interests lies within a national
setting. Rather than an appeal to a dynamic evolution of historical forces, Petersen's idea of change proposes instead the violent response of a
"nueva voluntad" ("new will") to the perceived weakness and immobility in a generation that has run its course, that this "anquilosamiento [de
la generación anterior] fuerza a la juventud a la sucesión" ("stagnation
[of the previous generation] forces the youth to succession," 145). Thus,
for Ortega, individuals find themselves in history and through it come
to an understanding of their circumstances and historical mission, what
they can or cannot accomplish. For Petersen, the generation emerges as
an aggressive process, to impose itself upon history through its leaders,
called *führers* ("caudillos").

Petersen strongly discredits "[e]l viejo y completamente anticuado
principio de los períodos con influencias extranjeras [. . .] lo más opues-
to al principio de las generaciones" ("the old and completely antiquat-
ed concept of literary periods with foreign influences [. . .] the most
opposed to the idea of literary generations," 153). The period concept
dilutes the expressive impetus that can emerge only from strict unity
within the group. This is where the role of the "tipo directivo de la generación" ("leadership of the generation," 159) is decisive, in which the
leader attracts his followers and thus "completa la impresión de unidad
de generación que se hace visible desde fuera" ("completes the impression of generational unity that becomes externally visible," 159). Indeed,
the failure to achieve cultural unity characterizes a weak nineteenth century whose "falta de unidad" ("lack of unity"), ironically, "hace surgir

fácilmente la impresión de una sucesión rápida de generaciones" ("gives
the impression of a rapid succession of generations," 160), thus confus-
ing issues even further by dispersing the efforts of generations. The continuity between generations is thus a negative one, since "el espíritu de
los viejos participa, mediante su fracaso, en la formación de una nueva generación" ("the spirit of the old participates, through its failure,
in the formation of a new generation," 163). The underlying historical
paradigm is dysfunction, cycles of momentary or apparent victory followed by inevitable failure. The principal expression of historical consciousness is a will to triumph over the chaos and failure of historical
succession that in turn threatens the existence of the generation itself
as a nation-centered phenomenon. Petersen's ideas are unmistakably
influenced by anti-democratic proclivities in Germany acquiring a decisive momentum at the very moment of his essay. This suggests that it is
a proto-Nazi document, that it shares great sympathy with the national hysteria sweeping the German nation at precisely this moment. This,
however, also strongly suggests that Petersen's essay is far from the superior and objective model for literary historiography that Salinas claims
for it in 1935, by which time it was—or should have been—evident that
the need for a dictatorial, disciplining *führer* to guide the literary generation is an extreme position.

The role of raw will as superior to anything in history or nature is
also central in Petersen's description of the literary generation. If what
is inherited from the previous generation(s) is a factor in the formation
of new generations, its most significant role is in response to rather than
compliance with "heredity." Petersen uses the analogy of the family that
typically features the coexistence of generations—father, son, grandfa-
ther—to turn the idea of an inheritance from the past completely around.
Just as a "familia no pued[e] sostener durante varias generaciones el caudillaje como una magistratura hereditaria" ("family cannot sustain during various generations the leadership as a hereditary magistracy") so
too in the literary generation "el necesario cambio de dirección se hal-
la en contradicción con el principio hereditario" ("the necessary change

of leadership finds itself in contradiction with the hereditary principle,"
165). He continues this theme in his remarks on the commonality of
birth in a generation, the one area in which he and Ortega are in clos-
est accord. Yet even here, Petersen suggests that there may be a deeper will beneath the apparent "golpe de dados de la naturaleza" ("toss of
the dice of nature," 167) underlying birth. If chance is the sole explanation for why men are born, Petersen questions why there exist such un-
explainable phenomena "como el aumento de las cifras de natalidad y el
predominio de los naciminetos masculinos después de guerras sangri-
entas, [que] nos revelan un régimen misterioso y una voluntad de com-
pensación que no es posible explicar racionalmente" ("like the increase
in the birth rate and the predominance of masculine births after bloody
wars, [that] reveal to us a mysterious regime and a will to compensation
that is not possible to explain rationally," 167). Clearly, even in the apparently neutral, "natural" category of date of birth there is an explanation
traceable to a human will to triumph over nature and natural forces: "Y la
misma voluntad se debe el que, cuando el tiempo está ya maduro, nace
siempre el genio que la época necesita" ("And the same will is applicable to the fact that, when the time is ripe, there is always born the genius that the period needs," 167). In the context of the German national
hysteria owing to the rise of Nazism, the reference to genius is also fully
applicable to political "genius." If German culture achieved superiority
under Goethe, so too it might again, in the agitations of the new generation. As Petersen states at a later point in his essay, "la sucesión de generaciones constituye [. . .] un problema histórico-cultural [. . .] que sirve
de base a la unión y a la interacción radical entre movimientos, concep-
ciones del mundo y programas de partido políticos y religiosos" ("The
succession of generations constitutes [. . .] an historico-cultural problem
[. . .] that serves as a base for the union and radical interaction among
movements, conceptions of the world and the programs of political and
religious parties," 190).

    As regards the educational experiences of a generation, Petersen em-
phasizes the creation of a national educational ideology. Much more im-

portant than the content of educational experience is the spirit of unity derived from sharing a common set of ideological values. Typically, therefore, the generation feels a kinship—"se sienten unidos por un mismo espíritu" ("they feel united by the same spirit," 171)—that transcends their need for close association in a physical or geographical sense. Petersen thus emphasizes the overcoming of geographical separations via the superior spiritual medium of commonly held national values. Indeed, when he speaks of the shared space of the generation the emphasis is on those aspects that serve to enhance the idea of a shared vital direction "que se presenta como unidad de destino de los individuos que se encuentran en la misma situación" ("that presents itself as a unity of destiny among individuals that find themselves in the same situation," 172). A shared space is not a neutral, a natural, or even a historical category, but rather an opportunity for the expression of a will to act within this space to achieve fundamentally a national destiny. The youthful element in every generation will be dissatisfied, therefore, with "ese principio de los viejos de que 'todo se repite'" ("that principle of the old that 'everything is repeated,'" 177). Indeed, the desire of youth is "su experiencia peculiar, su propia revolución, su ocasión genuina para actos heróicos" ("its distinctive experience, its own revolution, its genuine opportunity for heroic acts," 177). The sole vehicle of continuity between the will of generations to affirm a special destiny is the *führer*: "el caudillaje representa, dentro del antagonismo de los grupos de edad, un factor enlazador de generaciones y que hasta salta por encima de las generaciones" ("the leadership represents, within the antagonism of the groups of the moment, a uniting factor among the groups that stand out above generations," 179). Ortega's idea of history as a primary reality is thus decisively repudiated by the idea of the will of the strong leader.

Another determining factor for the literary generation is a generational language understood as a deeper phenomenon than mere changes in stylistic expression. This also has specifically to do with the initial moment of the literary generation, in which "[l]a nueva generación se encuentra por vez primera en su lenguaje. Todo el programa nuevo tiene que ser verbalmente nuevo para que prenda la mecha [. . .] tanto la fantasía verbal creadora como la actividad verbal receptiva, se presentan con la major viveza en los años juveniles" ("the new generation finds itself for the first time in its language. Every new program must be verbally new in order to light the fire [. . .] both creative verbal imagination and receptive verbal activity, that present themselves with the greatest liveliness in the younger years," 183). A generational language thus extends beyond a new and recognizable style. Style is a function of the primary agenda, the overturning of the older generation. Language as conceived by Petersen is thus an ideological weapon by which "el sentimiento orgánico de la generación más joven se configure, desde un principio, en una cierta dirección que se desvía de la antigua" ("the organic feeling of the younger generation is configured, from the beginning, in a certain direction that deviates from the older one," 185). Petersen's position in this regard must also be understood in opposition to long-standing European ideas of a universal language. There is a "universal" language, but it exists within the generation. A generational language is the most identifiable expression of a will to be different from those in an older group, whose language is out of date, indeed, no longer understood. Parody is thus the initial and enduring feature of any new generational language (185).

Present throughout his discussion yet specifically discussed in a separate category is the concept that the new generation emerges as a consequence of the "anquilosamiento de la vieja generación" ("stagnation of the old generation," 186). This also involves another failure, the moment when the older generation fails to understand the desires of the younger group. "Tanto a los viejos como a los jóvenes no les queda más remedio que ir a buscar la comprensión en los compañeros de edad" ("For the old as well as the young there is nothing that can be done except to find understanding among comrades of the same age"), which he goes further to state is a "comprehensión asegurada por una situación homogénea, por experiencias iguales, por una actitud en el mismo sentido y por una comunidad de destino" ("understanding assured because of a homogeneous situation, because of equal experiences, because of an common attitude and because of a community of destiny," 188). This also reinforces the idea of a generational language. The truest expression of language is in the communication of univocal meaning universally understood within groups but not across them. Language belongs to the generation, and not the contrary, leaving little or no room for alternative viewpoints.

It is from such a context, which at the dawn of the twenty-first century seems especially limited and ungenerous, that Salinas undertakes his interpretive commentary of Petersen regarding the suitability of these categories in relation to the generation of "1898." In the name of "la teoría de generación literaria elaborada en Alemania" ("the theory of the literary generation elaborated in Germany"), Salinas's conclusion that "no ofrece duda: hay una generación del 98" ("there can be no doubt: there is a generation of 98," 58) seems disingenuous in the context of Ortega's extensive and important writing over the preceding years. Given Petersen's pointed criticism of Ortega in his essay, to proclaim in 1935 to have "discovered" the precise means of defining "los perfiles exactos de un nuevo complejo espiritual perfectamente unitario que irrumpía en la vida española: la generación del 98" ("the exact outlines of a new spiritual complex perfectly unitary that erupts in Spanish national life: the generation of 98," 58) that Ortega more than anyone else had already made intellectually rigorous and compelling to Spanish criticism in precisely the opposite terms ("Los escritores de esa generación se diferencian tanto entre sí que apenas si se parecen en nada positivo. Su comunidad fue negativa" ["The writers of that generation are so different that they hardly resemble each other in anything positive. Their commonality was a negative one"])[13] is to add injury to the significant insult of bypassing him altogether in his commentary. Although Salinas's comparisons in relation to commonality of birth, education, and experiences largely coincide, as do Petersen's, with Ortega's views, his unconditional acceptance of the most questionable of Petersen's te-

13. José Ortega y Gasset, *Ensayos sobre la generación del 98* (Madrid: Revista de Occidente, 1981), 149.

nets—generational language and leadership—even to the point of devising ingenious interpretations to force these concepts to fit the generation of "1898" does not speak well for his capacity to understand that these are extreme positions. Salinas's contention that the largely symbolist innovation of Darío's *modernismo* "no es otra cosa que el lenguaje generacional del 98" ("is none other than the generational language of 98") misstates or overlooks Petersen's more radical concept of language, while his insistence on a generational *führer*, the fatherly figure of Nietzsche, even in the absence of anyone resembling a flesh-and-blood *caudillo* among these independent-minded writers—"Yo me atrevería a decir que todo el ambiente [. . .] de la época se advierte entonces la apetencia del caudillo, que el *führer* está presente precisamente por su ausencia" ("I would dare to say that the whole ambience [. . .] of the age is characterized by the desire for the strong leader, that the *führer* is present precisely because of his physical absence," 55)—is more revealing of his own sympathy for the Petersen model than any actual evidence or support for it. More disturbing than even these opprobrious aspects of his exposition is Salinas's insistence on the "nuevo complejo espiritual perfectamente unitario" ("new spiritual complex perfectly unitary," 58) of the generation of "1898." This position is in full consonance with Petersen's most intense conclusion that the generation reveals not only a unified expression of national will and values but "una unidad de ser debida a la comunidad de destino" ("a unity of being owing to a commonality of destiny," 188). Although studied in a separate literary sphere, the literary generation is ultimately not separable from science or politics. In this sense, the unity of which the generation is an expression is but one manifestation of the total national impetus to a unity of being, that is, a state of transcendence that surpasses time and space. Thus, there is an apocalyptic aspect to these "objective" considerations of literary generations. The strongly implied message of Petersen's position is that the time is coming when the phenomenon of the acceleration of generations will bring society to the point where it can no longer resist "la formación de la generación universal" ("the formation of the universal generation"), that the idea of a commonality of destiny "va creciendo la conciencia de generación en su expansión espacial y en su penetración social, así como se va acelerando la sucesión de las generaciones" ("augments the consciousness of the generation in its spatial expansion and in its social penetration, as the succession of generations continues to accelerate," 192). More so than in any meaningful relation to members of the generation of "1898," these statements are clear anticipations of the "apetencia del caudillo" that had captivated Petersen and Germany and that by 1935 was beginning to demand a "universal space" for its universal expression. Underlying Petersen's position, therefore, is an ultranationalism, indeed, a proto-Nazism, whose implications for Europe could not be fully imagined at the time of its publication.

The consequences of Salinas's essay for Spanish criticism are also unfortunate. From this apparently inconspicuous beginning, Laín Entralgo, Alonso, and others are quickly able to advance a strong concept of the literary generation in the first post–Civil War decade grounded in forceful appeals to a similarity of national literary purpose. Laín Entralgo's most theoretical yet least remembered book, *Las generaciones en la historia*—"concebido como una introducción metódica" ("conceived of as a methodical introduction," 9) to his seminal *La generación del noventa y ocho*—fully adopts Petersen's generational criteria.[14] Although by this date the generational leader is no longer called a *führer* but rather the "conductor" (*Las generaciones* 244), the Petersen-Salinas model provides the methodological underpinning for Laín Entralgo's subsequent expansions of the concept of a generation of "1898" centered exclusively in considerations regarding the history and problems of the Spanish nation. The generation is an "unidad producida por comunidad de destino, que encierra en sí una igualdad de experiencias y de fines" ("unity produced by a commonality of destiny, that contains within it an equality of experiences and goals," *Historia* 247). In the chapter titled "¿Generación del 98?" of *La generación del noventa y ocho* he also extensively quotes and

---

14. Pedro Laín Entralgo, *La generación del noventa y ocho* (Madrid: Diana, 1945); *Las generaciones en la historia*.

paraphrases Salinas's commentary on Petersen as a preliminary to his own less literary meditations on a conceptual basis for the generation of "1898." Laín Entralgo merges his critical discourse with Salinas's to reaffirm a strictly national literature guided by "'un nuevo complejo espiritual perfectamente unitario que irrumpía en la vida española: la generación del 98'" ("'a new spiritual complex perfectly unitary that erupted in the Spanish national life: the generation of 98,'" *Noventa* 60). By 1945, therefore, a less strident but fully orthodox version of Petersen's generational model has been recontextualized to reflect Spanish national values rather than to invoke the immoderate legacy from which it arises. This chapter is dropped from subsequent Espasa-Calpe editions (but included in the 1956 collection under the general title *España como problema*), possibly because by 1956 the generational concept has gained such authority in Spain that it no longer need depend upon the now problematical authority of the Petersen tenets. Thanks to Laín Entralgo, Alonso, and others, the concept has become fully integrated into a Spanish context.

By 1948, when Dámaso Alonso invokes the century's second major literary generation, the generation of "1927," in his sentimental account "Una generación poética (1920–36)" of the seminal event in its formation—the gathering in 1927 in Sevilla of most of the poets identified with this group to pay homage to Luis de Góngora on the occasion of the tercentenary of his death—there is no longer the need to justify the generation as a concept. Proceeding from the authority of Petersen, Salinas, and Laín Entralgo, Alonso simply affirms in terms that by now are quite familiar that "esos escritores no formaban un mero grupo, sino que en ellos se daban las condiciones mínimas de lo que entiendo por generación: coetaniedad, compañerismo, intercambio, reacción similar ante excitantes externos" ("those writers did not form a mere group, but rather in them were gathered the minimal conditions for what I understand as a generation: contemporaneity, comradeship, interaction, similar reaction to external stimuli," 667). As by this date it has become apparent to all of Spanish criticism, Alonso now needs only to invoke a

comfortable notion to claim, through his evocation of the many collabo-
rations and friendships among these poets, empirical evidence of a continuing generational agenda. From here, however, he makes the much
stronger assertion that the phenomenon of the close association of these
poets also signifies a commonality of thought and literary purpose. If
Salinas is sensitive to a spiritual, even priestly, reawakening in the generation of "1898," then Alonso's generation constitutes its like-minded
choir: "Magnífico coro, donde cada voz tiene su timbre, pero que, conjunto, se ofrece ante el altar, con una pureza de intención como segura-
mente no ha conocido nunca la literatura española" ("Magnificent choir,
where each voice has its own tone, but which, together, offers itself before the altar with a purity of intention that surely Spanish literature has
never known before," 675). This becomes an explicitly religious invocation in Laín Entralgo's understanding of the duty of a new generation
of literary critics whom he calls in the first edition of España como problema (1947) "los nietos del 98" ("the grandchildren of 98," 126) whose
mission consists in fostering this generational tradition.[15] Religious
belief—"la creencia en Cristo y en su Iglesia nos otorga una certidum-
bre respecto al último sentido de nuestros actos" ("the belief in Christ
and his Church bestows upon us a certainly with respect to the ultimate
meaning of our acts," 141)—and a national political structure that reaffirms such values—"la creencia en que España podía ser efectivamente
gobernada según este modo de concebir su entidad histórica" ("the belief that Spain could be effectively governed according to this mode of
conceiving its historical role," 143)—become integral to the generational legacy. Religious metaphor, but also the call to renewed spiritual practice, serves to moderate some of the harsher aspects of Petersen's discourse while keeping the original generational criteria fully intact.

In contradistinction to the political dimension integral to the Petersen model and prominent in Azorín's discussion of the generation of
"1898," Alonso fully disassociates the generation of "1927" from such
considerations:

15. España como problema (Madrid: Seminario de Problemas Hispanoamericanos,
1947).

No, no hubo un sentido conjunto de protesta política, ni aun de preocu-
pación política en esa generación. [. . .] Pero es el caso que tampoco lit-
erariamente se rompía con nada, se protestaba de nada [. . .] no hay ninguna discontinuidad, ningún rompimiento en la tradición poética. Puedo
decir más: no hay quiebra fundamental alguna [. . .] entre la revolución
modernista [de Darío] y la poesía de hoy, de 1948. (659)

No, there was not a group sense of political protest, nor even political
concern in that generation. [. . .] But the case is that neither did it break
literarily with anything, or protest anything [. . .] there is no discontinu-
ity, no breaking with the poetic tradition. I can say even more: there is no
fundamental break whatsoever [. . .] from the *modernista* revolution [of
Darío] and the poetry of the present day, of 1948.

More emphatic than Azorín's idea of a generational continuity with a
wider milieu and in consonance with Salinas's concept of a "complejo espiritual perfectamente unitario" ("spiritual complex perfectly unitary") is Alonso's strong idea of his generation's continuity and similarity within what by now is understood to be an unchanging national
tradition. Completely absent is Petersen's prewar notion of the apparent acceleration of the appearance of generations attributed to the dys-
functions of history. In Alonso, however, the most extreme aspect of Petersen's model, the idea of a "universal generation," has triumphed. The
generation of "1927" emerges as the like-minded continuation of a literary tradition "profundamente arraigada en la entraña nacional y española" ("profoundly rooted in the national Spanish constitution") decidedly unlike "otros movientos estéticos que pasan las fronteras por esos
años inmediatamente anterior al cuajar de nuestra generación" ("other aesthetic movements that cross the borders during the years immediately before our generation comes together," 661). The latter part of
the quotation clearly refers to the proliferation of avant-garde writing of
the 1920s and after, in which Alonso now claims his generation plays
no part. The strong view of similarity that emerges in the new generation, therefore, is actually the fulfillment of Petersen's model in an ideal sense. The Franco dictatorship provides the necessary conditions for
the "universal generation" and thus obviates the need to overthrow anything.

The view of an unchanging contemporary tradition is in perfect consonance with the state apparatus that emerges after the Civil War, a regime that is ideologically impoverished yet has a powerful if simple national plan of unity and a cultural isolation from Europe. As in Azorín's view of his generation, the generation of "1927" is not in opposition to a wider tradition, but rather continues the movement toward greater national and literary-cultural unity under Francoism. Also like Azorín, Alonso's view of his generation extends beyond a strict generational moment. If in Azorín's case it is to undermine the popular associations of his generation with political activity, in Alonso's it is precisely the absence of politics, the denial of his generation's participation in national political events and the international literary phenomena of the 1920s and '30s, that now allows literary history to be rewritten, apolitically and ahistorically. Alonso's presentation of his generation negates literary history. His understanding of the generation of "1927" marks the conclusion of contemporary literary development, the consolidation of a unified national literary style guaranteed in the unified political will of the Franco dictatorship. The deeper message of Alonso's apparently benign invocations is the paralysis of historical evolution whose "perfection" has already been achieved. The generational moment has extended to include the entire contemporary period and has triumphed to the point of surpassing historical literary evolution. By the middle of the twentieth century, therefore, the theoretical and practical basis for the study of contemporary Spanish literature in the context of the literary generation organized around a strong principle of similarity is fully established: Spanish literature is uniquely Spanish, faithful to its own largely unchanging tradition dissimilar to those of Europe.

There are certainly exceptions to this general rule in attempts to modify the generational model, much more so in relation to the generation of "1927" than the generation of "1898," the latter becoming very nearly an unquestioned reality as a consequence of the strong advocacy of Ortega as well as Laín Entralgo and others. In a 1955 discussion by Ricardo Gullón about the generation of "1927" (which he calls the generation of "1925"), there appears the first moderating response to the rigorous demands of the Petersen model. While outlining the problematical aspects of generational groupings, he also recognizes that a looser generational identification is justifiable.[16] Indeed, this has been typical of the attempts to modify the harsher aspects of the original generational format, to advocate greater flexibility within a fundamentally inflexible model somewhat along the lines of Ortega's more diverse model in an attempt to be more inclusive.

Luis Cernuda's 1957 essay in *Estudios sobre poesía española contemporánea* regarding his idea of a generation of "1925" represents a different type of effort to reorder the criteria for grouping.[17] Rather than to look to the age and experiences of the poets, his methodology centers in the chronology of the appearance of the first book of poetry. While this may seem innocent enough, this is actually a somewhat veiled response to Alonso's essay that as it establishes the idea of a generation of "1927" also creates hierarchies between the more mature poets, Guillén and Salinas, and a slightly younger group of somewhat marginalized talents that includes Cernuda, Manuel Altolaguirre, and others. In establishing his particular criteria, Cernuda is replying to Alonso by demonstrating that the "caudillo" of the generation, Jorge Guillén, is the last to publish his first volume of poetry. Cernuda's format, however, is also a choice between which talents to marginalize. Guillén and Salinas are considered apart from younger talents (that include Aleixandre, Lorca, and Alberti) who are considered sympathetic to the aims of European modernism, while Salinas and Guillén are not. Cernuda's position is historically significant in that it is the first to advocate a direct association of the generation of "1927" with European modernist writing.

Even though Cernuda's views are not incompatible with some of the conclusions developed in this study, his opinions, nevertheless, are in their own right just as ungenerous as Alonso's. Although Guillén and

---

16. Ricardo Gullón, "La generación poética de 1925," *Insula* no. 117 (1955): 3, 12; see also "La invención del 98."

17. *Estudios sobre la poesía española contemporánea* (Madrid: Guadarrama, 1957).

Salinas are certainly not sympathetic to surrealism and other avant-garde tendencies that identify with the political left, their poetry does claim a strong kinship with the more embracing concept of modernism devel-oped in this study. Thus, from the other end of the ideological spectrum, Cernuda demonstrates how easy it is to misuse the generational concept as a weapon of exclusion. In practical terms, Cernuda's outline of the agenda of his generation has not advanced his perspective but has con-tributed to the solidification of the idea that the literary generation is the sole vehicle for the historical grouping of contemporary Spanish liter-ature. For the sake of advancing a view favorable primarily to an even smaller group within an already restricted milieu, therefore, Cernuda ac-tually enhances the justification for the critical atomization that is the legacy of the generational paradigm.

The "grupo poético" approaches of the 1960s and 1970s put for-ward by Vicente Gaos and Angel González and slightly later by Juan Manuel Rozas and Gregorio Torres Nebrera, somewhat stronger re-formist attempts to transcend some of the harsher limitations of the Pe-tersen model, have actually served an opposite function by further vali-dating the authority of the generational paradigm even in the name of reforms and modifications. While recognizing the problematical no-menclature of descriptive terms such as the "Generación de Góngora," the "Generación de la Dictadura," or Jose Luis Cano's idea of a "Gener-ación de la amistad," the alternative name "Grupo Poético de 1927" has changed nothing. If anything, the older model remains as strong as ever, especially after having been given new life in the late Andrew Debicki's *Spanish Poetry of the Twentieth Century: Modernity and Beyond* (1994), which marks a full return to Alonso's conservative views of the generation of "1927." The persistence of such a state of affairs is the logical conse-quence of the absence of a positive concept to replace the authority of the generational paradigm.

Debicki's views in this regard are instructive of the persistence of loyalty to the generational model. Aware that the rest of the profession is investing heavily in an inclusive concept of modernism to tell the sto-ry of early contemporary European literature, he insists, as have a multitude of Spanish critics during the last half century, on maintaining an essential division between Spanish avant-garde writing (*ultraismo, creacionismo*), a "strand of modernity" whose "presence in canonical texts can hardly be discerned" (39) and another represented in the generation of "1927" that has nothing to do with *las vanguardias*: "The Generation of 1927 poets [. . .] immersed themselves in their literary tradition, fitted themselves into the dominant poetic represented by Juan Ramón Jiménez, and, rather slowly, wrote their poetry and criticism. Their first major books appeared in 1924 or later, when vanguardism was fading away" (33). This amounts to a paraphrase of Alonso's 1948 position. Debicki attributes such differences in evolution to "attitude and inclination [. . .] a preference for reading and writing in one's study and attending lectures at the Residencia versus participating in a shocking *ultra* event and spending time at vanguard cafes; an inclination to build traditions and give form to meanings versus an impulse to destroy them and undercut determinacy" (33). Such a peculiar notion is not unlike Petersen's explanation for why literary generations emerge, from a will within the group, in this case a will to conform to "tradition" rather than to overturn it.

Modernist tendencies outside of Spain, especially surrealism, offer unsatisfactory analogies with Spanish poetry, another restatement of Alonso. The fact that most Spanish poets reject the surrealist label is offered as proof that they are not modernist in any sense: "Aleixandre rejected automatic writing and asserted his belief in the poet's conscious creation; Cernuda minimized surrealism's effect on him. [. . .] These two poets spoke from within a prevailing symbolist perspective, even as their work presaged its erosion" (41). If there is an international flavor at all to the generation of "1927," it belongs to a nineteenth-century phenomenon—René Wellek acknowledges that standard conceptions of symbolism consider it "a coterie, a group, or possibly a school in Paris in the eighteen-eighties and nineties"—to which all the talents of the generation are simply made to fit.[18] Modernism seems hardly to exist, while symbolism is extended well into the 1930s, thus breathing new life

18. René Wellek, "What Is Symbolism?" in *The Symbolist Movement in the Literature of the European Languages*, ed. Ana Balakian (Budapest: Akademiai Kiadó, 1982), 18.

into Alonso's half-century old idea of an unchanging contemporary tradition.

A complementary position emerges in Derek Harris's *The Spanish Avant-Garde* (1995). For Harris as well, there is no Spanish participation in modernism, only a vague concept of a European avant-garde that Spaniards come to second- or even third-hand: "In Spain writers and artists [who] [. . .] felt the need to assert an individual identity apart from the dominating pressures from Paris [. . .] were functioning within borrowed horizons and seeking to adapt them to an indigenous circumstance" and such "writers were bound by the limitations of their native tongue, unless they chose to abandon it in favour of French, and no one who did so, made much impact on the chauvinist world beyond the Pyrenees" (2). The writers of the generation of "1898" are even worse, displaying "an essentially retrogressive attitude" (5). Harris strongly seconds Debicki's view of the most significant poetry of early contemporary Spain "as a continuation of symbolism based on the idea of pure poetry borrowed from Paul Valèry; poetry that eschewed any emotional, ideological, moral aims" (9). Also like Debicki, Harris acknowledges isolated expressions of "experimental" writing while noting that none of it resembles a sustained Spanish participation in vanguardism, so short-lived and fragmented, in fact, that one wonders what the fuss was all about.

Also in this prolix vein are even more revisionist positions that recall a cacophony of ultranationalistic, pro-Franco apologists of half a century ago. For example, C. Brian Morris's *Son of Andalusia: The Lyrical Landscapes of Federico García Lorca* portrays Lorca primarily as a regional talent, a "son of Andalusia" fully reminiscent of Alonso's civil war evocation of Lorca as "la expresión de lo español" ("the fullest expression of Spanishness").[19] This study concludes at the precise moment when Lorca is undertaking his modernist projects in earnest, and marks a return to the

19. C. Brian Morris, *Son of Andalusia: The Lyrical Landscapes of Federico García Lorca* (Nashville, Tenn.: Vanderbilt University Press, 1997); Dámaso Alonso, "Federico García Lorca y la expresión de lo español," in *Obras completas*, vol. 4 (Madrid: Gredos, 1975), 755–57.

type of jingoistic, reactionary criticism prevalent during the 1940s and
'50s, thus making Morris something of an honorary bisnieto in the Laín
Entralgo brotherhood of "98." Even more outrageous is Philip Silver's
Ruin and Restitution: Reinterpreting Romanticism in Spain (1997), which presents Luis Cernuda not as a modernist but as a "romantic" (not a neo-
romantic), advancing the idea that Cernuda epitomizes the flowering of
a "Spanish romanticism" precisely at the height of European modernism, a full century after historical romanticism's prominence in the rest
of Europe. Salinas adopted an identical position sixty years earlier in the
concluding essay of Literatura española: Siglo XX in calling Cernuda "el último grado de reducción a su pura esencia del lirismo romántico español" ("the ultimate degree of reduction to the pure essence of Spanish
romantic lyricism," 348). Once again, modernism seems not to exist.
The emphasis of all these prominent figures in Spanish contemporary
criticism is on "Spanishness," which they succeed admirably in defining
in terms that bear no relationship to more meaningful, historically relevant transnational "foreign contexts," which they fully denigrate.

In a hopeful vein are opinions offered over the past decade by Mainer/
Gracia (1997), Cardwell (1997), Geist/Monleón (1999), Bretz (2001), Kirkpatrick (2003), and Johnson (2003), more in consonance with my own positions developed in two earlier studies (1990, 1996).[20] The volume edited
by José-Carlos Mainer and Jordi Gracia features a manifesto titled "Contra el 98 (Manifiesto de Valladolid)" (177–78), along with a clarifying
statement by Richard A. Cardwell (173–75), that calls for the abolition
of the concept of the generation of "1898" and the merger of the study of
Spanish-speaking literatures (see also earlier attempts to modify the

20. Mainer and Gracia, En el 98 (Los nuevos escritores); Cardwell, "Los componentes del
fin de siglo"; Anthony L. Geist and José B. Monleón, Modernism and Its Margins: Reinscribing Cultural Modernity for Spain and Latin America (New York: Garland, 1999); Bretz, Encounters
across Borders; Susan Kirkpatrick, Mujer, modernismo y vanguardia en España (1898–1931) (Madrid: Cátedra, 2003); Roberta Johnson, Gender and Nation in the Spanish Modernist Novel (Nashville: Vanderbilt University Press, 2003); C. Christopher Soufas, Conflict of Light and Wind: The
Spanish "Generation of 1927" and the Ideology of Poetic Form (Middletown, Conn.: Wesleyan University Press, 1990), and Audience and Authority in the Modernist Theater of Federico García Lorca
(Tuscaloosa: University of Alabama Press, 1996).

concept by Butt, Pearsall, Fox, and Ribbans).[21] It does so not in behalf
of a recognizable or standard period approach but rather—and, again,
in keeping with the original generational model—in a time frame that
lasts about fifteen years. Cardwell's attack against "las fáciles y erróneas
etiquetas de modernismo y 98" ("the superficial and erroneous labels
of modernism and 98," 175) is framed as an appeal for the creation of
yet another literary generation, premised in the Spanish language if not
around national frontiers. Although a hopeful trend in that it questions
the hitherto unassailable idea of a generation of "1898," this position is
certainly not original or even as generous as earlier assessments in this
context (for example, Ricardo Gullón's *Direcciones del modernismo* and the
Geist/Monleón anthology). In a manifesto condemning generational groupings, the concept that is to take the place of the generation of
"1898" is another, yet more spectacular, Hispanic literary generation.

Mary Lee Bretz's important discussion of "Spanish Modernism" in
*Encounters across Borders: The Changing Visions of Spanish Modernism, 1890–
1930* (2001) takes a position similar to Mainer/Gracia and Cardwell as
well as the general line in Geist/Monleón in that her "modernist" focus, notwithstanding the temporal reference in her title, also lasts about
twenty years. Bretz excludes writers "whose major corpus appears in the
1920s and later" in part "because the relationship between modernism
and the vanguardist literature of the 1920s continues to puzzle critics
and is even more problematic in the case of Spain" (22). Although I admire this study, in the final analysis it is not about the modernism that
the rest of the profession has long maintained reaches its pinnacle only
after 1920, the chronological moment when the most important avant-
garde groups also make themselves visible (with the exception of the futurists and the dadaists, the major avant-garde manifestos are written af-

21. See also José-Carlos Mainer, *La edad de plata* (Madrid: Cátedra, 1981). See also
earlier attempts to modify the concept: Butt, "The 'Generation of 98'"; Priscilla Pearsall,
"Azorín's Myth of the Generation of 1898: Toward an Esthetic of Modernism," *Revista Canadiense de Estudios Hispánicos* 11 (1986): 179–84; E. Inman Fox, "Hacia una nueva historia literaria para España," in *Dai Modernismi alla Avanguardie*, 7–17 (Palermo: Flaccovio Editorie,
1990); Geoffrey Ribbans, "Some Subversive Thoughts on *Modernismo* and the Generation of
98," *West Virginia Philological Papers* 39 (1994): 1–17.

ter 1920). In fact, it also amounts to another generational approach to Spanish literature that focuses on the very years in which the generation of "1898" is dominant. In spite of its great breadth, modernism for Bretz is primarily a prose phenomenon. Poetry—for most scholars of modernism, poetry is the dominant genre of modernism—and theater are hardly mentioned. Roberta Johnson's *Gender and Nation in the Spanish Modernist Novel* (2003) is also an important contribution to genre studies, but modernism, mentioned in passing but a few times, is largely a word inserted in the title.

Susan Kirkpatrick's *Mujer, modernismo y vanguardia en España* (1898–1931) (2003) marks a major step forward in that the concepts *modernismo* and *vanguardia* are used instead of the generational nomenclature in order to carve out a space for early twentieth-century Spanish women authors, undoubtedly the most egregious victims of the generational paradigm. A significant aspect of the Petersen literary generation model is the prominence of the generation's "carácter racial" ("racial character," 189). This is not an overt aspect of the generational discussion in Spain since, again, Laín-Entralgo's and Alonso's discussions come in the 1940s after the discrediting of the powerful racist doctrines that held sway in Germany and elsewhere. However, a fundamental aspect of both pre–Civil War generations is their full exclusion of at least part of the "race," women writers, from these groupings. Indeed, the early contemporary canon, until only the last few years, has not included women writers at all even though critical accounts of the nineteenth century feature a number of important women writers (Cecilia Böhl de Faber, Gertrudis Gómez de Avellaneda, Carolina Coronado, Emilia Pardo-Bazán, and Rosalia de Castro). Kirkpatrick's study focuses on this "lost generation" of women writers that includes María Martínez Sierra, Carmen Baroja, Carmen de Burgos, and Rosa Chacel. The exclusion of women writers is not yet the case, for example, in 1931, before the more rigorous concept of the literary generation emerges, when Gerardo Diego includes Ernestina de Champourcín and Josefina de la Torre in his famous poetic anthology that features a varied array of contemporary poets, many of whom, rightly or wrongly, have also been subsequently forgotten. These significant female poets disappear for sixty years, since only within the last decade have they been rediscovered. Indeed, the much more prominently resurrected Rosa Chacel is invoked in a recent Editorial Cátedra edition of her important *Estación. Ida y vuelta* as "no sólo [. . .] la escritora del 27, sino [. . .] la única persona de este grupo que se ha mantenido fiel al desafío propuesto por Ortega en *La deshumanización del arte*" ("not only [. . .] the one female writer of 27, but [. . .] the only person of this group who remained faithful to the challenge proposed by Ortega in *The Dehumanization of Art*," 20). To enter the canon even today, one must do so through the continuing authority of the literary generation whose elitist legacy has served to atomize an entire field of study. If women's writing during the early contemporary period can be fully validated only by comparison to an exclusive "men's club," then it is not enough simply to be recognized as a writer worthy of serious critical attention, since women writers must at some point also pass a "generational" test.

The literary generation "tradition" has created a situation in Spanish literature in which the part defines the whole. Writers who do not fit the generational pigeonhole do not fare well. Most notable in this regard are Ramón Gómez de la Serna and, in a less obvious sense, Juan Ramón Jiménez, among many others. Just as Azorín's initial list of writers included in the generation of "1898" has been considerably pared down, so too a similar phenomenon has taken place in the generation of "1927" regarding Manuel Altolaguirre, Emilio Prados, Juan Larrea, and others who have been relegated into a second tier. The clear pattern has been to make premature and more definitive selections of the "fittest" invariably defined as the most similar. This is clearly not a healthy state of affairs for Spanish literary criticism in the context of continuing trends in the larger profession to acknowledge greater diversity. The generational legacy hastens the writing of "definitive" literary history and makes revisionism much more difficult.[22]

22. For a related discussion, see Jonathan Mayhew, "Poetry, Politics and Power," *Journal of Spanish Cultural Studies* 3 (2002): 237–48.

Even more disquieting is the fact that being named to membership in a literary generation, while it may assure an early place in the Spanish canon, has not increased the visibility or reputation of any of these writers in a transnational context. With the possible exception of Federico García Lorca, probably owing more to his tragic assassination than to an appreciation of his writing, there is no Spanish literary figure of the first half of the twentieth century who commands a wide name recognition outside the Spanish-speaking world. Even the most prominent works of contemporary canonical Spanish writers are infrequently translated, if at all. Contemporary criticism cannot make a compelling case for the more universal appeal of its greatest writers if it continues to study them from unproductive perspectives.

The fragmentation of early contemporary Spanish literary history, however, does find certain parallels in the wider profession as regards positions that continue to privilege nation- or metropolis-centered avant-garde groups over a more inclusive concept of transnational modernism. In the context of the present discussion, the variety of European avant-garde groups may be said to correspond, in loose analogy, to literary generations in their own right, especially since these individual avant-garde parts are also often approached, especially in the case of surrealism, as if they were the whole. As the provocativeness of the avant-garde has diminished as a consequence of greater critical understanding, the usefulness of "modernism" as a more generalized period concept has become more evident in the wider profession, especially over the past quarter century, in the sense that it can encompass seemingly radical modes of expression within a bedrock of criteria that fosters much greater inclusiveness among what had been approached earlier as heterogeneous phenomena. With the exception of Kirkpatrick, none of the above-mentioned recent Spanish studies, however, makes room for such developments. Eysteinsson voices the popular, and, indeed, authoritative opinion that the choice is no longer between modernism and the avant-garde. The avant-garde is more fully contextualized and situated, autonomously yet firmly, within modernism:

Some critics may only be satisfied if they can pronounce a clear-cut division between the two terms. Certain workable points of distinction are certainly an advantage. But rather than enforce a rigid separation, I find it a good deal more critically stimulating and historically challenging to work on the assumption that while texts such as *Ulysses*, *Der Prozeß*, *Nightwood*, and *The Cantos* are modernist works, they are also avant-garde in their nontraditional structure and their radicalized correlations of form and content, and that while the avant-garde movements are historical phenomena in their own right, they are also salient motors of modernism. (178)

As literary criticism adjusts its methodologies to the more important goal of historical and cultural understanding, the concept of a separate, nation-centered or otherwise fragmented avant-garde no longer suffices, just as a literary generation, or group, also fails to provide an adequate grounding for early contemporary Spanish literature. For the idea of the avant-garde to become truly profound, it requires a broader cultural context. Indeed, this has been the sad fate of *ultraismo* and *creacionismo* in Spain: to be consistently identified by Spanish critics with short-lived phenomena and minor talents "whose presence in canonical texts can barely be discerned." This, of course, is a political statement, the inevitable fate of any literary movement that does not find a more stable context from which to be studied. Spanish critics historically have tended to emphasize the most eccentric aspects of modernist production and thus to make comparisons from which it has been facile to conclude that Spanish writers did not emulate other European modernists, that Spain did not participate to any significant extent in modernism or the avant-garde but affirmed instead its own unique national tradition. Although the advocacy of a greater convergence between Spain and modernist Europe continues to find obstacles in the persistence of critical attitudes in the larger profession that associate modernism with "pointless rites" or extremist politics, or that continue to advocate essential differences between the avant-garde and modernism, there is strong evidence to suggest that such perspectives are in full decline. It is the illumination of such a literary critical paradigm in relation to Spain to which the subsequent chapters of this study aspire.

CHAPTER 2

Modernism and Spain

Aesthetics, Ideology, Tradition, Subjectivity

The unwillingness of Spanish criticism to consider an expansive concept of modernism as a viable aesthetic standard for early contemporary literary history has had adverse consequences for literary appreciation as well as for the standing of Spanish authors and texts in relation to other European writing. The aim of this chapter is to develop an artistic-ideological framework for a Spanish modernism that as it identifies a pertinent agenda also seeks to integrate this model with a revitalized concept of the "Spanish tradition." From this perspective, the most important area of interaction between Spain and an international modernist movement centers in the issue of subjectivity, what can be called modernist elaborations of fresh subjective models. As in the case in the renaissance, which witnesses the creation of a new sensibility, the most ambitious affirmative contribution of modernism is the creation of its own version of a "new man."

A broader and more inclusive context for modernism begins with a brief overview of historic evolutionary patterns in Europe. A productive area for comparison is the degree to which a "realist" aesthetic—values of mimesis, symmetry, orderliness, rationalism, and even scientism—competes with more eccentric styles that extend and modify this dominant paradigm. The manner in which earlier historical patterns have been characterized—the gradual extension of the renaissance into the baroque in contrast to the much more abrupt shift from neoclassicism to the heterogeneous eruptions of romanticism[1]—is relevant to a fuller understanding of modernism. In relation to nineteenth-century realism-naturalism, modernism manifests itself in a rather complex fashion, displaying an evolutionary aspect of more gradual innovation and departure from realist conventions and values, as well as displaying more radical proclivities, which at the height of such experimentation often calls for the overthrow of mimeticism altogether. It is useful to understand modernism's emergence and consolidation, therefore, from the perspective of both predominant traditions of historical literary evolution.

There is a substantial transition period between the initial stirring of modernism in the latter part of the nineteenth century, which many now date from between 1850 to 1870—specifically, in the work of Baudelaire and Flaubert and in Matthew Arnold's celebrated lectures on "modernity," as well as, slightly later, in Rimbaud and Nietzsche—and its most authoritative presence around the time between the two world wars, often referred to as "high modernism," as even more distinctive forms of literary expression gain fuller public attention. Accompanying the more aggressive aspects of modernism's revolutionary eruptions, therefore, is a much longer evolutionary trend that builds throughout the second half of the nineteenth century. Even earlier, however, romanticism's abiding interest in the psychological dimension of the human constitution—which effectively serves to finish the work of the renaissance and the enlightenment, to extend the "autonomous thinking subject" as consolidated in the triumph of the European middle class that consequently comes to regard itself capable not only of self-definition but of psychological individualization—signals a prelude to what later becomes a marked tendency to differentiate between multiple dimensions of "reality": outer vs. inner, public vs. private, and, eventually, con-

---

1. See especially Ronald Paulson, "Goya and the Spanish Revolution," in *Representations of Revolution (1789–1820)* (New Haven: Yale University Press, 1983), 286–387, in relation to Spain.

scious vs. unconscious. Perhaps as much as any other factor, the hegemonic dispositions of late-nineteenth-century middle-class culture very
much aware of its own modernity motivates dissenting responses to
what is progressively understood as an ideology of "completeness" and
a growing cultural-aesthetic impasse between bourgeois society and a
new mode of art and artist, succinctly characterized by Luis Cernuda in
"La gloria del poeta":

> Oye sus marmóreos preceptos
> Sobre lo útil, lo normal y lo hermoso;
> Oyeles dictar la ley al mundo, acotar el amor, dar canon
>   a la belleza inexpresable,
> Mientras deleitan sus sentidos con altavoces delirantes;
> Contempla sus extraños cerebros
> Intentando levantar, hijo a hijo, un complicado edificio
>   de arena. [. . .]
> Esos son [. . .]
> Los seres con quienes muero a solas.[2]

> Listen to their marmoreal precepts
> On the useful, the normal and the beautiful
> Listen to them dictate the law to the world, limit love, canonize
>   inexpressible beauty,
> While they delight their senses with delirious loudspeakers;
> Contemplate their strange brains
> Trying to raise, child by child, a complicated edifice
>   of sand. [. . .]
> Those are the ones [. . .]
> The beings with whom I die alone.

Eysteinsson's characterization of the "interruption" of realism as modernism's fundamental aesthetic principle (202–3) implies that modernist art—and as Cernuda here laments—can never achieve complete autonomy from the dominant tradition of realism. Thus, it should not be
surprising that, even as the more radical aspects of modernist art continue to attract critical attention, those zealous endeavors invariably fall

2. *La realidad y el deseo*, ed. Miguel J. Flys (Madrid: Castalia, 1982), 117.

short of stated or implied goals. Modernism is a multivalent movement whose aesthetic projects range from the relatively modest to the openly experimental. Nevertheless—position papers and manifestos notwithstanding—the conventions and ideology of realism remain the primal scene from which modernist views of new dimensions of the human constitution begin.

The conflicts within modernism itself also underscore its incapacity to realize the more radical forms of expression that many had envisioned, which suggests that modernism is perhaps more succinctly characterized in an aesthetic sense as adaptive, rather than independent, of realism and that divergences in expressiveness are better characterized as degrees of departure—that is, *nonessential* differences—from such norms. The challenge for criticism of the early contemporary period—and this is especially the case in a Spanish context—is to resist the temptation to focus on what are often spectacular avant-garde failures and instead to embrace a more extensive milieu of modernist texts. As Richard Murphy has examined at length, what often parade as comprehensive accounts of the avant-garde are almost invariably quite limited in scope, the most egregious example being Bürger's influential treatise premised almost entirely on dada/surrealism and largely ignoring the remaining preponderance of the avant-garde, much of which does not conform to his thesis. Ironically, the greatest difference between the approaches to the fragmented history of early contemporary Spanish literature, owing to the prominence of the literary generation, and attempts to theorize the avant-garde is not their scope or their approaches to literary history but simply the fact that the Spanish avant-garde continues to be considered inconsequential while other European forms of "national" expression are postulated as decisive. Both "traditions" are better served by acknowledging that nationally defined movements belong to a more inclusive phenomenon.

As Richard Sheppard has noted, it is also less productive to approach modernism in terms of overly specific "characteristics" which may or may not be evident in given varieties of modernist writing.[3] Similar prob-

3. Sheppard, "The Problematics of European Modernism," 2.

lems have arisen in criticism of the baroque and romanticism, which many scholars have long considered to be overburdened by a bewildering array of often contradictory "defining features."[4] Since the critical focus on modernism has also emphasized the particular, the continuing attractiveness of nation-centered approaches is understandable, as is the fact that few Spanish critics have been interested in linking Spanish writing of the early contemporary period to a transnational context. Nevertheless, the tremendous flowering of writing in Spain from before 1898 to 1936—that is, precisely during the plenitude of modernism elsewhere in Europe—demands to be approached with greater conceptual rigor, as part of a multidimensional, multinational phenomenon.

An "aesthetics of interruption" is also suggestive of the incapacity of modernist form to sustain itself without recourse to wider structure, a sustaining ideological context that situates it in a quest for a "better" modernity while it grapples with the conventions of realism, the mimetic tradition that has prefigured it. A significant impetus for an awareness of structure emerges from early-century theories of semiotics (Peirce, Saussure) that consolidate preexisting notions (as early as the eighteenth century, e.g., Edmund Burke) that language is a convention-determined construction. The emergence of semiotics as an instrument of literary appraisal (Russian Formalism, Jakobson)—and early seminal tracts proposing that modernism is about the creation of myth (Eliot), another type of structure, or the abandonment of historicity-temporality in favor of "spatial form," a synchronic structure (Frank)—serves to advance the emergence of a formalist aesthetics, the most influential expression of which is Anglo-American "New Criticism." During the middle decades of the twentieth century, a modernist canon is established primarily on the authority of the concept of the literary work as a discrete, autonomous structure, or "verbal icon" (Wimsatt). The momentary tizzy of "synchronic structuralism" (Barthes, Levi-Strauss, Lacan, Todorov, et al.) quickly defers to a much easier-to-accept "poststructuralism," a loose version of Derridean "philosophical deconstruction" that ensures

4. See Lovejoy, "On the Discrimination of Romanticisms"; Wellek, "The Concept of 'Romanticism.'"

the preservation of the "interpretive imperative" of the New Criticism (Miller, Hartman) while replacing its iconophilic bent with a severe form of iconoclasm (De Man). This continuation of such a formalist agenda gives rise over the last two decades to diverse feminist, "new historicist," neo-Marxist, and "cultural" criticism that as it has largely succeeded in supplanting formalism also has advanced the concept of postmodernism, at the expense of the modernist canon. The seemingly unassailable status of any number of modernist masters has been diminished to at least some degree by their alleged or actual associations with rightist politics, sympathies, or beliefs with which formalist criticism never concerned itself.

Early semiotics in the context of modernist production of literary signs stops well short of endorsing the post-structuralist depiction of literary expression as a "free-play of signifiers." Referentiality, or at least a hybrid form of it, is pivotal to the goals of all forms of modernist expression in that signs are not considered ends in themselves but rather the means to achieve fuller expressive meaning—whether univocal and precise as in Pound's imagism or extended and seemingly indeterminate in the language of surrealism. For this reason Charles Sanders Peirce's tripartite configuration of a semiotic order—based on his concepts of "symbol," "icon," "index" and strongly premised on degrees of referentiality, in contrast to the solitary linguistic minimal unit of Saussure, "the sign," which has dominated contemporary semiotics and whose more recent proponents have been generally unconcerned with the question of referentiality—is more advantageous in providing a structural basis for approaching the multivalent aesthetic agenda of modernism. Peirce's "symbol" is analogous to Saussure's "sign" since the symbol's status and meaning is fully conventional. The "icon" or "natural" sign, which present-day orthodox semiotics does not recognize (see especially Eco; Barthes is the notable exception),[5] achieves its meaning by virtue of a comparison, which involves reference to an extra-linguistic source. The

5. See especially Umberto Eco, *A Theory of Semiotics* (Bloomington: University of Indiana Press, 1979); Roland Barthes, *Image, Music, Text*, trans. Stephen Heath (New York: Hill and Wang, 1977), is the notable exception.

"index" indicates the proximity, direction, or location of its referent. Demonstratives and personal pronouns are linguistic indexes, yet also included in this category are a variety of physical objects as well as visual and/or sonorous phenomena—weathervanes are indexes of the presence of wind, thunder of lightning, smoke of fire, and other indexes are fingerprints, some types of photographs, and so on. The index is thus a special instance of representation that has an intimate relationship with various domains of referentiality. Without intending to join a debate about the legitimacy or illegitimacy of Peirce's system that, certainly among contemporary semioticians, does not seem to hold much currency, I do believe that such an ordering of "signs" does, indeed, correspond to the understanding of a great many modernists who are deeply concerned with questioning the boundaries between conventional representation and more immediate and direct forms of expression for which the Saussurean model does not account. It is thus not inappropriate to understand modernist aesthetics from the perspective of the succinct formal grid provided by Peirce, whatever the current thinking about the "nature" of signs happens to be.

All varieties of modernist expression are challenging a representational paradigm that dominates European literature and art for four hundred years, the perspectival model, that is, what an autonomous free-thinking subject, one pair of eyes, perceives situated in a specific space-time and from a specific distance. The vogue of impressionism in the late nineteenth century presages the limitations of subject-centered representation. Among many examples is Monet's series of the Rouen Cathedral (1892), in which the artist believes it necessary to render, on multiple canvases, acts of vision under a variety of conditions of empirical lighting, to express the greater fullness of a subject that a single perspective is inadequate to convey. This is a prelude soon thereafter to cubism's overturning of perspective to refute long-held aesthetic opinions that painting is strictly a spatial medium, whereas poetry, literature, is by "nature" temporal.[6] Cubist paintings are not projected from a single

6. See G. E. Lessing, *Laocoön: An Essay on the Limits of Painting and Poetry*, trans. Edward Allen McCormick (Baltimore: Johns Hopkins University Press, 1984).

point of view at one precise moment, but rather require the viewer to re-assimilate an apparently fragmented object or landscape in the imagina-tion and thus to convert the previously instantaneous activity of viewing into a type of "narrative." Vision cannot occur as a discrete act; rather, referentiality is achieved primarily through the retrieval and reconstruc-tion of the painting's subject in an inner, mental realm, that also be-comes a meta-artistic parody of mimesis.[7] The cubist painting demands a "doubled" reality since the viewing subject does not simply receive a pictorial content but also must reassemble the painting in more familiar, referential, conventional terms in order to see it fully.

Analogously, the most typical modernist literature challenges the temporality of writing. Eliot's defense of Joyce's *Ulysses* in "Ulysses, Or-der, and Myth" critiques the realist-naturalist novel's incapacity to con-front the degradations of a chaotic modern order that Joyce supplements by providing it with a mythic structure.[8] Joyce's novel is not situated in time or history but in a superior structure, the Homeric myths that un-derpin European culture and provide a sense of order that the exter-nal world cannot do. Eliot's decisive influence on subsequent criticism is epitomized in Joseph Frank's "Spatial Form in Modern Literature," which touts Eliot's capacity to suspend the temporality of language, and thus to interrupt "the process of individual reference temporarily until the entire pattern of internal references can be apprehended as a unity."[9] Reading a modernist text, analogous to the viewing of a classical paint-ing, effects a "transformation of the historical imagination into myth—an imagination for which time does not exist" (60). Forty years later Jameson represents the modernist sensibility

> as a fragmentation of the psyche and of its world that opens up the semi-autonomous and henceforth compartmentalized spaces of lived time over against clock time, bodily or perceptual experience over against ra-

---

7. See Johanna Drucker, *Theorizing Modernism: Visual Art and the Critical Tradition* (New York: Columbia University Press, 1994), 46–53.

8. T. S. Eliot, "Ulysses, Order, and Myth," *Dial* 75 (1923): 480–83.

9. Joseph Frank, "Spatial Form in Modern Literature," in *The Widening Gyre: Crisis and Mastery in Modern Literature* (New Brunswick: Rutgers University Press, 1963), 13.

tional and instrumental consciousness, a realm of "originary" or creative
language over against the daily practice of a degraded practical speech
[. . .] and of the growing independence of the various senses from one
another—in particular the separation of the eye from the ear.[10]

This, in effect, is a succinct conceptual restatement of Eliot's early formulation of what the new art is about. What changes is the view that the
"passionate private languages" of modernism are innocent. Upon "en-
tering the field of force of the real social world [they] take on a [. . .]
wholly unsuspected power" which, in the aftermath of world political
events left "many of them quite genuinely shocked to discover the things
for which the words really stood" (Fables 177).

Modernists tended to be "anti-liberal" that is, political rightists or
leftists (or sympathizers) who had lost faith in the "democratic center."
The pervasive aggressiveness in modernist expression—whether by a fascist Ezra Pound or a Stalinist Rafael Alberti—is a function of the need to
create a new model of being in the world. Integral to the affirmation of
a "second reality," invariably conceived as superior to the middle-class
version, is the giving over of oneself to unconventional forces. Force expresses itself in a strongly willful, active aspect, frequently in an exalted, aggressive consciousness dedicated to refashioning the literary, and
sometimes social, reality in which he/she is obliged to reside. Yet equally
prominent is a corollary aspect that ascribes agency to supra-personal,
telluric, or historical forces against which personal will is largely ineffec-
tual. Modernists participate in a literary agenda that accommodates both
the *fabbro*, the willful maker, a craftsman of alternative "worlds," and the
visionary *vates*, who seems to occupy transcendent perspectives. The collapse of the bourgeois medium of mimetic, empirical space cedes to the
production of a meta-literary "space," not a space at all in any conventional sense of the word, but an artistic substitute where the personal
struggles to express new understandings of subjective positions are situated. Since all modernist production is to some degree meta-literary, the
development and evolution of this phenomenon is central to any account

10. Jameson, *Fables of Aggression*, 14.

of modernism. Spain is no exception, and meta-literariness extends to all modernist works in all genres, indeed, intensifying as the early twenti-eth century progresses. It most certainly includes most of the writers tra-ditionally identified with the early-century literary generations as well as many others. The realist concept of a unified reality to which the writer must confine the scope of art is progressively rejected.

Mature expressions of this phenomenon—via a type of poetics—are offered by, if we are to believe Dámaso Alonso, the so-called tradition-minded talents of the generation of "1927." Instructive in this regard are Luis Cernuda's "Palabras ante una lectura" (1935), his introduction to the first edition of La realidad y el deseo, and private correspondence in 1928 between Pedro Salinas and Jorge Guillén regarding the forthcoming appearance of the first edition of Cántico. The attitudes revealed here un-derscore the artificiality of generational groupings since their aesthetic-ideological differences are quite sharp. Cernuda's often difficult per-sonality, his public homosexuality, and his blistering attacks, in essays and/or in his later poems, against Alonso, Aleixandre, and Salinas clash sharply with the idea of a "generación de la amistad" and the view of a homogenized, gentlemanly, professorial, even conservative group of ar-tistic colleagues and friends.

In a letter of 1928 to Juan Guerrero, Cernuda proclaims that "es cier-to: hay una segunda realidad. ¡Tanto como yo la he deseado! Mas ahora sólo tengo la forma. Si llego a poseerla algún día" ("it's true: there is a second reality. Just like I have desired it! But now I only have the form. If only I could possess it one day").[11] "Palabras ante una lectura" recounts Cernuda's experience in the first edition of La realidad y el deseo, his in-capacity to resist an all-consuming force, likened to Moses' experience of the burning bush, "un poder daimónico" ("a daimonic power"), to which he ascribes an aggressive agency in his life and art: "la poesía [. . .] no es sino la expresión de esa oscura fuerza daimónica que rige el mundo" ("poetry [. . .] is but the expression of this obscure daimonic

11. James Valender, "Cuatro cartas de Luis Cernuda a Juan Guerrero (1928–1929)," Cuadernos Hispanoamericanos, no. 315 (1976): 53.

force that rules the world").[12] His experience with this force brings him
to the conclusion that "la realidad exterior es un espejismo" ("exterior
reality is a mirage," 872) and that he finds himself ultimately in the role
of mediator between antagonistic realities. The poet is a type of daimon,
a creature who inhabits the ordinary world yet who has periodic contact
with this "poder indefinido y vasto que maneja nuestros destinos" ("undefinable and vast power that controls our destinies," 874). In a variation
on Eliot, Cernuda understands that his mission is to formulate a personal myth that embodies the elite status and desolate understanding of the
modern—that is, the modernist—poet. Anecdotal, temporal life experiences become occasions to shape "myth," a "segunda realidad" far superior to the bourgeois phantoms with whom he is condemned to reside (recall "los seres con quienes muero a solas"). Cernuda's poetry is
strongly meta-literary in that it is concerned with revealing an alternative
reality that the bourgeois cannot acknowledge.

A quite different attitude finds expression in the first edition of
Jorge Guillén's *Cántico* as succinctly expressed in Pedro Salinas's private
assessment in a letter written slightly before the volume went to press.
Guillén's poetry exemplifies the willful act of fashioning

> Un mundo. [. . .] Un mundo como no lo tiene hoy nadie. Tuyo, inven-
> tado, erigido con materiales nuevos e intactos. Mejor, materiales cono-
> cidos pero pasados por algo lustral, por un medio clarificador. [. . .] Ni
> sentimentalismo, ni misticismo, ni realismo. [. . .] Mundo selecto, es-
> cogido. [. . .] No del verso, no de la técnica, no como creen los necios,
> sino del cosmos nuevo, de la vida en poesía.[13]

> A world. [. . .] A world like nobody has today. Yours, invented, con-
> structed with new and intact materials. Better still, familiar materials
> but passed through something lustral, through a clarifying medium.
> [. . .] Not sentimentality, or mysticism, or realism [. . .] A select, chosen
> world. [. . .] Not of verse, or of technique, not like the idiots believe, but
> of a new cosmos, of a world of poetry.

12. Luis Cernuda, *Prosa completa*, ed. Derek Harris and Luis Maristany (Madrid: Barral, 1975), 875.
13. Andrés Soria Olmedo, ed., *Correspondencia (1923–1951). Pedro Salinas / Jorge Guillén*
(Barcelona: Tusquets, 1992), 90.

In sharp contrast to Cernuda's impotent attempts to deal with a force that dominates his existence, Guillén's poetry is produced by a much different force, an active, aggressive consciousness, in order to bring forth an alternative "world" also incomprehensible to the horde of "necios" incapable of understanding that aesthetics ("la técnica") is but a means to display an elite intellect, a qualitatively different type of dominant subjectivity that has fashioned a "cosmos nuevo" by means of art.

While these poets are dedicated to similar goals—the elaboration of a superior meta-literary reality—the means of production are exactly opposite. Force is a fashioning tool for Guillén, whereas for Cernuda it is the summoning agent of a poet subservient to its demands. What they share in common, however, is the idea that force is responsible for the emergence of a "new world," a "new reality," and a "new man," new subjective models. Generally speaking, Cernuda's experience of daimonic power forces him into greater contact with the desolate, public world of ordinary reality against which he incessantly recoils, while Guillén remains faithful to his elaborations of a superior, elitist, private world that rarely portrays him in social settings. More significant than the fact that Cernuda and Guillén also reflect political attitudes that make them more than simply "liberal" or "conservative" in the conventional sense is that these attitudes reflect differences in the more important modernist enterprise of superseding bourgeois subjectivity. To refer to the general title of Pablo Neruda's poetry of this time, *Residencia en la tierra*, modernists, indeed, tend to regard themselves more as "residents" of the planet with alienated, divided allegiances rather than as "citizens" loyal to their ordinary historical circumstance. The modernist's allegiance is firstly to his/her "ideological" intuitions of the expansive and extended experience of a superior alternative reality, or, falling short of that exalted goal, at least to a more truthful exposition of the insufficiencies and ugliness of such an existence. As I shall discuss below, the positive agenda of modernism that makes it more than the expression of ingenious "pointless rites" is the bringing forth of new, unconventional, and antibourgeois models of subjectivity.

Before turning in earnest to this issue of the "Spanish tradition" in the context of modernism, it is necessary to examine other aspects of modernist expressive possibility that present more formidable interpretive challenges. If an "aesthetics of interruption" may be characterized by "meta-literary effects," one of the more intensified expressive pathways of such an aesthetic is profitably characterized as a type of iconic, or "hieroglyphic," expression (Peirce's second type of sign), which historically and generically finds greater expressive strength in the poetry of the later 1920s and '30s. Although it is not essentially different from earlier expressions, the hieroglyphic mode adapts conventional language to a new context in which traditional referentiality has apparently been rendered inoperative. Readers are confronted with syntagms that, while they form recognizable phrases and sentences containing subjects, verbs, and objects, initially convey little in the way of conventional meaning. Like the viewer of a cubist painting, the reader is required to assume a much more active role, this time in order to decipher what on the surface may seem to be an incomprehensible jumble. Language, however, continues to function in the same manner as conventional, public modes of speech and writing. What is significantly different is that there is a wholesale displacement of conventional signifiers from signifieds. This means that the modernist is embracing not a concept of "free play," but rather an aesthetic position that demands an imaginative reorientation on the reader's part in order to discover—that is, to decipher—the code or pattern of signification that will allow the structure of conventional language to function in its accustomed sense, albeit in a new referential context of an "inner space" or "geography." The difference between the hieroglyphic mode and meta-literary expression is that language becomes even more hermetic in the sense that the reader's disorientation is also "geographic."

Indeed, modernist hieroglyphics typically features the creation of an unconventional if identifiable "geography" or "world," more extensive and more visually elaborated articulations of meta-literariness that often express themselves, if not as a "cosmos nuevo" then perhaps a "cosmos *extraño.*" The location of all such spaces or geographies is invariably a private dimension of consciousness, or unconsciousness. The hieroglyphic mode, therefore, represents an intensification of earlier intuitions of a "second reality" or "private world" because it often not only confuses the conventional reader at the level of communication but also situates him/her in a bewildering alternate locale often described in detailed physical terms. The most ingenious manifestation of this phenomenon in a Spanish context is in the poetry of Vicente Aleixandre, whose elaborate geographic circumstances in his production of the 1920s and '30s are actually psychic locales from which sounds, images, and words are portrayed as being communicated to the poet from an unsuspected and unidentified source. Even more interestingly, the poet himself assumes a role that parallels that of the uninformed reader and thus presents himself in a disoriented and confused posture in relation to this strange discourse that he must also decipher with great difficulty. Beginning with *Pasión de la tierra*, Aleixandre initiates an extended dialog with an incomprehensible yet personalized creative-destructive force that is also credited with teaching him a new language in "El amor no es relieve" ("Love Is Not a Relief"): "Tu compañía es un abecedario" ("Your company is a reading primer," 96).[14] His inner geography acquires "relief," that is, a spatiality that is analogous to conventional space, in proportion to his capacity to extract meaning from unconventional expressions embedded in what is often portrayed as a domain of planeness. The structure of language is the same whether it refers to external or internal "geographies." The difficulty lies in adapting the conventional system to a hitherto unsuspected set of meanings. Thus, even in this apparently autonomous "second reality," there remains a continuing dependence on the "ordinary" system, albeit in extraordinary circumstances.

The hieroglyphic mode marks the dismantling of conventional generic divisions as the realms of the visual and the verbal—eye/ear and space/time—acquire a different "nature" that nevertheless reveals a hid-

14. Vicente Aleixandre, *Obras completas* (Madrid: Aguilar, 1968), 96.

den, secret order and system of conventions. Among numerous Spanish expressions of such an awareness is Rafael Alberti's "Los ángeles
sonámbulos" ("The Sleep-Walking Angels") in *Sobre los ángeles*, where the
eyes and the ears, organs of human perception / consciousness, acquire
autonomy and assume an altogether different function: "Ojos invisibles, grandes, atacan. [. . .] / [. . .] oídos se agrandan contra el pecho.
/ De escayola, fríos, / bajan a la garganta" ("Huge, invisible eyes attack
[. . .] / [. . .] ears aggrandize themselves against my breast. / Cold, plas-
tered, they descend to the throat," 356).[15] Previously complementary, eye
and ear now become antagonists that assume a new function at a different site of production, the throat, a locale of involuntary utterances
that speak to the reality of both a new artistic sensibility and a different
understanding of new subjective dimensions. As suggested in the idea
of the hieroglyph, this mode of expression also marks an intensification of visuality as symbolic conventions are adapted to new contexts. It
thus presents a certain analogy with the Peircian model of semiotics—in
contrast to the Saussurean model that features only strictly conventional signs—in that symbolic expression acquires a striking iconicity. As in
Peirce's understanding of the icon, meaning is produced by means of a
comparison. This comparison is effected, however, by the conscious efforts of the reader to translate one conventional system—ordinary language—to a new form of "nature." Rather than a comparison of signs in
relation to an external order, however, the comparison is undertaken in
the vividly pictorial context of an "inner" geography.

The concept of hieroglyphics, nevertheless, is also relevant to more
rationally articulated modes of expression, for example, the imagism of
Ezra Pound and colleagues, which is developed at length in Pound's appropriation of Ernest Fenollosa's idiosyncratic understanding of Chinese writing in *The Chinese Written Character as a Medium for Poetry*. Chinese
writing is conceived as a type of picture writing and not an expression of
a convention-determined system. This provides an analogy for the type

15. Rafael Alberti, *Poesía* (1924–1967) (Madrid: Aguilar, 1972).

of expression valued by Pound, a return to a primitive and much more direct, verb-oriented system that lies in sharp contrast to what he considers a degenerated Western writing dominated by the copula "to be" that has drained language of its original active, action-oriented role. In Pound's imagism there is an active disassociation of the visual and the verbal. Words lose their association with sound and become more fully related to images, not the copied images of nineteenth-century realism, but unique and more valuable "primary apparitions." The desire becomes to transcend the phantom reality embodied in the copy premises of conventional representation. In the context of his "generation," Jorge Guillén, in a reminiscence in El *argumento de la obra*, invokes Pound's imagism to characterize, in his opinion, the dominant mode of poetic expression after World War I: "El nombre americano *imagists* podría aplicarse a cuantos escritores de alguna imaginación escribían acá o allá por los años 20" ("The American term *imagists* could apply to a number of writers of some imagination that were writing here and there during the 20s") because his milieu was interested in a "realidad [. . .] no reduplicada en copias sino recreada de manera liberrima" ("reality [. . .] not duplicated in copies but created in the freest manner," 20).

Arguably the most extreme if nonetheless logical progression of the aesthetic movement away from mimesis in modernism expresses itself as an intention to transcend the mediation of language altogether. In this mode, the intention is to surpass the conventional circumstance of literary language as a secondary or borrowed medium from the structure that produces public discourse in the form of spoken language. The goal is to break through to a primary mode of communication that can only be described as an epiphanic mode of "presence," the moment when creative intention or thought corresponds exactly to written expression. This is the expressive mode most often associated with surrealist "automatic writing," which is purported to arise without the intervention of consciousness and exterior reality in order to communicate directly with an "under-reality" understood, again—as modernists typically understand the "second reality"—to be a superior domain. Indeed, Rosalind

Krauss considers surrealist automatism as the principal aesthetic means to convey an even more important existential-ideological tenet, that literary presence is inseparable from the phenomenon of the experience-expression of the presence of "full being":

> Automatism may be writing, but it is not, like the rest of the written signs of Western culture, representation. It is a kind of presence, the direct presence of the artist's inner self. This sense of automatism as a manifestation of the innermost self, and thus not representation at all, is also contained within Breton's description of automatic writing as "spoken thought." Thought is not a representation but is that which is utterly transparent to the mind, immediate to experience, untainted by the distance and exteriority of signs.[16]

However, Krauss's further association of automatic writing as analogous to photography—as with the production of fingerprints, photographic images are manifested "automatically" on a revelatory medium "as an imprint or transfer off the real [. . .] a photochemically processed trace causally connected to that thing in the world to which it refers" (110)—parallels Peirce's classification of some types of photographs as indexes, that is, not actual "presences" but rather "traces of presences," indicators that lead or point in a direction toward a referent. Thus, arguably, the most revolutionary aspect of modernist expression, had long been anticipated by Peircian semiotics. This analogy, however, is important in completing the semiotic structure into which modernist aesthetic positions may be situated as well as to associate such positions with an ideology guided by the desire to formulate new models of greatly expanded subjective possibility. The desire for presence—typically envisioned as epiphanies or secular versions of "eternity" where conventional time-space is nullified—becomes a progressively more important theme of modernism even though for many such a possibility may be only a distant nostalgia (Cernuda, Alberti) or tragically conceived as an impossibility from the outset (Lorca). At a thematic level if not as a lit-

16. Rosalind Krauss, "The Photographic Conditions of Surrealism," in *The Originality of the Avant-Garde and Other Modernist Myths* (Cambridge, Mass.: MIT Press, 1986), 96.

eral aesthetic option, the question of presence in relation to existence, or "being," is fundamental. It is here again where Spanish contributions to modernism in the development of new subjective models intersect explicitly with Europe.

It is also here where the weight of the "Spanish tradition" in Peninsular critical thinking makes such a thesis most difficult to advance. It will be necessary, therefore, to examine this issue in some detail, from a less isolationist perspective, in order to suggest that for early contemporary writers it is an informed consciousness of the "Spanish tradition" that allows Spain to participate in the "positive" agenda of modernism, as a true partner and not as another "imported" phenomenon. To varying degrees, the case continues to be made by many Hispanists (see, more recently, Parr) that every Continental literary period from the renaissance onward is in some sense "foreign" to Spain, that is, distant from the evolving discourse of modernity in the rest of Europe while ever faithful to its own "unique" tradition, perhaps even more so in the early contemporary period.[17] The need to stress Spanish national values and differences becomes almost a requirement as Francoism makes itself their defender as well as a vigorous repudiator of internationalism. The postwar climate for literary criticism is thus not favorable for adopting critical arguments that align Spanish literature with a wider European milieu.

Paralleling Laín Entralgo's and Alonso's advocacy of nation-centered literary generations during the late forties are "uniqueness" positions in Golden Age studies that emerge in earnest slightly thereafter. The most exemplary of such arguments is Alexander A. Parker's seminal essay on the *comedia*, which establishes the direction for early modern criticism for decades. Although certainly well intentioned, Parker's thesis is that Spanish plays from this period require special guidelines to be appreciated by contemporary audiences: theme is more important than action or

17. See, more recently, James Parr, "A Modest Proposal: That We Use Alternatives to Borrowing (Renaissance, Baroque, Golden Age) and Leveling (Early Modern) in Periodization," *Hispania* 84 (2001): 406–16.

"character drawing," which as a consequence makes "realistic verisimili-
tude" irrelevant; and principles of poetic justice and dramatic causality,
used in plot construction in a manner that clarifies the moral purpose of
these plays, assure closure (706–7).[18] Reading early modern Spanish literature is thus a much more cumbersome activity than reading plays from
the rest of Europe, which have achieved a high degree of realism. Europe
has been able to "eliminate" conventions in order to make its literature
seem more "natural." Spanish literature, however, requires the reader to
learn a complicated set of special conventions that in turn imply that such
works are more "primitive." The representational values of Europe have
achieved a level of realistic expressiveness that makes reading effortless
by comparison.

Early modern Spanish literature, according to this line of reasoning, is burdensome and overloaded while it also lacks something fundamental. Although there are many objections to Parker's methodology,
the most significant is that he is making a comparison based on the values of the late-nineteenth- and early-twentieth-century stage, whose primary emphasis is, indeed, realistic "character building" grounded main-
ly in psychology. The standard explanation for such glaring differences
is that Golden Age Spain is a theocentric culture still largely medieval in
outlook and thus incapable of portraying the "new man" of the renaissance, whose secular values have liberated him and allowed him to consider himself an autonomous "free thinker." This still relatively new yet
decisive shift in Europe that creates the early versions of the "autonomous thinking subject," therefore, is alien to Spain, still dedicated to the
idea that full human subjectivity can never be achieved; the human subject is invariably less than "full." The possibility of fullness exists as a
consequence of an intimate association with a structure of salvation that
leads to a "second," incomparably superior reality that has been divinely
instituted. Parker's thesis is thus grounded on the concept of a funda-

18. A. A. Parker, "The Spanish Drama of the Golden Age: A Method of Analysis and
Interpretation," in *The Great Playwrights*, vol. 1, ed. Eric Bentley (New York: Doubleday, 1970),
706–7.

mental "lack" in characters not authorized to function as "subjects" by a theocentric ideology.

Yet Golden Age literature is full of characters who are free thinkers. A much simpler explanation for the differences between Spain and a more secular-minded Europe is that whereas Europe seems dedicated to portraying secular subjectivity, the "new man," in a rather positive light, Spanish writers by and large disapprove and dedicate themselves to critiquing such an attitude. This suggests, therefore, that the differences between Spanish and European literary characters arise on both sides of the Pyrenees from a strong awareness that this "new man" exists, the contrast being that for Spanish writers he is understood in negative, indeed monstrous, terms, whereas in other parts of Europe he is much more likely to be conceived of as heroic.

An alternative hypothesis, therefore, begins by revisiting the modern era from the point of view that Spanish ideological differences with Europe promote what all ideology dedicates itself to advancing: the notion that a specific point of view is not simply one of many but rather "better" than others. The "Spanish point of view" does not merely present itself to its true believers, but also replies to European positions, dialectically. Spanish positions are not "alien" from Europe—in early modern literature or in subsequent periods—but rather in theme and content, and especially in many of its greatest literary and artistic achievements, are taking informed issue with the direction toward which this "new man" is leading European culture. What is important in a discussion of modernism is that the Spanish positions throughout modern literary history resist the evolutions of the European "autonomous thinking subject," whose hegemonic triumph in the nineteenth century becomes one of the principal motivating factors for the emergence of modernism, which, in the aftermath of over three hundred years of protracted Spanish engagement with this issue, also begins to reject the autonomous thinking subject. The early contemporary period, perhaps ironically, witnesses the return of the rest of Europe to a discourse that in Spain had been ongoing since the Golden Age. This also serves to explain why signifi-

cant numbers of writers from one of the least "modernized" nations of
Europe can enter into modernism as integral partners in what ultimately
becomes another struggle to bring forth a *new* "new man." Modernism
can, indeed, be viewed from a variety of perspectives, significant among
which is Europe's rapprochement with a long "tradition" of consistent
Spanish attitudes toward this central theme in its agenda.

A brief account of representative Spanish viewpoints throughout
the modern era concerning the insufficiencies inherent in the European
"autonomous thinking subject" will serve to illustrate this idea more fully. A quite significant contribution to European cultural studies over the
last quarter century—initially propounded by Michel Foucault and refined thereafter by Timothy J. Reiss—has contrasted a premodern epistemological model with attitudes that emerged subsequently and became
dominant by the nineteenth century. According to Foucault, the decisive
turn from a medieval, theocentric mode of understanding premised on
analogical thinking toward the "discourse of modernity" based on de-
ductive reasoning begins in the sixteenth century. For premodern understanding, which Reiss characterizes as a "discursive exchange within the
world,"[19] recourse to the referential world is fundamental to the production of any type of certain knowledge, which is effected only with great
difficulty. Foucault characterizes this analogical mechanism as an unstable, almost interminable process in which

> resemblance never remains stable within itself; it can be fixed only if it re-
> fers back to another similitude, which then, in turn, refers to others; each
> resemblance, therefore, has value only from the accumulation of all the
> others, and the whole world must be explored if even the slightest of anal-
> ogies is to be justified and finally take on the appearance of certainty.[20]

In sharp contrast to an organizing principle of "sameness" is the modern system centered around a new principle of "identity and difference,"
which Reiss more succinctly characterizes as a "reasoning practice upon

---

19. Timothy J. Reiss, *The Discourse of Modernism* (Ithaca: Cornell University Press,
1982), 30.
20. Michel Foucault, *The Order of Things* (New York: Vintage, 1970), 30.

the world" (30), a mode of ratiocination in which the human mind frees itself from referentiality in order to perform operations upon the external world. This fundamental epistemological shift allows for the emergence of the intellectual structure responsible for constituting "modernity"—that is, its successive redefinitions from the sixteenth to the twentieth centuries—via a revolutionary expansion of knowledge.

Fundamental to Foucault's and Reiss's concept of a discourse of modernity is autonomous, "free-thinking" subjectivity. The movement away from dependence on the experiential world toward an outlook in which the "world" becomes the vehicle by which to perform intellectual operations upon it is impossible without the construction of a subjective position aware of a distinctness and separation from one's physical circumstance, in the classic statement of renaissance art theorist Leon Battista Alberti, that there is "a definite distance for seeing."[21] In art and literature, the "superior" imitative models from the renaissance onward are directly attributable to the invention of one-point perspective, which brings forth a "new man" whose subjectivity allows him to use signs in a different way. If premodern representation depends upon, as Foucault says, "the sign and its likeness [. . .] nature and the world [. . .] intertwine[d] with one another to infinity, [to] form for those who can read it, one vast single text" (34), the "new artist," like his counterparts in other areas, becomes an active manipulator of signs that belong to him as the consequence of a much expanded imagination-consciousness that allows him to produce a multitude of autonomous versions of the world.

While Spanish writers reveal an intimate familiarity with the values of the discourse of modernity, their responses to the variations on European representational themes throughout the modern era are less than fully accepting of it. Indeed, they are often distinguished by resistance to it, yet more importantly, by a willingness to engage, dialectically, their reservations about modern literary paradigms embodied in the ideology of autonomous subjectivity. In opposition to the "thinking subject" is a

21. Leon Battista Alberti, *On Painting*, trans. John R. Spenser (New Haven: Yale University Press, 1966), 57.

premodern "structural" model of consciousness that does not recognize
a "clear and distinct" separation from the world and that considers such
a "definite distance for seeing" as a source of error and even delusion. In
fact, the enactment of such differences in relation to the question of subjectivity constitutes the major focus of the most important early modern
Spanish masterworks—Don Quijote, La vida es sueño, El burlador de Sevilla,
the picaresque novel, and many others. All of these works feature similar situations in that the protagonists find themselves, at least initially, at
the margins of society for whatever reasons. The successful characters,
however, are able to find their way toward the social and moral mainstream, while the unsuccessful ones remain at the periphery or suffer an
even harsher fate.

Foucault's interpretation of Don Quijote, prominently featured in The
Order of Things, considers Don Quijote's madness as an embodiment of
premodern thinking, a nostalgia for an earlier time when a system of si-
militudes and resemblances guided the production of knowledge that
must now confront the windmills of an intractable, implacable reality in
which words

> are no longer anything but what they are; words wander off on their own,
> without content, without resemblance to fill their emptiness [. . .] The
> written word and things no longer resemble one another [. . .] there has
> opened up a field of knowledge in which, because of an essential rupture
> in the Western world, what has become important is no longer resem-
> blances but identities and differences. (48–50)

I believe, however, that precisely the opposite takes place in part 1
since in reading the long-discredited books of chivalry to great excess
Don Quijote incapacitates himself to engage in a discursive exchange
within the world and instead performs ludicrous reasoning practices. He
fills his imagination with words and images that have no basis in referentiality and thus alienates himself from the all-encompassing structure,
the "great text of the world," in effect, willing himself into the madness
of a self-created, subjective consciousness, the consequence of a devotion to a discourse of "difference," which leaves him without an "identi-

ty." Don Quijote parodies the new discourse of modernism by embracing values inspired in his counterparts in Europe in order to become a monstrous caricature of the type of autonomous subjectivity that Cervantes and his Spanish colleagues consider to be the foundation stone of error and delusion. As a "free-thinking subject," Don Quijote denies himself the capacity to participate in the discourse of salvation. Foucault's reading is even more infelicitous in relation to part 2, a major motivation of which is to restore the madman to sanity by having him return to the world and to remember his real name, Alonso Quijano. Only by adjusting his intellectual position can Don Quijote undertake the type of "reading" that will bring him redemption and give his life positive meaning.

Like most contemporary interpreters of Cervantes' masterpiece, Foucault's interest in Don Quijote stops at part 1. There are, however, a number of prominent Spanish characters who also begin at the alienated margins yet who do not succeed in reincorporating themselves into the mainstream. Principal among these are the pícaros (Lázaro, Buscón, Guzmán) whose names are also the titles of the books in which they relate their unhappy life stories. Like Don Quijote, the pícaro is an ingenioso, a man of wit who confides in his own free-thinking subjectivity only to outwit himself. Frequently associated with unstable watery mediums—Lázaro claims to be "remando a buen puerto" ("rowing to a safe port"), Guzmán writes his story as a galley slave, Buscón travels the sea to the New World to begin another unhappy chapter of his life—these characters delude themselves by their subjective perspectives in order to expose untenable lives built on a sea of "difference," a self-engendered discourse that keeps them at the margins.

Spanish resistance to the type of subjectivity that these characters exemplify is also prominent in the comedia. Examples abound of characters whose excesses of detached, self-absorbed thinking and imagining lead to delusional antisocial consequences. Calderón's wife murderers in El médico de su honra and El pintor de su deshonra, who seize upon flimsy circumstantial evidence to avenge imagined offenses against family honor, as well as prosperous villagers in Calderón's El alcalde de Zalamea and Lope's Villano en su rincón, who represent for practical purposes an

incipient middle class unwilling to be governed by established laws and/
or authority, are further indications of the social confusion and personal
delusion that accompany the appearance of a "new man" in Europe. The
most powerful manifestations of the monstrous consequences of "reasoning practices upon the world," however, are developed in Calderón's
La vida es sueño and Tirso's El burlador de Sevilla.

La vida es sueño parallels Don Quijote in that the "monster" Segismundo progresses from extreme marginality toward an affirmation of his
proper role in his society by means of adjustments to his understanding of the world. Made monstrous because his father, King Basilio, im-
prisoned him at birth and thus made him unable to engage himself with
the world, Segismundo finds that his considerable education is ineffec-
tive because his knowledge is groundless and therefore incapable of providing him an understanding of the all-encompassing structure with
which it needs to be integrated. Even more monstrous than Segismundo
is his father, who by means of deluded "reasoning practices"—his private, subjective determination that he can penetrate mysteries reserved
for a higher power—produces a human creature who can think as an autonomous subject only apart from a structure that requires active participation with the natural and social world. It is by means of experiences
initially understood as "dreams" that Segismundo discovers the capacity
to affirm the values of "discursive exchange within the world" and thus
to surpass his father's intellectualizations and to affirm a transcendent
structure that leads to an ultimate truth:

> Lo que está determinado
> Del cielo, y en azul tabla
> Dios con el dedo escribió,
> De quien son cifras y estampas
> Tantos papeles azules
> Que adornan letras doradas,
> Nunca mienten, nunca engañan.[22]
> (v. 3162–68)

22. Pedro Calderón de la Barca, La vida es sueño, ed. A. E. Sloman (Manchester: University of Manchester Press, 1961), v. 3162–68.

What is set in heaven,
And which is on a tablet of blue
Is written by God's finger,
From whom come the ciphers and imprints,
The many blue pages
That golden letters adorn
Never lie, never deceive.

Affirming a "better reality," Segismundo's message speaks as well to all of Europe: the "new European man" is the real monster.

Tirso's depiction of Don Juan Tenorio in El burlador de Sevilla delivers the most forceful message of all since his protagonist embodies the discourse of modernity to the fullest extent imaginable. Paying only lip service to the existence of a structure ordained by God as the proving ground of redemption, Don Juan uses his wit and intellect to commit repeated acts of treachery. God is so offended by Don Juan's unrepentant state of mind that He intervenes directly to punish an anarchic subject who threatens the entire fabric and structure of society because he embodies a different set of values. Of all the brilliant Spanish characters that could have inspired replicas by other authors only Don Juan, and spectacularly so, captivates the literary, philosophical, and psychological imagination of Europe. Part of the reason for this is because Tirso's character so closely corresponds, in his capacity for "autonomous free thinking," to values that in Europe are worthy of emulation rather than condemnation. As Europe progressively invests in the rational thinking subject, Spanish reservations about its "dark side" continue. If as Foucault describes, Europe abandons the structural model of premodern consciousness, Spain does not, yet not primarily because of a continuing resistance to secularism.

Spanish participation in the Enlightenment—represented here in Fray Benito Feijoo and Goya—extends the consistent Spanish position of dialectical opposition to the European construction of a rationalist model of autonomous subjectivity. Prominent among the topics of discussion in the Age of Reason is the nature and scope of what by mid-century is reason's most prominent counterpart, the imagination, which becomes a progressively more important topic during the eighteenth century, especially in the context of pronouncements on the nature of the sublime by influential thinkers such as Kant, in *The Critique of Judgment* and *Observations on the Feeling of the Beautiful and Sublime*, and Burke, in *A Philosophical Enquiry into the Origin of Our Ideas of the Sublime and the Beautiful*. The high valuation of the "natural sublime" by these and other thinkers is another significant occasion for the strong enhancement of autonomous subjectivity since the colossal, form-defying nature of the sublime—and the delight that is integral to its experience—is accompanied by the aggrandizement of the scope of the imagination and, therefore, of human autonomous subjectivity as well. The imagination now becomes a partner of the intellect rather than to continue in its premodern subservient role. These philosophical enhancements of the capacity for "free thinking" prepare the way for an even greater role for the imagination during romanticism. Significantly, Spanish thinkers continue to resist these enhancements and the progressively greater independence of the human subject from the referential world.

The most systematic Spanish advocate of the virtues of reason is Feijoo, who understands that his intellectual mission is to expose errors of all kinds, a primary source of which lies in the newer ideas regarding the imagination as an active, coequal partner of the intellect. The most significant source of error is the imagination and its false products: idols of the mind, ungrounded images that disengage the intellect from the wider structure of the world. Indeed, as he advocates the importance of reason, Feijoo continues to adhere to the traditional epistemological model of the "rational soul" consisting of the intellect, will, and memory. In this model, the imagination is primarily a conduit that communicates external perceptions to the understanding in order for judgments to be made. Feijoo's objection to an enhanced role for the imagination is that it separates the human subject from direct observation and experience in order to favor the represented image or idea. Thus, for example, he describes Descartes's mind as being "de una imaginación vasta y elevada"

("of a vast and elevated imagination") that "duda de todo, hasta la existencia de Dios y del mundo" ("doubts everything, even the existence of
God and the world").[23] He and others have abandoned the experiential
world and the structural model of being for the "arbitrarias ideas" ("arbitrary ideas") of the imagination. The means to avoid error is thus to
"rendirse a la experiencia, si no queremos abandonar el camino real de
la verdad; y buscar la naturaleza en sí misma, no en la engañosa imagen
que de ella forma nuestra fantasía" ("give oneself over to experience, if
we do not want to abandon the real road of truth; and to search for nature in itself, not the deceptive image of it that our fantasy forms").[24]

Feijoo's warning about the role of imaginative excess in the creation
of a new and monstrous subjectivity is echoed strongly, if eccentrically, in
Goya, whose fullest exposition on the role of the imagination in relation
to reason is found in Los caprichos, especially the celebrated self-portrait
accompanied by the phrase "El sueño de la razón produce monstruos"
("The sleep/dream of reason begets monsters").[25] This series offers
strong testimony to Goya's disenchantment with both the Enlightenment version of reason and the unchecked imagination that produces a
fragmented consciousness incapable of affirming its stability and autonomy. Goya subverts traditional epistemology by denying the understanding a role. His vision here is more than simply modern, it is "modernist"
in the sense that it decries the supremacy of the paradigm of "reasoning
practices upon the world." Like the unfortunate characters from Gold-
en Age literature whose autonomous subjectivity condemns them to ever
more severe alienation from the world, Goya as a character in a picture
book and as a person heralds the unreasonableness of a rationalist doctrine that cannot account for his lived experience. As another exemplary
instance of Spanish dialectical engagement with Europe, Goya's radical
leap into the "modern" in the process invalidates the conventional dis-

23. Fray Benito Jerónimo Feijoo y Montenegro, Obras escogidas. Biblioteca de autores españoles, vol. 56 (Madrid: Atlas, 1952), 131, 64.
24. Feijoo y Montenegro, Obras escogidas, vol. 142, 340.
25. See C. Christopher Soufas, "'Esto sí que es leer': Learning to Read Goya's Los Caprichos," Word and Image 2 (1986): 311–30, for a fuller discussion.

course of modernity. His vision is grounded in an awareness of the monstrous constitution of the autonomous European subject. At the moment of the triumph of the middle-class political revolutions, Goya does not celebrate its victories but rather heralds the inadequacy of its ideology to interpret human experience. Goya is thus a precursor to what will eventually become prominent a century later as modernists throughout Europe begin to perceive, rather belatedly in comparison to Spain, the unreasonableness of modern doctrines of subjectivity.

Spain's minimal participation in romanticism is represented by José Zorrilla's *Don Juan Tenorio*, a play often cited for its "modernity" because of its many departures from realist conventions. It nevertheless continues the Spanish tradition of resistance to European subjective models. The play, in fact, offers a brilliant reply to the now institutionalized values of European subjectivity as they related to the discourse on the sublime and the beautiful. By the mid-nineteenth century, the figure of Don Juan had been fully appropriated by Europe and had certainly captivated the collective imagination. Zorrilla presents his audience in *Don Juan Tenorio* a character who fully embodies the most salient aspects of what Kant calls the "feeling of the sublime"[26] and who is resisted and ultimately transformed by a character, the virginal and delicate Inés, who is consistently connected with the very terms that Burke uses to describe the "beautiful." Given this perspective, the play is not so much about Don Juan's improbable salvation but rather, at the level of legend and imagination where this character is most real for nineteenth-century audiences, about a redress of the imbalance between the subject values ordered around romantic concepts of the sublime and the beautiful. If the sublime affirms an aggressive, dominating, masculine form of monstrous subjectivity that fully affirms Goya's vision of the human constitution, then the antidote is certainly a strong dose of "the beautiful," a tempering element to such a self-begetting form of subjectivity, which Zorrilla provides in a play that, among other things, reaffirms the "Spanish tradition."

26. See C. Christopher Soufas, "The Sublime, the Beautiful, and the Imagination in Zorrilla's *Don Juan Tenorio*," MLN 110 (1995): 302–19.

Even toward the end of the nineteenth century, Spanish consciousness of and resistance to what is by now the fully hegemonic bourgeois
subject—that is, a mode of being that has acquired "naturalness," that
has transcended ideology and is aligned with the "objective" discours-
es of science—continues its dialectical critique. More significant than
Pardo Bazán's rebuff of the deterministic aspects of naturalism in "La
cuestión palpitante" ("The Burning Question") are the novels of Benito Pérez Galdós, whose most notable characters reaffirm the consistent
Spanish position evident since the Golden Age.[27] Whether sympathetic or not, most of Galdós's characters who persist in an attitude of performing "reasoning practices upon the world" are singularly unsuccessful. The downfall of Isidora Rufete of *La desheredada*, Ramón Villaamil of
Miau, and the merciless usurer Francisco Torquemada of the trilogy bear-
ing his name is their intellectual detachment from the world, their pro-
pensity to wrap themselves in their own isolating subjectivity that leaves
them ill-equipped to deal with the vicissitudes of their lives. Isadora's
obsession that she is a displaced heiress leads her to identify herself with
premises—quite similar to the heroines of popular novels—that guide
her progressively into self-deception and, when reality fails to conform
to her imagined idea, eventually to a dissolute life. Likewise, the unfortunate Villaamil, dismissed from his job only a couple of months before
he can collect his pension, also devises pathetic, if entertaining, mental
strategies that nevertheless lead to progressively more ungrounded fan-
tasies and, finally, suicide. The supreme materialist Torquemada does
not suffer poverty, but when a crisis arises that money cannot resolve,
the death of his son whom he had imagined to be a genius destined to
save the world, Galdós makes it clear that Torquemada becomes the victim of his own misguided self-importance, bitter and resentful toward a
world whose only meaning is a material one.

Ultimately, Galdós's characters are not tragic but, as the modern
representatives of a consistent Spanish attitude and "tradition," delud-

27. See Luisa Elena Delgado, *La imagen elusiva: lenguaje y representación en la narrativa de
Galdós* (Amsterdam: Rodopi, 1999), 11–30, for a related discussion.

ed, done in by their incapacity to acknowledge the world. The exemplary counterpoint to these characters is the servant Benina of *Misericordia*, who suffers the cruel injustice of being discharged from the family she so faithfully has served and kept together as the fortune of her mistress improves. Yet it is also clear that Benina, even though she eventually becomes a beggar, will certainly endure because she does not live exclusively in her consciousness. Like her counterparts, she is a "thinking subject," yet one who believes in other dimensions of "reality." However rich and original his characters may be, Galdós's writing at the very moment that modernism is beginning to assert itself, also reaffirms the "Spanish tradition," which, from the perspective of subjectivity, at no time during the modern period conforms to the conventional European model. As late-nineteenth- and early-twentieth-century European writers and artists become disillusioned with the self-satisfaction of the middle-class subject, modernism emerges to offer its own critiques that in relation to Spain actually mark a turn toward consistent Spanish positions throughout the course of its modern literary history.

If contemporary criticism is at somewhat of a loss to offer "positive" accounts of the contributions of modernism, perhaps tired of its verbal disruptions that today seem to some critics like rather meaningless word games, not to mention its often extremist ideological affinities, there seems little doubt that if a case is to be made for an affirmative agenda for this period it would seem to center around the issue of subjectivity. Judith Ryan has commented that by the end of the nineteenth century empiricist subjective models grounded primarily in sense perceptions were already undermining the idea of the middle-class subject.[28] The growing awareness of what Ryan terms "the vanishing subject" thus becomes the basis for more intense explorations of alternative models during modernism.[29] Analogous to the renaissance project of bringing forth a "new man," therefore, a spectrum of artistic interests dedicated to new modes

28. See also, from the perspective of class and gender, Bretz, *Encounters across Borders*, 347–440.

29. Judith Ryan, *The Vanishing Subject: Early Psychology and Literary Modernism* (Chicago: University of Chicago Press, 1991), 13–22.

of being in the world—that is, to the creation of another "new European man"—arises in modernism. In relation to middle-class norms, these efforts parallel the Spanish tradition to a great extent. While the rest of Europe must come to a somewhat abrupt and often alienated awareness of the insufficiencies inherent in its most important cultural product that is now understood as stifling and empty, Spanish writers who never fully invested in this ideology are poised in relation to Continental movements, as during no time in modern literary history, to continue a critique that elsewhere has only just begun.

From the Golden Age to modernism, free-thinking autonomous subjectivity has been consistently portrayed in all the great characters and stories from the Spanish tradition as monstrous. The great Spanish characters have nearly always been cerebral types who parody their European counterparts' capacity for free thinking. Excessive thinking detached from one's social circumstance invariably leads to disastrous consequences for the individual and for his/her milieu. Those characters who can free themselves from their monstrousness do so because they recognize their interconnectedness within a structure much greater than themselves. The unsuccessful characters—who take the law into their own hands, who murder their wives, and the like—deceive themselves as they respond to mental scenarios that have no basis in reality. As they embrace a misplaced faith in reasoning practices in the face of a world capable of easily overturning all theories, enlightened or otherwise, about the proper scope of the workings of the autonomous rational mind, they become monsters. The antidote to the monster position harkens back invariably to a modernized version of a premodern model invoked here as a "structural" model of consciousness in which reasoning practices alone are never sufficient to bring about a desired resolution to a character's dilemma.

As modernists throughout Europe begin to reject the bourgeois subject and search out alternative positions, they typically embrace two predominant alternatives that correspond quite remarkably to the longstanding Spanish "monster" and "structural" models. Arguably, the most productive agenda of modernist literature is the exploration of the evolutions which take place in relation to bourgeois subjectivity and to which Spanish models have much to contribute. Johanna Drucker characterizes a popular subjective model of modernism as fundamentally the psychoanalytic subject, "constantly in formation, psychically dynamic, open-ended and complex," and further, that this "subject as such is never complete, whole, or intact: it is split from the very outset between self/other, conscious/unconscious."[30] With the ascendance of the structural models of Freud, Jung, and others, the ego-centered subject is progressively understood as simply a public referent, part of something much more significant. "Being" is not centered in consciousness, and if there is indeed a core of being, it resides in a much wider structure. The modern structural models of consciousness, however, are not essentially different from the premodern structural model replaced by the "thinking subject" during the renaissance. The greatest difference between these constructs, of course, is the domain of being. Taking its clues from the romantic notion of the natural sublime, that sphere in modernism becomes an "oceanic" unconscious from which the "island" of consciousness emerges. In premodern terms, of course, this area was to be encountered, via one's faithful reading of the "great text of the world," in the realm of eternity. Full being did not reside in an earthly domain or in a subjective consciousness, but rather in the "second," superior reality. Thus, for many modernists as well as the premodernist, being is not consciousness-centered but resides in a structure.

The other pathway during modernism lies in affirming versions of what in the Spanish tradition is consistently portrayed as "monstrous" subjectivity, the invariably unflattering parody of middle-class "free-thinkers." This expresses itself during modernism in the also prominent tendency of many early contemporary writers to reject the supremacy of the unconscious and structural subjectivity and instead to infuse their works with characters and/or personae who dedicate their efforts

30. *Theorizing Modernism*, 109, 100.

to affirming the fullness of being on their own terms. This position may well be understood as a reaction to the more expansive structural model. In practical terms, this position represents an intensification, sometimes quite extreme, of the consciousness-centered bourgeois model of the nineteenth century. The appeal here is also to force, yet in the special sense that what is ascribed in structural models to unconscious-irrational force becomes instead a reassertion of the intellectual will in order to affirm in consciousness what structural models suggest lies beyond any such conscious control.

This phenomenon is also prominent in many early contemporary Spanish masterpieces, in variant forms, either in affirmation of the experience of epiphanic moments of "full being" or in the form of an aggressive, willful subject position. What Eliot, Pound, and, after them, the early apologists for the new art proclaim is modernism's will to create timeless, "eternal" myths in opposition to history is, in fact, part of a more ambitious project, the creation of a "new man" whose beliefs, values, and perspective on the world repudiate middle-class norms. This rather violent bifurcation of the nineteenth-century subject model is shaped, however, by the fact that in both positions the role of force is central: on the one hand the raw force of the unconscious, on the other the force of the will-intellect. Subsequent chapters will examine the extensiveness of Spanish participation in this central dimension of the aesthetic-ideological agenda of modernism, in all genres and, as outlined above, in all expressive modalities, while also following, as much as possible, a chronological progression.

CHAPTER 3

From the Labyrinth

The Spanish Modernist Novel and the "New Man"

In the introduction to a recent edition of *Estación. Ida y vuelta*, in which
the editor designates Rosa Chacel as the female writer most worthy
of keeping intellectual and artistic company with the "Generation of
1927" ("la escritora del 27" ["the female writer of 27"]),[1] Chacel pays
homage to the major talents of the early-twentieth-century Spanish
novel, most of whom had been prominently identified with the "Generation of 1898":

> Unamuno proyectaba la sombra de su persona [. . .] Valle-Inclán
> era un ejemplo de riqueza y complejidad verbal [. . .] Baroja con-
> quistaba con la simpatía de sus personajes antipáticos [. . .] Ramón
> [Gómez de la Serna] [. . .] ocultaba el horizonte con su volumen
> [. . .] Estas eran las anfractuosidades de la vertiente literaria: de los
> caminos llanos no hay por qué hablar. (74)

> Unamuno projected the shadow of his person [. . .] Valle-Inclán
> was an example of verbal richness and complexity [. . .] Baroja con-
> quered with the sympathy of his unsympathetic characters [. . .]
> Ramón [Gómez de la Serna] clouded the horizon with his literary
> volume [. . .] This was the upside of the literary slope: concerning
> the lower there's no need to say anything.

1. Rosa Chacel, *Estación. Ida y vuelta*, ed. Shirley Mangini (Madrid: Cátedra,
1989), 20.

Since these figures are writing at the moment that modernism is achieving prominence elsewhere in Europe, Chacel's opinion also provides an
appropriate point of departure for a discussion of the modernist novel
in Spain. Later in her remembrance of a work that after more than half
a century is finally achieving recognition, Chacel maintains that the central motivation of her novel is to examine the private intricacies of a character that she identifies simply as an "ente pensante" ("thinking subject," 80) and that her novel represents "[lo que] pasa en la mente de
un hombre. [. . .] El encadenamiento de las ideas, imágenes, sentimien-
tos [que] conduce a decisiones, aclara o agrava dudas, ahonda abismos,
enreda o desenreda laberintos, etc." ("[what] happens in the mind of
a man. [. . .] The linking together of the ideas, images, feelings [that]
lead to decisions, clarify or aggravate doubts, deepen abysses, entangle
or disentangle labyrinths, etc.," 80). Chacel is also sketching here the
primal scene of the Spanish modernist novel, the dilemmas and opportunities presented to characters in quite familiar company with protagonists from the "Spanish tradition": cerebral, thought-obsessed heroes/
anti-heroes who must deal with a seemingly labyrinthine reality that is
primarily the construct of their own monstrous intellects.

The novels chosen for discussion—Baroja's El árbol de la ciencia (The
Tree of Good and Evil, 1911), Unamuno's Niebla (Mist, 1914), Gómez de la Serna's El novelista (The Novelist, 1923), Valle-Inclán's Tirano Banderas (1926),
along with Chacel's Estación. Ida y vuelta (Season/Station: Round Trip, 1930;
perhaps the most notable among a group of experimental works by
young novelists including Antonio Espina, Francisco Ayala, and Benjamín
Jarnés)—are exemplary of the evolution of the Spanish modernist novel.
From a strictly formal perspective, these works impressively fulfill Eysteinsson's requisite criterion that a work identified as modernist will be engaged, to varying degrees, in interrupting the realist illusion. Indeed, all
of these novels are splendid examples of modernist meta-literariness. Yet
despite their considerable formal innovation, they are perhaps more important as meditations, revealing portraits of the modern dilemma and
the crisis confronting the pivotal cultural construct of European moder-

nity, the autonomous thinking subject—Chacel's "ente pensante"—from an individual and collective perspective at the outset of the twentieth century. As such they also participate in the much broader and ongoing Spanish reflections on the appropriate constitution of human subjectivity.

The crisis of the "autonomous thinking subject" calls into question the very concepts of human autonomy, the role of thinking, and the processes of thought; indeed, conventional ideas of subjectivity as the guiding definitions of the late nineteenth century are progressively understood no longer to suffice. Perhaps nowhere is the dilemma of the "new man"—the new modernist man—better represented than in Baroja's El árbol de la ciencia.[2] This novel has never been associated with modernism. Rather, it has been consistently identified with the guiding nationalist ideology ascribed to the "Generation of 1898." It strongly critiques a spiritual malaise in Spain, one of consequences of the ignominious defeat in the war with the United States. It despairs of a political solution to Spanish social problems, while it seems to be obsessed with a desperate search for the means to regenerate national values and virtues. Indeed, perhaps more than any other, this novel seems to embody the values that Salinas and Laín Entralgo so closely associated with "los perfiles exactos de un nuevo complejo espiritual perfectamente unitario que irrumpía en la vida española: la generación del 98" ("the exact profiles of a new and perfectly unitary spiritual complex that erupted in Spanish national life: the generation of 98").

Yet the nationalistic interpretation of this novel is not satisfying. The lamentable demise of the protagonist, Andrés Hurtado, may just as well be attributed to his remaining in Spain instead of seeking his fortune beyond the Pyrenees. Indeed, Hurtado's friend Fermín Ibarra, whose entrepreneurial ideas are soundly rejected in Spain, is able, and rather easily so, to secure patents and financial backing for his ideas in other parts of Europe. Arguably, this could also have been Hurtado's fortune (his

2. Pío Baroja, El árbol de la ciencia, ed. Pío Caro Baroja (Madrid: Caro Raggio / Cátedra, 1985).

materialistic friend Julio Aracil also becomes, in Madrid, a rich "society" doctor). Yet rather than to emulate this type of character, Hurtado, progressively disillusioned with the largely unrewarding and often sordid practice of medicine, instead withdraws from public life into himself. Eventually, he makes his living by translating articles from French medical journals. Indeed, this allegedly most Spanish of novels is infused with almost constant references to things European: Hurtado's decrepit science professors' name-dropping of famous European scientists with whom they were allegedly fast friends; the competition with French wines that eventually helps sink the economy of Alcolea del Campo (Andrés's provincial medical post); European capital that allows Spaniards like Ibarra to start a lucrative enterprise; and scientific and medical advances that Hurtado submissively reports, secondhand, to the Spanish medical profession.

More evident, however, is the pervasiveness of what prove to be troubling and problematical European ideas, especially when Andrés discusses the natural-ethical order of things with his uncle and mentor Iturrióz. This is particularly prominent in the novel's fourth part, which consists entirely of a philosophical exchange at the uncle's house, in which it becomes very difficult to understand who is speaking or advocating which position at a given moment. This purposeful confusion of the reader, the blurring of the discursive space in the colloquy between the two "thinking subjects," reiterates a more somber, debilitating, and, eventually, tragic confusion in the consciousness of Andrés Hurtado. Above all others, he is the one character who struggles to affirm a consistent position—to uncover what is repeatedly referred to as "una fórmula de vida" ("a formula for life")—regarding his geographical, political, and intellectual circumstances that closely corresponds to "modern" ideas, the then-current vogue of deterministic, sociologically oriented writing identified with French naturalism. From the outset, Hurtado identifies with such a position: "Hurtado era enemigo de la burguesía [. . .] partidario de los escritores naturalistas" ("Hurtado was an enemy of the bourgeoisie [. . .] a partisan of the naturalist writers,"

39). Indeed, he demonstrates a disposition to embrace uncomplicated explanations of the structure of reality. At one point Andrés is strongly attracted to the "genio trascendental" ("transcendental genius") José de Letamendi, who advocates the fanciful notion that "la vida [. . .] es una función indeterminada entre la energía individual y el cosmos, y que esta función no puede ser más que suma, resta, multiplicación y división, y que no pudiendo ser suma, ni resta, ni división, tiene que ser multiplicación" ("life [. . .] is a indeterminate function between individual energy and the cosmos, and that this function cannot be other than addition, subtraction, multiplication and division, and that unable to be addition, subtraction, or division, it must be multiplication," 69). He becomes quickly disillusioned of finding "algo que llegase al fondo de los problemas de la vida" ("something that would get to the core of life's problems," 70). Above all, Hurtado desires intellectual clarity, a position that will allow him to contemplate, understand, and interpret the social and moral reality he must confront. What he hopes for, therefore, is actually something akin to the perspective of the typical narrator of a naturalist novel, that is, a thesis or rational formula from which to explain the workings of reality. This, of course, is something that Andrés invariably fails to attain as the Spanish social reality proves resistant to any hypothesis about its constitution and functioning.

As much as it portrays the Spanish political-moral circumstance at the end of the nineteenth century, El árbol de la ciencia, therefore, also functions as an extended parody of the premises of the naturalist novel. Here a supposedly "objective observer" of the slice of life chosen as its subject—in the manner of Claude Bernard's clinical methodology, himself a doctor like Andrés—is instead victimized and left progressively confused and desperate by virtue of his very observations. In his pursuit of ciencia, the comprehensive yet formulaic explanation of reality, Hurtado achieves precisely the opposite of what he covets, discovering instead the same confusion, degradation, and mortality of his counterparts in the biblical story of Genesis from which the novel takes its title. Indeed, the more Andrés struggles to attain an objective view of things, the more bewilderment he encounters. Yet Hurtado's "anarquismo espiritual" ("spiritual anarchy") is more than spiritual. It also displays physical symptoms: "La vida era una corriente tumultuosa e inconsciente donde los actores representaban una tragedia que no comprendían [. . .] Estos vaivenes en las ideas, esta falta de plan y de freno, le llevaban a Andrés al mayor desconcierto, a una sobreexitación cerebral contínua e inútil" ("Life was a tumultuous and unconscious current where actors represented a tragedy that they did not understand [. . .] These swings in ideas, this lack of a plan or restraint, carried Andrés to the greatest uneasiness, to a continual and useless cerebral over-excitation," 84–85). The failure to achieve the sense of an "objective distance" to cushion him from an unforgiving reality progressively leads to his own deterioration, in a moral yet also in a physical sense, something akin to brain fever.

Closely paralleling the progressive collapse of Andrés's sense of existential-intellectual space is the novel's principal aesthetic strategy characterized by the narrator's incessant violation of the customary realist-naturalist mode of rigorous narrative detachment from the principals and their predicament. The narrator of El árbol de la ciencia does not properly observe and represent but rather interprets for the reader via an interminable succession of explicit interruptions of conventional expectations of "objective" novelistic narration. Andrés finds himself in the same predicament as "[e]l estudiante culto, [que] aunque quisiera ver las cosas dentro de la realidad e intentara adquirir una idea clara de su país y del papel que representaba en el mundo, no podía" ("the cultured student, [who] even though he wanted to see the things in reality and tried to acquire a clear idea of his country and the role that it represented in the world, could not," 41). Yet the reader is also repeatedly denied clear and unimpeded observations of Hurtado in favor of a pattern of unrelenting interpretive interruptions of the narration from a narrator incapable of performing, or unwilling to perform, a conventional function. The events of this novel do not exist independently of the narrator but rather are communicated in hybrid form. The reader almost invariably receives them as commentary, strongly biased commentary, and not as "objective" observations. Narration and interpretation are constantly intertwined, their separate functions blurred and confused to such an extent that the reader can hardly be said to receive "narration" in any customary sense. It is a further irony that the reader's knowledge of a protagonist obsessively committed to the type of empirical understanding that had been the hallmark of the realist-naturalist novel is communicated almost exclusively via a narrative mode that emphatically repudiates such an approach. The sense of narrative distance and empirical objectivity, hallmarks of the realist-naturalist novel, become instead the collapse of distance and the blurring of the boundaries between narrative subjects and the objective means of their representation. This novel, in the final analysis, tells the story of the collapse of hope of a protagonist who in an ideological-intellectual sense is fully invested in an epistemology that had been premised on the capacity of the human consciousness to achieve an "objective" position, the expectation to remain above the possibility of such a catastrophic disintegration.

More than any single motivating factor in Andrés's struggle for *ciencia* is his steadfast conviction that such knowledge and understanding can come only with a sense of distance and detachment from his empirical circumstance. Baroja underscores this explicitly at the conclusion of the first section, in which Hurtado encounters a character by the name of "hermano Juan" ("brother John"), a charitable cleric who ministers to the infirm yet whom Andrés considers repulsive because he seems so attracted to suffering and squalor:

> Andrés comprendía el otro extremo, que el hombre huyese del dolor ajeno, como de una cosa horrible y repugnante, hasta llegar a la indignidad, a la inhumanidad; comprendía que se evitara hasta la idea de que hubiese sufrimiento alrededor de uno; pero ir a buscar lo sucio, lo triste, deliberadamente, para convivir con ello, le parecía una monstruosidad.
>
> Así que cuando veía al hermano Juan sentía esa impresión repelente, de inhibición, que se experimenta ante los monstruos. (91)

> Andrés understood the other extreme, that a man would flee from another's pain, like a horrible and repugnant thing, even to become indignant, to the inhumanity; he understood that one would avoid even the idea

that there was suffering around one; but to go looking for the dirtiness, the sadness, deliberately, to live with it, seemed to him a monstrosity.

Thus when he would see brother John he felt this repellent impression, of inhibition, that one experiences in front of monsters.

Perhaps the most significant irony of the novel is that the outlook that Andrés obsessively embraces in order to distance himself from people like Juan, "monsters" who entangle themselves in the suffering of others, leads him inexorably along this very course and to the eventual realization that there is no place—given the terms of his peculiar nomenclature—where he can avoid the type of "monstrous" circumstance he abhors. Hurtado's own "dream of reason," his quest to achieve the equivalent of the detached, scientific, observational perspective of nineteenth-century naturalism, creates instead the monstrous conditions whereby the raw materials of reality progressively unsettle and disrupt the domain of thought itself.

As the novel's last sentence ("había en él algo de precursor" ["there was in him something of a precursor," 303]) makes clear, Hurtado presages the emergence of a new man on the European scene, a "modern" attitude that exposes the shortcomings inherent in the conventional order of things. The name "Andrés Hurtado"—from the Greek ἄνδρας, "man," and from hurtar, "wounded," "hurt," but also "hidden away"—epitomizes an attitude, as long as the "Spanish tradition" itself, that at the outset of the twentieth century has become the harbinger of tragedy. Andrés's progressive withdrawal from an intractable modern world brings him to a perverse reenactment of the position of "hermano Juan." The elimination of distance between sufferer and healer, progressively enacted in the novel in Andrés's tortured consciousness, produces an even more serious disease as Hurtado moves inexorably inward, into himself and the confused labyrinth of his tortured intellect. However, not only Andrés suffers from this affliction; seemingly everybody in the novel experiences a similar one. For example, the deluded bohemian Villasús refuses to "sell his conscience," but not his daughters, to live a "life of art." La Venancia's "extraña filosofía" ("strange philosophy," 122) affirms that the rich deserve their wealth and, moreover, the poor deserve their poverty, while the prostitutes whom Andrés examines are infected not only with syphilis but also with "el espíritu de la esclavitud" ("spirit of slavery," 266), which justifies their status to themselves, in their minds. Attempts to systematize thinking, to philosophize, and to defend a consistent ideological position pervade every level of this society. Indeed, Baroja's parody of European rationalist doctrines manifests itself most resonantly in the specific "thinking subjects" in whom these "principles" have been conceived and made monstrously incarnate. Andrés Hurtado, however, is different from the others who use their "philosophies" to insulate themselves from despair. His ever-deepening involvement with European ideology and his progressively more desperate quest to find an intelligible explanation for the workings of a reality far more complex, irrational, and aggressive than he could ever imagine, eventually claim him as their thought-obsessed victim. Andrés encounters forces in the world that all hoped-for "fórmulas de vida" prove inadequate to confront. The crisis of the European thinking subject incarnate in Andrés Hurtado becomes at this juncture yet another occasion to reaffirm, in the "Spanish tradition," the essential inadequacy and monstrousness of this approach to life. Hurtado's desire for expansive understanding and intellectual clarity cedes to progressive disorientation, confusion, and solipsistic despair, which culminates in his suicide.

The themes of intellectual obsessiveness, incomprehension, confusion, self-doubt, and suicide are also prominent in Unamuno's *Niebla*,[3] in which, as Chacel has suggested, the "sombra de su persona" is nowhere more evident. In relation to *El árbol de la ciencia* it reaffirms and intensifies the recognition of the hollowness of conventional European subjective models, revisited here in the tragic, yet also comic, Augusto Pérez. While the ever-serious Andrés Hurtado's many experiences progressively expose him to the seamy side of modern life and while Augusto is a sheltered and rather pampered *señorito* who never ventures far from home, both are nevertheless quite similar in their capacity for extended and excessive intellectual speculation that ultimately brings

3. Miguel de Unamuno, *Niebla*, ed. Mario J. Valdés (Madrid: Cátedra, 1985).

them to doubt their status as autonomous subjects. The incapacity to achieve intellectual clarity is reflected at the formal level in both works via the significant disruptions of the narrative space. The constant interruptions of the narrator in El árbol de la ciencia continue in spectacular fashion in Niebla with Unamuno's appearance as a character in his own work. This and other disruptions of conventional novelistic expectations underscore the precariousness and undependability of the intellectual process for protagonists for whom freedom of thought and action prove elusive. As Pérez's friend Victor Goti explains: "pensar es dudar y nada más que dudar [. . .] no se piensa sin dudar" ("thinking is doubting and nothing more than doubting [. . .] one cannot think without doubting," 252). Yet in the same breath he qualifies his statement by asserting as well that "es la duda lo que de la fe y del conocimiento, que son algo estático, quieto, muerto, hace pensamiento, que es dinámico, inquieto, vivo" ("it is doubt that faith and knowledge, that are something static, quiet, dead, make thought, that is dynamic, unquiet, alive," 252). To be able to consider that one is alive in a meaningful sense, therefore, virtually requires doubting that such is the case, which means, paradoxically, that the most productive form of thinking is that which leads not to clarity but to confusion. Doubt, the offspring of thought, also becomes the primary source of human vitality and, paradoxically again, the very source of resistance to despair, the logical outcome of doubting one's permanence and presence in the world. The type of thinking most worthy of the name eventually leads to befuddlement and confusion: the amorphous niebla, reality in its barest and most truthful form. Yet from here there also arises a dissatisfaction that becomes the basis for a defiant resistance to feelings of hopelessness, resignation, and absent existence. Although Augusto Pérez's struggle ultimately brings his life to an end, it nevertheless leads him beyond Andrés Hurtado's intellectual blind alley to the purported source of his confusion, where he is able to confront, and to confound as well, his averred creator.

If in the final analysis to think is to become confounded by what one thinks, it also provides the capacity to confound others in just the same way, as a consequence of the resentment at having been confounded and bedeviled by the processes of thinking in the first place. To be in the world, therefore, means not only to be able to endure the humiliation and impotence of understanding that one's existence offers no certain course but also to bring others into this vortex as well. As Victor Gotí in the prologue, speaking on behalf of Unamuno, declares: "Y si nos han arrebatado nuestra más cara y más íntima esperanza vital" ("And if they have taken from us our most precious and most intimate vital hope")—that is to say, the fundamental human intellectual desire for self-understanding, the capacity to validate one's subjective position in relation to an expansive circumstance—"¿por qué no hemos de confundirlo todo para matar el tiempo y la eternidad y para vengarnos?" ("why not confuse it all to kill time and eternity and to get our vengeance?" 103). The modern confusion that ensues as the consequence of the indefensibleness of previously foundational rationalist principles also constitutes the only principle, the only hope, that one can cling to in the defense of one's existential position, which, when all is said and done, can affirm no position at all. In the intellectual ground that is the *niebla*, truth is the labyrinth and thus also an aspect of a formless phantom.

In what may be considered something of a reply to the situation that develops in El *árbol de la ciencia*, in which the will to clarity leads Andrés Hurtado to a desolate and progressively desperate confusion, the only appeal to the corrosive hopelessness that makes suicide seem a rational alternative becomes precisely the contradictory imperative of a conscious struggle to "confundirlo todo." What distinguishes it is the steadfast will to continue and, indeed, to enlist others to the camp of confusion. Hurtado's enduring will to clarity becomes in *Niebla*, therefore, a "clear" and persistent will to confusion. The only "rational" response to the crisis of the European rational tradition is, indeed, to prolong and intensify this profound sense of confusion. To acknowledge the collapse of the sense of distance between thinking subject and the objective world, therefore, one must affirm a new formula. To continue to think in the conventional sense for the "new modern man," therefore, means that it is no longer possible to affirm that "I am." The structure of thinking has the consistency of mist.

Unamuno poses the question of subjectivity in terms of the location of being: does it reside exclusively in consciousness or does it find fuller expression in the embrace of a wider structure? Given the fundamental contradiction with regard to the products of thinking, it is not surprising that the answer seems to be less than clear. While this novel, or *nivola*, has more than its share of less than admirable characters, especially considering the subsidiary cast (such as Paparrigópulos) in the intercalated stories, the most negative and least likeable of all is clearly the character of Unamuno himself. In the "Post-Prólogo" he grows indignant at the prologue writer, Victor Goti, who offers the opinion that Augusto Pérez does, indeed, commit suicide and is not simply eliminated as Unamuno, the author-creator of his story, has ordained: "debe andarse mi amigo y prologuista Goti con mucho tiento en discutir así mis decisiones, porque si me fastidia mucho acabaré por hacer con él lo que con su amigo Pérez hice" ("my friend and prologue writer Goti better tread lightly in quarreling with my decisions, because if he annoys me too much I will wind up doing to him what I did to his friend Pérez," 107–8). Unamuno plays the role of a vengeful god who, if he does exercise his "libérrimo albedrío" ("most free will," 107) as he claims, does so cruelly at the mortal expense of his character-creation, who is denied both his expectation of an autonomous existence and a freely arrived at decision to end it. The dilemma, however, extends as well to his creator-author, who ultimately possesses no more authority than his creature. As Goti's remarks, infuriating to Unamuno, in the prologue make clear, the capacity to impose a definitive conclusion to this narrative that reflects the "clear" intentions of an autonomous creative will is also a casualty of a new and "modern" mode of writing, a *nivola* and not a novel. The true protagonist is not Augusto Pérez or Miguel de Unamuno but the *niebla* itself, the structure of thought and consciousness that is always and simultaneously in formation and in collapse, an ultimate reality that is primordially formless.

The recognition that modern subjectivity is grounded in little more than a mirage revisits the scene of the subject as well in the "Spanish tradition" that tends to equate the idea of autonomous consciousness with monstrosity. Unamuno is decidedly in line in this regard in that try as he might to affirm a larger structure in which to situate thought and consciousness, such an avowal is invariably thwarted. This structure is conditioned upon the presence of a subject desperate to affirm something beyond itself yet always frustrated by the fact that structure and subject are of the same nebulous consistency. Augusto Pérez's dilemma and that of his author are ultimately that their subjectivity is tenuous at best since they are both trapped in a system whose limits coincide with the limits of consciousness. Clarity of thought, therefore, is anathema since only in confusion, or the will-to-confusion, can these limitations to any degree be circumvented. Human effort, therefore, must be directed toward reestablishing the notion that there is something beyond the "clarity" of solipsism that at every turn threatens to overthrow this hope. The most fundamental human aspiration in the modern age, therefore, must be to resist the monstrous excess of self-propagation to the exclusion of everything else.

Unamuno's position here represents a modification and perhaps a parody of attitudes that became prominent in Europe in the preceding century, in which monstrosity becomes associated with the idea of a self-propagating vital power, "that rather than something gone awry during formation, monstrosity was the result of the formative capacity."[4] The monster theme taken up by Kant in an aesthetic sense to refer to those things that exceed representation considers that the monstrous describes an entity whose life force is greater than the matter in which it is contained (434). Thus rather than something that malfunctions during the course of its production, monstrosity is associated during romanticism with "overexuberant living matter" (438) that extends itself beyond its natural borders in order to affect a much wider sphere. The idea of the monstrous is closely related to the more familiar concept of the sublime, which is in

4. Denise Gigante, "The Monster in the Rainbow: Keats and the Science of Life," *PMLA* 117 (2002): 434.

turn instrumental in the development of modern theories of the imagination that, like monstrosity, are characterized by self-generation and self-
aggrandizement, or as Kant puts it in *Critique of Judgment*, the "extension
of the imagination by itself."[5] As Francis Ferguson has noted, "the in-
creasing attenuation of authorial subjectivity" in all accounts of the sublime is upheld especially by Kant, who "explicitly establishes the sublime
as an arena of aesthetic experience in which authorial intention is total-
ly irrelevant."[6] Unamuno's stance in *Niebla* corresponds well to the self-
procreative capacity of the monstrous that, as with the sublime, eventually brings the effacement of the initiating agent. Monstrous growth is
dynamic and aggressive but also self-consuming. Unamuno in the role
of monstrous creator—a self-creator—can propagate a world only with
versions of himself and, consequently, can destroy or take vengeance
on himself only when he proclaims his intention to "confundirlo todo,"
which, among the many paradoxes of this work, also heralds the nega-
tion of intention. Exercising his will to eliminate Augusto Pérez is effectively to embrace solipsism and to expose further the distance between
the possible solace of confusion and uncertainty and the certain deso-
lation of realizing the destructive consequences of thinking and inten-
tionality. In his extratextual decision to validate the contention that he
and not Augusto Pérez is the agent of this character's destruction, Unamuno reenacts the "original sin" of this mode of approaching the world.
To validate his interpretation of events over those of others is to embrace
the concept of clarity and the idea of the finality of thought. Yet to do this
is to turn his back on the only possibility for even the illusion of salvation, which can only come from confusion.

The suggestion in the title of Baroja's novel becomes explicit in *Niebla*: to taste the fruit of the tree of wisdom, of good and evil, is to find
oneself isolated, trapped in a labyrinthine predicament in which the only
consolation is the dubious knowledge that such confusion can be shared

5. Immanuel Kant, *Critique of Judgment*, trans. J. H. Bernard (London: Macmillan,
1914), 108.
6. Francis Ferguson, "A Commentary on Susanne Guerlac's 'Longinus and the Subject
of the Sublime,'" *New Literary History* 16 (1985): 296.

by, if not necessarily with, others. This sentiment is touchingly under-scored in the epilogue that features the lament of Augusto's dog Orfeo, a creature whose relationship to his master parallels at a "microcosmic" level that of Augusto and his creator. Orfeo's observations invoke anoth-er biblical story, the tower of Babel, that underscores the impotent con-sequences of thinking about things best left unthought:

> Cuando el hombre aúlla, grita o amenaza le entendemos muy bien los demás animales. ¡Como que no está distraído en otro mundo! [. . .] Pero ladra a su manera, habla, y eso le ha servido para inventar lo que no hay y no fijarse en lo que hay. En cuanto le ha puesto un nombre a algo, ya no ve este algo, no hace sino oír el nombre que le puso, o verlo escrito. La lengua le sirve para mentir, inventar lo que no hay y confundirse. Y todo es en él pretextos para hablar con los demás o consigo mismo. Y hasta nos ha contagiado a los perros. (297)

> When man howls, shouts, or threatens we the other animals understand him quite well. When he is not distracted in some other world! [. . .] But he barks in his own way, he speaks, and this has served to invent what isn't there and not to notice what is there. As soon as he assigns a name to something, he ceases seeing it, he only hears the name he has given it, or sees it written. Language serves only to lie, to invent what isn't there and to confuse you. Everything is a pretext to talk to others or himself. And he's even infected the dogs.

Thinking, consciousness is a sickness, a contagious disease. It unites humanity in the sense that the human condition is ultimately that of a shared solitude. Like the loyal Orfeo and his master, humanity also in-variably finds itself in movement from, toward, and between "la niebla de que brotó y a que revertió" ("the mist from which he sprang and that to which he reverted," 300).

Valle-Inclán's *Tirano Banderas* also seems to be about movement (rebellion against a ruthless dictator), inexorable social movement and revolution in the fictional Latin American country of Tierra Caliente.[7] While seeming to offer a panoramic view of the corrupt structure of Lat-in American society, the prominence of expatriate Spaniards ("gachu-

7. Ramón María Valle-Inclán, *Tirano Banderas* (Madrid: Espasa-Calpe, 1972).

pines") among the ruling clique, and the social tensions that underlie the unrest and violence in the great expanse of colonized territory imbued with Spanish and European cultural values, this novel ultimately turns upon causes and effects that have little to do with the many issues facing postcolonial Spanish America. *Tirano Banderas*, in fact, is not about national aspirations or the expansive possibilities that a new regime may open for the citizens of Tierra Caliente but rather quite the opposite: the bankruptcy of the individual and collective imagination, stagnation, and immobility. At the center of this morass is the assemblage of characters who combine to produce a collective reincarnation of monstrous subjectivity, beginning with the dictator Banderas yet extending to virtually everyone in this wretched "sucesión de imágenes violentas y tumultuosas" ("succession of violent and tumultuous images," 55) constituting Tierra Caliente.

Banderas presents a monstrous physical countenance often compared to a mummy whose head "parece una calavera con antiparras negras y corbatín de clérigo" ("looks like a skull with black glasses and a cleric's collar"); he has acquired the habit of constantly chewing coca leaves that produce "siempre una salivilla de verde veneno" ("always a little spittle of green poison") that dribbles down his chin. The adjective most consistently employed to describe him is "inmóvil" ("immobile," 40). Indeed, except for the defection of the Coronelito de la Gándara to the forces of Filomeno Cuevas and Zacarías el Cruzado's murder of the pawnbroker Quentín Pereda to avenge the death of his son, the greater part of the novel consists simply of physical descriptions of characters, locations, or trivial conversations, all in a state of general inactivity and immobility. The iconic dimension of the novel is striking, especially in comparison to *El árbol del la ciencia* and *Niebla*, which provide almost no information about the physical appearance of the principals or the physical scenarios they inhabit. The novel's strong visual dimension is accompanied with the division of the novel into multitudinous "parts," "books," and numerical chapters—also grouped in a numbering pattern that alludes to quasi-mystic theosophical "magic numbers." In addition, the intricate vocabularies drawn from virtually all the many regions of the Spanish colonial empire enhance the illusion of immobility in that it serves to interrupt the reader's movement through the text, effectively isolating one episode/section/chapter from the next. This specialized vocabulary, often perplexing to Latin American readers and Spaniards alike, is both a visual and an intellectual impediment to easy comprehension of what is ultimately a series of trivial scenes related to a coherent whole only by the principals' relation to Santos Banderas. The real action takes place during the prologue and epilogue as the local ragtag army composed of Cuevas's serfs and Gándara embarks upon its mission and, at the appointed hour, storms Banderas's palace, where the dictator's defenders offer scant resistance and the dictator is killed. His severed head is then placed on a spike for all to see.

What seems to have transpired is that Cuevas's rather small group of hired hands accomplishes in a few minutes what the official revolutionaries—whose leadership, the "Cuartel General del Ejército Revolucionario" ("Revolutionary Army Headquarters," 35), located in the remote mountains—had not been able to do for years. In fact, the first argument that Gándara has with Cuevas is over the latter's unwillingness to follow orders from a central command, which produces an immediate rift between the two since Gándara, a professional soldier, claims special expertise in leading troops. The reason that Gándara defects is that, in spite of the fact that he is one of Banderas's most competent lieutenants, the dictator decides to honor a complaint against Gándara for having broken, while drunk, a few glasses that were worth almost nothing but were the property of Doña Lupita, a camp follower and Banderas loyalist of long standing. As fate would have it, Gándara is warned of his impending arrest by another Lupita, called "la Romántica" because she is a prostitute. He then escapes to join the rebels. Although the reason that the second Lupita is able to warn Gándara is likely the loose lips of another client of hers and associate of Banderas, Nachito Veguillas, and not as Lupita believes, that she has a vision of what is happening in her capacity as a "medium of the present," these trivialities set up a chain of events that tips the balance of power. The rebels, who infiltrate the All Saints/Day of the Dead festival ongoing during the time of the novel, have a surprisingly easy task of overthrowing Banderas. In fact, perhaps the only casualty besides Banderas's daughter (whom the tyrant kills to spare her the degradation of being raped by the victors) is Banderas himself. The dictator's soldiers shoot into the air rather than at the attackers, and the once mighty dictator falls in a matter of minutes. With Gándara certain to become more prominent in the new regime, if not to be Banderas's actual replacement, it is also clear that the "new" Lupita will take the place of the old woman in the new hierarchy. As Banderas laments to the old camp follower on the eve of his overthrow: "¡Doña Lupita, por menos de un boliviano me lo habéis puesto en la bola revolucionaria! [. . .] Doña Lupita, la deuda de justicia que vos me habéis reclamado ha sido una madeja de circunstancias fatales: Es causa primordial en la actuación del Coronel de la Gándara" ("Doña Lupita, for less than the pittance of a *boliviano* you have put him into the revolutionary party! [. . .] Doña Lupita, the debt of justice that you have demanded from me has become a web of fatal circumstances: It is the primordial cause in the action taken by Colonel de la Gándara," 215).

The inconsequential causes upon which the change of regimes ultimately turns underscores both the radical fragility of this society and the horrifying prospect that literally anything—in the present cycle, breaking a few glasses—can become a "causa primordial" in a disastrous chain that leads to "circunstancias fatales." This disproportionality between cause and effect is further highlighted in the story of Zacarías el Cruzado's family as the *tumbaga*, the supposedly valuable ring that the otherwise penniless Gándara gives him to help him escape, is recognized immediately by Quintín Pereda as belonging to Gándara, who had pawned it previously many times. As a consequence Pereda cheats Zacarías's wife, offering her a pittance, and then denounces her to the police, who take her off to jail, leaving their child behind to be eaten, no less, by pigs. After Zacarías understands what has happened, he exacts vengeance by ringing his lariat around the *gachupín*'s neck and dragging him to his death. In the novel's bewitching circumstances, in which literally everybody is strapped for cash—"bruja" ("broke") is the word most commonly used—the failure of the ring to generate value accentuates a more fundamental problem in Tierra Caliente with regard to all mediums of exchange. They simply do not function according to conventional expectations. The ring's true worth is as an icon/index of its bankrupt owner. Ownership cannot be transferred, and the ring's consequent value as an economic commodity is naught because it remains exactly what it is, self-contained and self-referring, with its ultimate worth actually negative since the consequences of having it in one's possession prove catastrophic.

A similar pattern of negative cause-and-effect relationships exists with virtually every character, social class, and political tendency in Tierra Caliente, consistently interpreted by friend and foe alike as referring to a "first cause," invariably negative, an origin that is not the recent or even the remote past of Tierra Caliente but rather Spanish and European. The temporal setting of the novel is All Saints/Day of the Dead, November 1–2, at some point in the mid-1870s during a time when the liberal (and homosexual) Emilio Castelar is prime minister of Spain, yet after the first Spanish Republic, which is followed by the Bourbon Restoration, the Second Carlist War, and a return to a much greater conservatism. The narrator, however, invariably locates the coming together of the effects of multiple "first causes" in a remote time and place. The many allusions to the close relationship between the present-day Tierra Caliente and a long history of repeated spectacles in the same place but at different times begins in the novel's first moment: "San Martín de los Mostenses, aquel desmantelado convento de donde una lejana revolución había expulsado a los frailes, era, por mudanzas del tiempo, Cuartel del Presidente Don Santos Banderas,—Tirano Banderas—" ("San Martín de los Mostenses, that abandoned convent from where a long ago revolution had expelled the friars, was, as a consequence of the movements of time, Headquarters of President Don Santos Banderas,—Tirano Banderas—" 39).

The same evening, at the Circo Harris, while imploring his audience to "escuchar las voces de las civilizaciones originarias de América" ("listen to the voices of the originary civilizations of America," 72), the verbose orator of the opposition forces, the apparently socialist Doctor Alfredo Sánchez Ocaña, rails against the evils of bourgeois Europe, which he portrays as under attack globally by all people of color ready to "destruir la tiranía jurídica del capitalismo, piedra angular de los caducos Estados Europeos" ("destroy the judicial tyranny of capitalism, cornerstone of the decrepit European States"), the same "colorless" race that includes the "criollo rancheros" ("creole ranchers") such as Filomeno Cuevas, who only extend the life of "la sórdida civilización europea, mancillada con todas las concupisencias y los egoísmos de la propiedad individual" ("sordid European civilization, stained with all the greed and egoisms of private property," 74). Yet unlike many a doctrinaire ideologue, Sánchez Ocaña's ultimate take on the new revolutionary order is subject-centered, much more "spiritual" than political:

> el ideal de una nueva conciencia [. . .] más que revolucionarios políticos, más que hombres de una patria limitada y tangible, somos catecúmenos de un credo religioso. Iluminados por la luz de una nueva conciencia, nos reunimos [. . .] para crear una Patria Universal [. . .] donde se celebre el culto de la eterna armonía, que sólo puede alcanzarse por la igualdad entre los hombres. (74–75)

> the ideal of a new consciousness [. . .] more than political revolutionaries, more than men in a limited and tangible fatherland, we are the catechumens of a religious credo. Illuminated by the light of a new consciousness, we gather [. . .] to create a Universal Fatherland [. . .] where the cult of eternal harmony is celebrated, that can only be achieved by equality among men.

Later that night, at Santa Mónica prison, the reader discovers the deeper source of such grandiloquence, Don Roque Cepeda, the revolutionary leader who hardly seems so.

Cepeda is a theosophist and mystic more intent on contemplating the cosmic order than economic inequality and class distinctions:

> buscaba en la última hondura de su conciencia un enlace con la conciencia del Universo. [. . .] Para Don Roque, los hombres eran ángeles des-

terrados [. . .] Las almas, al despojarse de la envoltura terrenal, actuaban
su pasado mundano en límpida y hermética visión de conciencias puras.
Y este círculo de eterna contemplación—gozoso o doloroso—era el fin
inmóvil de los destinos humanos [. . .] Cada vida, la más humilde, era
creadora de un mundo, y al pasar bajo el arco de la muerte, la conciencia
cíclica de esta creación se posesionaba del alma, y el alma, prisionera
en su centro, devenía contemplativa y estática. (174)

he searched in the ultimate depths of his consciousness for a connection
to the consciousness of the Universe. [. . .] For Don Roque, men were ex-
iled angels [. . .] Souls, upon becoming removed from the earthly covering, acted out their worldly past in the limpid and hermetic vision of pure
consciousness. And this circle of eternal contemplation—pleasurable
or painful—was the immobile end of human destinies [. . .] Every life,
even the most humble, was creative of a world, and upon passing under
the arch of death, the cyclical consciousness of this creation took possession of the soul, and the soul, prisoner in its center, became contemplative and ecstatic.

Don Roque's revolutionary "conciencia nueva," spiritual rather than political, is actually a modern version of the other-worldly mysticism made
famous in the Spanish sixteenth century by Santa Teresa and San Juan de
la Cruz. Don Roque's vision, which understands human life as a cyclical
migration and return of the soul to a contemplative, static point of origin, actually coincides with that of Banderas in that both men idolize immobility. This so-called revolutionary agenda is thus ultimately grounded in the definitive absence of movement.

Descended from a Spanish-European origin, Tierra Caliente has already fulfilled this vision to a stunning degree. Literally everybody and
everything, and especially the economy, is paralyzed. If Cepeda considers that all life longs to return to a static, self-contemplative immobility, the characters actually portray this. Bereft of a transcendent dimension, these characters are nevertheless "pure presences," in their
monstrous physicality, fully what they purport to be. To a remarkable degree Roque's idea of the theosophic paradise has already been realized.
It is not at all surprising that the tyrant and the revolutionary, as near
mirror reflections of each other in an ideological sense, should ultimate-

ly agree to a cease-fire and a cessation of revolutionary agitation. Tierra Caliente is premised on a bedrock concept: immobility. With its economy paralyzed and its native population in a perpetual state of stupefied intoxication, its ruling classes have become interchangeable parts of a constantly changing monster that as it changes remains ever the same, as Banderas himself points out: "La Humanidad, para la política de estos países, es una entelequia con tres cabezas: El criollo, el indio y el negro. Tres Humanidades. Otra política para estos climas es pura macana" ("Humanity, for the politics of these countries, is an entelechy with three heads: The Creole, the Indian and the Negro. Three Humanities. Any other politics for these climes is pure silliness," 48). Both Banderas and his enemies conceptualize their culture as "eternal" and already "full," which every apparent change only reconfirms. In the final analysis, the immobility over which Banderas has presided remains intact. To remove him from power, to place his severed head on a stick for all to see, is not change at all because in Tierra Caliente "revolution" is, paradoxically, constant and unchanging. As likely the sole casualty in what is, literally, a *coup*, the change of heads of government actually reaffirms an unchanging, immobile order.

Don Roque's dream of a "new man" is also a mirage tainted, like everything else, by the ideology of immobility that has mesmerized the citizens of Tierra Caliente. The "new world" becomes the site where the old European world and its inadequate construct of consciousness, premised on autonomy and completeness, is exposed. This doctrine, however, is decisive in Roque's dream as well as in La Romántica's claims as a "medium of the present." Eternity, like time and history, exists in an ever-present present. Likewise, Valle-Inclán's intricate, composite vocabulary displays a denseness, an impenetrability, and thus a presence that directly mirrors the opaqueness of his characters. Language and characters are more like hieroglyphs that collectively embody a common meaning: in Tierra Caliente presence, the fullness of being, is hollowness, the fullness of absence; movement in the name of revolution brings the exact opposite, immobility, embodied in the tyrant himself

"inmóvil y taciturno, [. . .] una calavera [. . .] agaritado en una inmovili-
dad de corneja sagrada [. . .] mirando las escuadras de indios, soturnos
en la cruel indiferencia del dolor y de la muerte" ("immobile and taci-
turn, [. . .] a skull [. . .] posed in the immobility of a sacred crow [. . .]
looking at the squads of Indians, silent in the cruel indifference of pain
and death," 40). The new is old, and the old is new. The monster subject
finds new breath and gasps its last in Tierra Caliente.

In sharp contrast to the static backdrops of *Tirano Banderas* is Ramón
Gómez de la Serna's *El novelista*, whose constant and abrupt shifts in locales and subject matter brings together in one work multiple "novels,"
in reality fragments of novels, whose common denominator is that they
are the products of the same fertile novelistic imagination.[8] Consequently, the title is fully appropriate. This ambitious and challenging novel, in
the context of those examined thus far, is also profitably interpreted as a
meditation upon and reply to these writers and the positions they have
taken in relation to the question of subjectivity. Recalling Baroja's rest-
less protagonist Andrés Hurtado is Andrés Castilla, the surname being
a rather pointed reference to Hurtado's vast yet ultimately constricting
domain of activity, as is the title in relation to *Niebla*, which, ostensibly
about a new theory of the novel, is actually about a specific novelist. Both
these writers—and others from the "Generation of 98," Valle-Inclán and
Azorín—are points of departure for a wide-ranging meditation on the
contemporary novel and the type of artistic sensibility that the times require in order to circumvent their becoming a breeding ground for monsters.

A statement that has been used to characterize Gómez de la Serna's
attitude to novel-writing—"Toda obra ha de ser principalmente biográ-
fica y si no lo es, resulta una cosa teratológica" ("Every work must be
principally biographical and if it isn't, something monstrous results")[9]—
certainly suggests that the theme of monstrous subjectivity, and how to

8. Ramón Gómez de la Serna, *El novelista* (Madird: Espasa-Calpe, 1973).
9. Ramón Gómez de la Serna, *Una teoría personal del arte. Antología de textos y éstetica y teoría del arte* (Madrid: 1988), 62.

avoid it, is also prominent in Gómez de la Serna's thinking. Throughout the work there are specific "novels" whose content focuses on monstrosity, beginning with Cesárea, a character whose name also titles her
novel, identifying her as having had a caesarian birth. Later in the "novel," *Pueblo de adobes*, reminiscent of an Azorín setting in "un pueblo de
Castilla dotado de detalles inacabables" ("a Castillian town endowed
with unending details," 156), features a "ser monstruoso de cerebro em-
pedrado" ("monstrous being with a pock-marked face," 164), Engra-
cia. Finally, there is the story of the conjoined twins Dorotea and Gracia, who live in a house "lleno de objetos teratológicos para soportar la
teratología de aquellas hermanas" ("full of monstrous objects to com-
plement the monstrosity of those sisters," 226). In relation especially to
writers such as Baroja and Unamuno, Gómez de la Serna's above-cited
assertion is particularly noteworthy. It would seem that in contradistinction to the "biographical" Ramón, Unamuno and Baroja may be considered "autobiographical." The difference between autobiography and bi-
ography is one of distance. In the autobiographical mode there is much
less distance between author and character. Indeed, there is a distinct
possibility that distance will disappear altogether, as in Augusto Pérez's
confrontation with the character Unamuno in *Niebla*. Baroja's Hurtado
fares little better as his physical circumstance becomes progressively cir-
cumscribed, making his space, in the final analysis, almost exclusively a
mental one.

Yet these more experimental forms of the novel are hardly different from the conventional realist-naturalist novel that, even at the time
El *novelista* appears, still remains influential. In both types of novel, the
same relationships between subject and object obtain. This is underscored in the chapter entitled "El enemigo de las novelas" ("The Enemy
of Novels"), in which Andrés Castilla engages in a discussion with another type of novelist whose ideal is not art but rather "science," to write
novels like an "hombre de ciencia" (110). This "enemy" is something of
a petulant embodiment of the naturalist narrator who invokes the methods of science in order to make his observations of reality appear to be

case histories, sociology instead of art. Castilla is so upset with his adversary that he shows him the door. In contrast, he advocates an expanded range of possibilities for novelistic subjects ("la novela es el factótum de la vida" ["the novel is a factotum of life," 111]) and does not relish the thought of a novel "hecha para los médicos y los aceleradores de su velocidad o su telefonía" ("made for doctors and the accelerators of their speed or telephony," 111). Similar positions emerge in his trips to other countries, especially France, where he has occasion to speak with the great novelist Remy Valey, who seems clearly enough to be a surrogate for Proust and whose novels take shape "en mi propia habitación, que es donde hay que dar con las cosas, no en la vida" ("in my own room, that is where one comes across things, not in life," 184).

Likewise, when he visits England and chats with Ardith Colmer—the allusion here is less clear, perhaps to Joseph Conrad and/or others—since Castilla "tenía envidia de aquellas novelas oscuras y psicológicas" ("was envious of those obscure psychological novels"), something that Andrés, being "el gran novelista de las novelas con luz" ("the great novelist of the novels with light," 172), is apparently incapable of emulating. In his return to his writing of the improbable novel titled El faról 185 (Street Lamp 185), about the life and destiny of a street lamp, the reason for the reticence to explore psychology becomes clearer, as expressed by the street lamp's observation about the true nature of reality: "La realidad [. . .] es sordomuda y ciega, y no piensa nada [. . .] Nosotros percibimos como nadie el silencio y el vacío de pensamiento que hay en la naturaleza durante la noche" ("Reality [. . .] is deaf-mute and blind, and doesn't think anything [. . .] We perceive better than anybody the silence and emptiness of thought that there is in nature during the night," 173–74). In the realist-naturalist novel and its meta-novelistic successors, the illusion of structure is invariably provided by the consciousness of the novelist. What has happened over the course of the contemporary era is that the dividing line between the novelistic thinking subject and a fundamentally unstructured, unthinking objective reality has been breeched, not only by the likes of Baroja, Unamuno, and others but by the very na-

ture of the generic components that have come to produce the contemporary novel. The discovery and exploration of psychology has moved the
novel inward, and finally into the subjective consciousness of the novelist.
In relation to the statement that the failure to remain "biographical" produces monsters, the novel has, indeed, become instead "autobiographical," and monstrous, in that the domain of the novelistic object has been
appropriated by a thinking, subjective consciousness that has contami-
nated it with the structure of its own thought. The failure to approach reality as an objective entity, the collapse of the unthinking external space of
reality into the realm of the subject, has produced the novel of monstrosity, that has simply followed an inherent tendency present at the outset to
its inevitable end.

If a novel-*nivola* such as *Niebla*, an extreme example of the collapse
of space, is "teratological" because the novelist becomes caught up in
the very confusion he creates, making him effectively transparent and all
but erasing the distinction between subject and object, then the antidote
is the strong reaffirmation of space. By embracing a variety of concrete
spaces, Andrés Castilla is able to write and thus to make room for himself. Novel-making must involve interaction and conflict between the
novelist and an objective, autonomous space. To assure that the "biographical" does not become "autobiographical" and monstrous, that the
personality of the novelist does not dominate the artistic scene, novels
must affirm the novelist but not his person. The writing of novels should
reflect not identity themes but rather the centrality of the creative circumstance. Anything less limits novelistic possibilities.

The antidote to monstrosity is the recognition of a larger structure
upon which the individual consciousness can avail itself to surpass the
solipsism inherent in the meta-novel. An equal temptation, however,
is to embrace the structure of reality in all its raw and undifferentiated
complexity and confusion. If *Niebla* portrays the monstrous excesses of
subjectivity that leaves no space for anyone, Gómez de la Serna recalls its
presence in the chapter appropriately titled "Vuelta a la nebulosa" ("Return to the Mist") to portray "una novela en que la vida entrase sin tes-

is y sin ser sectorizada ni demasiado individualista" ("a novel in which
life enters without a thesis and without being sectored or too individu-
alized") in order to communicate that "la vida tiene una unidad comple-
ja, precipitada, revuelta que había que intentar dar en su propia tesitura
[. . .] Hay que dar la sensación de ese variado aburrimiento en que consiste la vida y en medio del que sin aislación alguna están los más diverti-
dos acontecimientos" ("life has a complex, precipitous, scrambled unity
that it has to try to give in its own state of mind [. . .] It is necessary to
impart the feeling of this nuanced boredom of which life consists and
in the middle of which without any isolation whatsoever are the most
entertaining happenings," 117). Although Castilla's notion may well
be true, his representational strategy—in a novel that is titled *Todos (Everyone)* and that consists of a paragraph each about a seemingly endless
stream of persons who happen to be occupying the novelist's field of vision—leads nowhere. He promptly aborts his project: "No, no podía ser.
[. . .] La nebulosa se traga las novelas y por el deseo de dar capacidad a
la novela la perdía en la masa cosmogónica, primera, desprovista de formas, de géneros, de salvedades, de excepciones, de concreción [. . .] El
novelista rompió las cuartillas de *Todos*, novela vana, hija del deseo estéril de la universalidad y de la totalidad" ("No, it could not be. [. . .]
The mist swallows up novels and through the desire to give breadth to
the novel he lost it in the cosmogonic mass, first, lacking form, material, qualifications, exceptions, concretions [. . .] The novelist tore up
the manuscript of *Todos*, foolish novel, a daughter of the sterile desire
for universality and totality," 124). Ramón thus understands that the attempt to acknowledge the complexity of the structure of reality brings
with it the possibility for equal excesses. The capacity to navigate the labyrinth thus requires a dynamic compromise between the subjective and
the objective. To embrace either extreme is to affirm labyrinthine confusion and monstrosity.

   The climax to Andrés Castilla's novelistic career is represented in
two stories about monstrosity and obsession, *Las siamesas (The Siamese
Twins)* and *El biombo (The Folding Screen)*, that appear very near the end of

this repertoire of "novels." The monster theme is evident in the situation of the conjoined twins, less so with regard to the prominence of the folding screen that, in fact, is the real protagonist of that story. In the context of Gómez de la Serna's meditations, the conjoined twins, named Gracia and Dorotea, are also the embodiment of a situation, or at least a potential circumstance, that the novelist must confront every time he contemplates writing a novel. Andrés Castilla thinks of the sisters as one monstrous entity, "aquella doble novia de su fantasía" ("that double lover of his fantasy," 231), which points to the problem of authorial subjectivity that in the making of a novel always runs the risk of becoming conjoined to the product of his imagination. The problem is always one of space or distance, the necessary distance between subject and object as well as the expanded possibilities for novelistic subjects within this space that are vital for viable products to emerge. In fact, the problem of the attenuation of space, symbolized in this segment in the composite body in which the twins find themselves and from which they cannot escape, is not recent, having been present throughout the period of the novel's dominance in nineteenth- and twentieth-century Europe, a crisis point in the appearance of the godlike omniscient narrator.

If anything, this type of narrator in Gómez de la Serna's mythology, perhaps corresponding to a one-eyed monster, is the prototype of the monstrous creation that Andrés Castilla dedicates himself to avoiding. In this context, therefore, the experiments of Baroja and Unamuno do not represent a break with the traditional novel of realism but rather are simply clearer manifestations of a tendency already present. All these types of novels are, in a sense, meta-novels in that all of them portray the progressive collapse of space. Bringing a thesis to the novel, as is the case with the naturalist novel, is to diminish novelistic possibilities as surely as Unamuno's *Niebla* ultimately collapses space, to the extreme of eliminating everyone except perhaps himself from the scene of the representation. Gómez de la Serna's novel instead refuses to narrate from a position of omniscience in order to affirm the other side of the novelistic equation: the need for space and distance. Indeed, throughout the novel

Andrés Castilla is accompanied by another, unnamed narrator who sets the scene but who does not write any of the novels, and, in turn, others often narrate Castilla's stories. All these types of novels are, in the final analysis, "fratricidal," as the plot of *Las siamesas* also reveals, in that the progressive incapacity to differentiate subject and object leads invariably to violence, upon the novel itself.

The last "novel," *El biombo*, ostensibly about the disconcerting effects that a folding screen exerts upon a variety of different characters, attempts to establish a symbolic presence in these narrations for the hitherto unmentioned yet fully integral component of the subjective equation. The function of the folding screen is to divide one space into two and in the process to enhance the illusion of the separateness of such spaces. In a conceptual sense, however, the screen may be understood in the role of the barrier that maintains the separation between binary combinations (recall Unamuno's ridicule of them in *Niebla*).[10] In short, the function of such entities embodied concretely in the screen can be said to be pivotal in the sense that before the presence of the screen the relationships inherent in a given space were understood much differently. As the narrator explains what happens when he brings the screen to his own home: "comenzaba el biombo a crear esa dualidad adversaria que crea de un lado la luz y del otro la sombra, de un lado la vida y del otro la muerte" ("the folding-screen began to create that adversary duality that creates from one side light and from the other shadow, from one side life and the other death," 261). As events proceed, the screen is ascribed an agency that it obviously does not possess and that eventually leads the narrator to imagine as he returns home one day that there is someone behind the screen, whom he suspects is his wife's lover, and toward whom he proceeds with a pistol. Upon discovering no one yet realizing that he was more than ready to commit violence, he decides to do away with the screen, and at this point the story ends.

This rather extended vignette is climactic in the sense that it brings

10. Unamuno, *Niebla*, 105–6.

into physical focus all the elements of the artistic formula. One's attitude toward "dividers" is at an artistic level one's capacity to situate oneself in the modern debate, to declare one's allegiance to a subjective space as Baroja, Unamuno, and others have done, to the monstrous and meta-novelistic, or to an expansive notion of a multivalent reality that holds the promise for success, and failure, in the furtherance of novelistic possibilities. Castilla and his narrator merge their voices at the novel's conclusion to proclaim

> pues hay mil aspectos de lo real en sus mareas movidas por lo fantástico que hay que perpetuar [. . .] se podría decir que está bien que existan todas las novelas posibles y que alguien tenía que tramar las que aparecieron viables [. . .] Hay que decir todas las frases, hay que fantasear todas las fantasías, hay que apuntar todas las realidades, hay que cruzar cuantas veces se pueda la carta del vano mundo, el mundo que morirá de un apagón. (287)

> that there are a thousand aspects of the real in its ups and downs moved by the fantastic that must be maintained [. . .] one could say that it is good that there exist all the possible novels and that someone had to give shape to those that seemed viable [. . .] One must say all the sentences, one must fantasize all the fantasies, one must note all the realities, one must cross as many times as one can the map of the vain world, the world that will die from a power outage.

Gómez de la Serna is certainly aware of the choices facing novelists at the apogee of modernism. Although his novel about novels and novel writing is certainly "meta-novelistic," it achieves this status in a manner different from that of his contemporaries. There is a structure to reality that the novelist must uncover. One cannot fulfill the obligations of a novelist by retreating into a fantasy. Fantasy is also outside ourselves.

As affirmed by Gómez de la Serna and, indeed, all the writers discussed thus far, creating the Spanish modernist novel, among other things, is a constant struggle between writing about someone or something and writing about oneself. Continuing this exploration of the relative importance of self and circumstance—subject or structure—in the creative process is Rosa Chacel's *Estación. Ida y vuelta*, the last of the novels under discussion to be published and thus perhaps a work in a position to take advantage of what is, by 1930, both from Spain and the rest of Europe (Chacel specifically mentions the influence of Joyce's *A Portrait of the Artist as a Young Man* in her endeavor) a considerable body of dialogue on what the modern novel is and should be. Chacel's is a portrait of young men and women, not necessarily artists, whose passage from one season of life to another—youth to adulthood—is paralleled by the physical passage from station to station and back again in a journey by train. Along the way she offers her self-critical reflection on life's important passages as well as a meditation on the modernist novel as it also moves into a new phase.

In her retrospective introduction to the novel of 1974, Chacel explains that she does not give her characters names—she calls the significant characters *él* and *ella*—so that they will not achieve coherence "más que mediante la exactitud rigurosa de las secuencias" ("more than by the rigorous exactitude of sequences," 80), which will require the participation of the reader. The novelist further asserts that this novel is about what takes place "en la mente de un hombre que [. . .] se ha debatido con su circunstancia externa [. . .] y que, espectador de sí mismo, trata de salvarse salvando de ella—de su total, racional, homogénea esencia—lo que prevalece como verdad" ("in the mind of a man that [. . .] has debated with his external circumstance [. . .] and that, a spectator of himself, tries to save himself saving from it—from its total, rational homogeneous essence—what prevails as truth," 80). Although steeped in the phenomenological credo of Ortega y Gasset, it is not warranted, however, that Chacel should be regarded a "disciple."[11] Chacel's novel is an exploration of subjective possibilities to expand upon the modernist meta-novel and to surpass its appetite for self-absorption. A work about self, circumstance, and the creative means to confirm them both, it complements Gómez

11. Shirley Mangini overstates the case in "Women and Spanish Modernism: The Case of Rosa Chacel," *Anales de la literatura española contemporánea* 12 (1987): 17–28; Kirkpatrick, *Mujer, modernismo y vanguardia en España*, 262–83, offers a compelling argument for Chacel's independence.

de la Serna's response to the subject-centered meta-fiction of Baroja and Unamuno. Although Chacel's novel is itself intensely meta-novelistic, its ultimate goal is to explore a different venue in order to bring the relationship between subject and object, self and structure, into clearer focus, which—and this is the irony upon which this novel turns—is ultimately unstable and unclear.

The three parts of this short novel—and there is, I believe, something of an analogy here to be made with the three *salidas* of Don Quijote since these forays also represent a journey into error and confusion yet nevertheless conclude in a redemptive return—each mark an exploration of what it means to be an "ente pensante" ("thinking subject," 80) in the modern age and, equally as important, what is entailed in writing about such subjects in a manner that will not diminish or deform them. Chacel introduces her hero, *él*, in the 1930 prologue in terms that echo Gómez de la Serna: "Aunque no coincide con casi ningún hecho de mi vida, le considero autobiográfico, y aunque él empieza a vivir ahora, es el reflejo una realidad mía ya lejana" ("Although it does not coincide with almost any fact of my life, I consider him autobiographical, and although he begins to live now, he is the reflection of my own reality now far away," 85). Even though he is something of an absence, *él* nevertheless dominates the first part of the novel, whereas there is a succession of female subjects, the precise qualities of whom are difficult to distinguish. Although the reader knows nothing about *ella* except that she is *él*'s *novia*, that, along with him, she is a university student, and that she inhabits an apartment in the same building as her beloved, one can certainly suppose that *ella* may well be something of what, at the time, was known as a "mujer nueva" ("new woman"), not necessarily a feminist but logically, in a Spanish context, a "modern woman." At the same time, it is also quite possible that she could be nothing of the sort. It is exceedingly difficult to know anything significant about this couple except that as the school year passes their love affair becomes more important than their studies ("había llegado el tiempo de faltar a clase" ["the time had come to skip class," 94]) and their conventionality.

At about this time, él becomes much more introspective about ella and the meaning of their relationship as he also begins to become conscious of what he begins to call his "egoism," a term that also recalls Joyce's *Portrait*. El's will to affirm his subjectivity is given free rein in the first part, which, along with what can be surmised from fragmented anecdotes, mostly in relation to ella, provides the groundwork for a theory of personality and existential possibility. Ella becomes associated with other women who either live in the apartment house—including Anita, the only character in this section with a proper name, who is the apparent murder victim of her *novio*, the watermelon seller adept with a knife, and who disappears from the women's consciousness at the moment of her violent end. Yet much more intriguing to the couple is the shadowy presence of someone called the "chica del velito" ("girl of the veil," 95), about whom there emerge contradictory details. The religious connotation of wearing a veil is countered by the assertion that she is a "falsa virgen" (96). She and "ella" are "hermanas de día" (95), born on the same day, and her picture appears in the newspaper shortly thereafter in what seems to be the society section, announcing her debut into society, while the caption is said to read "Joven intoxicada" ("Drunk young woman," 98), which may well be the other side of the coin, a candid photograph of an upper-class young lady misbehaving. These rather unsettling experiences serve to make the couple aware of a "velo de distancia" ("veil of distance," 97) between them and slightly later what "él" terms "la zona de la distancia" ("zone of distance," 101), a mental space in which one becomes aware of one's existence.

What has been happening in this first section, in fact, is an extended act of separation as what originally is presented as *nosotros* becomes él and ella, who evolve into more mature and autonomous personalities and who begin to confront the consequences of that relationship. As él becomes aware of his entry "de lleno en esa primera juventud" ("fully into that first youth," 100), he takes note that "[n]ecesitábamos nuestra ida aparte, nuestra independencia" ("we needed our trip apart, our independence," 102), that ella is also changing: "me daba cuenta de que iba con una mujer" ("I was becoming aware that I was going with a woman," 103). He begins to see her as doubled, multiplied, and much more complex. The ultimate meaning of the visit of the "chica del velito" is the realization that "ya era hora de dejar de ser pequeñas" ("it was time to stop being little," 106), that "su dualidad, su multiplicidad, si la hubiese, era [. . .] como esas cajas japonesas que se cierran unas en otras [. . .] la mayor llena de la pequeña; más bien llena de pequeñas" ("her duality, her multiplicity, if that were it, was [. . .] like those Japanese boxes that close inside of each other [. . .] the biggest full of the smallest; or rather full of all the smaller ones," 107).

This brings *él* to an extended meditation on repetition, that only through the multiplicity of repetition does he become aware of the nature of form and shape. He gives the example of the repeated pattern of a leaf in wallpaper, a form that would have never registered had it been only the unique "original." This, in turn, leads to a generalization about the instability of all forms, including, and especially the "*pose* de ahora, en su timidez pensativa" ("*pose* of the moment, in her pensive timidity") of *ella* that "avanza siempre al primer término, hasta hacerme sentir a veces la impresión de que le ha crecido, de que se le ha hecho más curva y de que es dentro de ella donde tiene esa pesadumbre interior" ("always moves to the foreground, to the point of making me feel at times the impression that she has grown, that she has become more curvaceous and that it is inside of her where she has that interior sorrow," 110). The more profound conclusion is that it is futile to speak of a fixed position: "Desde fuera no tiene explicación; [. . .] ya que toda posición es relación del individuo con el medio" ("From the outside there is no explanation; [. . .] since every position is the relationship between the individual and the medium," 111–12). To hope to discover form in any sense that pretends to be exact is to understand form as the consequence of a long sequence of events, likened to a road:

> ¡Un camino! Mejor que toda posición. Un camino largo, sin montañas limitadoras. [. . .] En los caminos no hay las rivalidades que en los puestos. Los que se sitúan hacen valer lo suyo, porque tiene lo suyo, saben

dónde empieza y donde termina lo suyo. Pero los que van por el camino
no tienen nada, pertenecen al camino, navegan en él siendo al mismo
tiempo su corriente. (112)

A road! Better than any position. A long road, without limiting mountains. [. . .] On the roads there aren't the rivalries that one finds in fixed
places. The fixed ones have their own validity, because they have their
own, they know where they begin and end. But the ones that go by the
road have nothing, they belong to the road, navigate on it being at the
same time its current.

El's insights on the intricacies of self and circumstance are complicated further by the presence of another element—"el chico" (114), the
child, the physical index of what is also involved in "knowing," or attempting to know, someone—in a scenario that has, up to this point,
comprised only two. The added element of the child requires him to
think now about the prospect of abandoning the liberating concept of
the "camino" in favor of a "posición": "El desenlace, el encasillamiento,
la clasificación de mi historia vulgar de mal estudiante que tiene un con-
tratiempo con la vecina y recurre a la burocracia, sin terminar el doctor-
ado. Todos verán con desprecio mi historia vulgar" ("The denouement,
the pigeonholing, the classification of my superficial history of bad student that has a mishap with the neighbor and has recourse to the bu-
reaucracy, without finishing his doctorate. Everybody will look upon my
ordinary history with contempt," 115). Concluding that self and circumstance are not discreet entities but rather interdependent, penetrable,
indeed, "pregnable," él resolves not to allow the physical consequences
of his amorous inclination to divert him from the understanding he has
achieved: "Tengo mi destino, que yo prefiero llamar camino [. . .] Yo no
veré mi Destino; mientras yo lo vea será camino [. . .] Claro que lo que
no he hecho, ni haré, es modificar mis direcciones por complacer a los
que miran" ("I have my destiny, that I prefer to call a road [. . .] I will
not see my Destiny; while I see it, it will be a road. [. . .] Of course what
I have not done, nor will do, is to modify my direction in order to please
those who are watching," 116–17).

Yet this is exactly what he does in this section's final moment in his encounter with a woman and her child, perhaps an unwed mother, whom he calls "la chica comunista" ("the communist girl," 117), in part because of her political affiliation but, more importantly, as a consequence of the chance union that the trio forms as they happen to stroll together, which nevertheless attracts the approving attention of passersby touched by what appears to be "la ternura de nuestra escena familiar" ("the tenderness of our familial scene," 118). This spontaneous representation, objectively false yet immensely gratifying, achieves its power because of the mutual participation of the players and their audience that appropriates them for such a role. The promise heralded in the experience of "aquella mañana comunistica" ("that communistic morning," 119) proves conclusively to él that there is a higher, better form of truth than that which he had understood during his egoistic phase: "Crear estos momentos que repercuten en las vidas de los demás, divergentes de la nuestra. Partículas de nuestra personalidad, que se nos lleva la sensibilidad ajena, que se irán desenvolviendo con ese poco de esencia nuestra, según las mil modalidades de los que las perciben. Esta es la verdadera vida" ("To create these moments that reverberate in the lives of others, different from our own. Particles of our personality, that an outside sensibility takes away, that will go entangling itself with that little bit of our essence, according to the thousand modalities of those that perceive them. This is true life," 119). It is toward the hope that the egoism-solipsism of youth can be surpassed, that "este comunismo unánime puede salvarnos del torpe instinto de propiedad" ("this unanimous communism can save us from the vile instinct of property," 119), that the following sections address. In essence, what is true is not a product of an act of consciousness but rather what can be shared, which until this epiphany had seemed labyrinthine to a thinking subject supposedly full and autonomous.

Since the first part of this novel was published separately, I believe that it is appropriate to consider it an autonomous episode to which the following sections respond. As the title of the novel suggests, the first part is, indeed, about an "estación," the passage from adolescence into adulthood. The subsequent sections, via the pretext of él's journey by train from Madrid to Paris and other French cities ("ida") and back again ("vuelta"), represent expansions upon themes that were prominent at the end of the first section. The second section is populated by a number of new characters, notable among whom are two French women who move into the apartment house, the thirty-six-year-old Julia and a younger woman, Julia's niece, referred to only as "la pantorrilla" ("the calf"), the part of her anatomy that seems to define her. What emerges in the second section is a further separation from the original intimate unit "nosotros" that began the novel. El becomes attracted to Julia but also to the idea of a therapeutic journey ("el viaje como una medicina" ["a trip like a medicine," 127]), to Paris, "la sede del sentido crítico" ("the center of the critical sense," 127), during which he has the opportunity to clarify further his thoughts on life, reality, and art, the boundaries between which become progressively blurred. In fact, what begins as something of an existential meditation concludes in an extended reflection on aesthetics (again, offering analogies with the progression in Joyce's *Portrait*). The second part, therefore, offers an intermediate step between él's earlier introverted egoism, his personal awareness of the limitations of such a perspective, and the novel's final section when another actor, a third-person narrator (in relation to él) takes over the narration in order to make some more definitive statement about the writing of modern novels.

   In an otherwise excellent discussion of this novel, Susan Kirkpatrick suggests that, however much it may strive to escape a restrictive provincialism, Chacel's novel is ultimately a representation of the "dilema del intelectual modernista español ante la peculiar e inconsistente modernidad del país" ("dilemma of the Spanish intellectual modernist in the face of the peculiar and inconsistent modernity of the country").[12] In my view, however, the round-trip journey from the cosmopolitan center of

12. Kirkpatrick, *Mujer, modernismo y vanguardia en España*, 297.

modern art is not a return to the "heart of darkness" but rather an attempt to wed the existential meditation about the infelicities of the solipsistic subject position that, in the Spanish tradition, has been consistently associated with monstrosity, to a theory of the art of novel-making that, in establishing a position for this work and this author in the Spanish tradition, also undertakes a critique of the European modernist novel as well. What begins as the self-absorbed philosophic-existential meditation of a masculine subject about the limitations of the autonomous thinking subject concludes in the third part in an aesthetic analysis of the contemporary novel, via a narrator who, if not Chacel herself, is certainly feminine. The aesthetic meditation actually begins in earnest in the second section. On his journey to the heart of contemporaneity and modernity in virtually all things, *él* centers his observations on the question of a satisfactory narrative perspective and the appropriate distance from which to narrate.

The dilemma of any subject-centered narration is precisely that raised by the question of distance: there is none, but if there were, the subject, as subject, would be erased. El is most reluctant to confront the contradictions of the subject-centered position: "repugnándome tanto la idea de sumergirme yo en su realidad [de los otros], no puedo menos de querer difundir en todos la mía" ("as disgusting to me as is the idea of submerging myself in their reality [of others], I have no alternative but to want to disseminate in others my own," 139). The blame rests with the idea of distance propagated by the realist novel: "Precisamente en lo de la distancia está la diferencia; porque no hay la misma de acá para allá que allá para acá. La infranqueable es sólo para los realistas, para los que argumentan que entre dos cuerpos no hay distancia cuando al pasar se toca, ¡aunque al tocarse hayan sonado a leguas!" ("Precisely in the idea of distance lies the difference; because it is not the same from here to there as from there to here. The insurmountable distance is only for the realists, for those that argue that between two bodies there is no distance when they touch in passing, even that upon touching they may have been heard for miles!" 140). The distinction that continues to be drawn between "objective" and "subjective" distances is thus the major impediment to an ideal form of expression that employs them both simultaneously:

> Tiene ahora para mí mi propia vida el problema complejo que tenían las casas de cartón cuando yo hacía el pequeño arquitecto. Por un lado, su construcción, la delectación de su forma; por otro, su hueco, el sacar de mí la suficiente vida para poblarlo. No sé en qué había más arrobamiento, si en la contemplación de su perspectiva, de los accidentes de su fachada, o en la de aquellos tabiques irrreales que componían la interioridad de su organismo, lleno en todos sus rincones de un alma que era la mía.
>
> Hay que resolverlo, hay que enfocar el total y ser capaz de llevarlo a cabo: de ¡realizarlo!, lograr una construcción sólida con todas las reglas del arte, donde puedan encerrarse las reglas íntimas, las normas informulables.
>
> La cuestión es ésa: compaginar, armonizar, logranado la máxima tensión de actividad intelectual. (142)

> For me my own life now has the complex problem that the cardboard houses had when I played architect. On one side, their construction, the delight of their form; on the other, their hollowness, extracting from myself sufficient life to populate it. I don't know in which was there more ecstasy, in the contemplation of their perspective, the accidents of their facade, or in those unreal walls that comprised the interiority of its organism, full in all of its corners of a soul that was my own.
>
> It is necessary to resolve it, it is necessary to focus on the whole and to be capable of carrying it through: of realizing it!; to achieve a solid construction according to all the rules of art, where the intimate rules, the unformulatable norms might also be enclosed.
>
> The question is that: to put in order, to harmonize, achieving the maximum tension of intellectual activity.

The issue that Chacel raises here is not parochial but lies at the heart of what type of expression modernists throughout Europe and the world are trying to achieve. Nevertheless, it attempts to integrate her thoughts on what a "new" novel can mean to Europe in the context of the Spanish tradition and its misgivings on the limitations of subjectivity and subject-centered art.

The novel's final section begins as *él* is still in France. The narrator, however, is now someone else—an authorial presence, perhaps Chacel herself—who occupies the position that *él* has had up to this point. Her presence is made manifest by fever, a form of delirium, that brings the narrator "back to her senses," literally. The narrator-Chacel begins remembering the couple who began the novel and her relationship to them. The role of *ella*, she recalls—and this is, indeed, the case in the first part—had quickly become transparent: "la imagen de la mujer acabó por desaparecer. No por irse, sino por confundirse con la de él, como una cosa que se traga, como una idea que se olvida" ("the image of the woman wound up disappearing. Not by leaving, but by becoming blurred with his, like a thing that is swallowed, like an idea that is forgotten," 146). This, indeed, is the problem of all subject-centered narration, as well as the dominant techniques of the realist novel and its modern progeny, the cinema. Their capacity for omniscient narration-vision, which in spite of being "omnividente, perceptora de todos los planos, de todas las faces" ("all-seeing, perceiving of all planes, of all phases") is also conceptualized as an "ojo desparejado" ("unpaired eye") that provides only a "mirada monocular" ("monocular view") (123), ideas that recall the Gongorine monster Polifemo with which Chacel's poetic contemporaries are rather engrossed in 1927 as she writes her novel, as well as Gómez de la Serna's anatomical anomalies recounted in *El novelista*, notably in the story of the one-eyed Beatriz (236–53). In fact, none of the modern representational vehicles—the novel, cinema (161–63), or theater (160–61)—are adequate mediums to express what it is that Chacel is interested in conveying, a narrative mode that will not obliterate one subject position by means of the presence of another, which is exactly what modern representation, albeit in a less-than-evident manner, has done all along. At the subjective level, the narrator wishes to represent, to convey memory, not as memory but as presence: "Lo que yo necesitaba era hacer acto de presencia para conmigo mismo. Claro que desde que decidí la vuelta empecé hacia mí. Pero sin la experiencia de los sentidos. [. . .] Entonces fue el recordar lo nunca visto, lo nunca sentido, con

su sabor inconfundible. El recordar sin idea de pretérito" ("What I needed was to make an act of presence for myself. Of course since I decided
the return I began toward myself. But without the experience of the senses. [. . .] Then it was remembering the never seen, the never felt, with its
unmistakable flavor. Remembering without an idea of past," 149).

An important recognition in the furtherance of her goal is to acknowledge the primacy of interpretation as opposed to the poles of
subjectivity-objectivity: "Acaso esto mismo es cínico, este interpretar,
este descargar la conciencia en la creación. Pero no, este interpretar es lo
único puro. La más aspera, la más intransigente disciplina mental, ahon-
dar en la investigación con apasionada templanza, hasta encontrar la in-
terpretacón de más luminosa complejidad" ("Perhaps this very thing is
cynical, this interpreting, this emptying of the consciousness in the creative act. But no, this interpreting is the only pure thing. The harshest,
the most intransigent mental discipline, to probe the investigation with
passionate restraint, until finding the interpretation of the most lumi-
nous complexity," 152). This leads to an ideal vision of the type of narration that she wishes to achieve: "Fluctuará mi 'yo' movedizo alrededor
del suyo firme. Pero llegaré a precisar, respecto a él, mi debida situación
y distancia. Encerraré su yo y el mío en respectivas copas cristalinas, desde donde se vean sin mezclarse. Y saltaré de una a otra, colectando lo
más escogido del yo y del él, sin confundirlos nunca" ("My moveable
'ego' will fluctuate around his firm one. But I will be able to determine
exactly, with respect to him, my proper situation and distance. I will en-
close his ego and mine in crystalline vessels, from where they will see
each other without mixing. And I will jump from one to the other, col-
lecting the choicest from me and him, without mixing them ever," 153).
Thus, as él is confronted with the news of the birth of his child via tele-
gram, occasioning his decision to return to Madrid and what seems to
be the acceptance of his adult role and responsibility as a father, the narration returns as well to the understanding of what has been undertaken
and why. A major aspect of this has been egoism: "Pescaba mi yo; Más
que pescarlo, lo rebuscaba. Mi yo no era entonces un pez ligero que na-

dase en agua limpia, yo lo buscaba en la baja marea [. . .] Y algo encon-
tré" ("I was fishing for my *ego*; But more than fishing, I was meticulously
searching. My *ego* was not then a fast-moving fish swimming in clear water, I was searching for it at low tide [. . .] And I found something," 154).
But it is something of a necessary egoism because of the equal realization
that the "objective," third-person narrative mode of realism possesses
"ninguna trascendencia" ("no transcendence," 158). Chacel's refusal to
give names to her characters is also a recognition of a more profound
form of subjectivity that resides not in a fixed position but rather within
a larger structure. There is ultimately no means to circumvent that structure, just as Chacel herself understands that her works and her characters "quedarán siempre cortadas, sin punto final, como si me faltase saber algo para rematarlas, como si necesitase cursar finales [. . .] Ellos
necesitan seguir una vida recta, confiada; aventurarse por un camino sin
ninguna dirección marcada" ("will remain always cut short, without a final point, as if I would be needing to know something more to complete
them, as if I needed to study the endings [. . .] They need to follow an
unswerving, confident life; to venture down a road without any marked
direction," 168). Egoism thus gives birth in a sense to its opposite, the
structureless structure that is an open road, of possibility: "Así partirá
de mi un árbol genealógico" ("Thus, there will spin off from me a ge-
nealogical tree," 168). Baroja's image of the "árbol de la ciencia" with its
bitter fruit is replaced here by the image and reality of new life. Refusing
to acknowledge essential categories, Chacel charts a course beyond the
monster subject and into the positive promise that awaits its progeny.

CHAPTER 4

Modernist Hieroglyphics

Geographies of Presence in the Poetry of Jorge Guillén
and Vicente Aleixandre

The "hieroglyphic mode" represents an intensification of the "aesthetic of interruption" fundamental to works identified as modernist. The much greater iconicity of the poetry of Jorge Guillén and Vicente Aleixandre—in comparison to the almost anti-pictorial settings of the previous chapter—reflects as well a distinctive mode of subjectivity that in some important respects parodies the dominant middle-class subjective model. Yet it is fully appropriate to poets whose "generation" has been strongly identified with Góngora and his unparalleled creation, the monster Polifemo. As one moves from familiar names if not actual physical descriptions that locate Baroja's Andrés Hurtado in turn-of-the-century Madrid and the Castillian countryside to the minimal backdrops across which Augusto Pérez scurries, the hybrid scenarios of Tierra Caliente, to the sketchy settings of the many "novels" of Gómez de la Serna's Andrés Castilla, and, finally, to the perplexing narrative trains of thought in Chacel's Estación. Ida y vuelta, it is clear that these geographies are intimately linked to a narrating consciousness that appropriates a public space in order to give form to a private, meta-novelistic vision. As they aggressively dedicate their poetry to the fabrication of private, hermetic worlds—unconventional geographies that require an uncommon sensibility to engage them—Guillén and Aleixandre intensify the course of these explorations to bring forth the most extended and pronounced manifestations of what I have been calling the "monster subject" in Spanish modernism.

Perhaps the most striking aspect of the subjective positions developed by these poets is that they represent radical distortions of the conventional model based on free-thinking and autonomy. Both poets parody this construct—without, of course, intending to do so—by extending the principal aspects of the conventional model to immoderate bounds. Free-thinking becomes intellectual aggressiveness and, quite often, intellectual violence to objects and landscapes, while autonomy metamorphoses into solipsism. What effectively happens is that alienation from the dominant bourgeois subjective pattern brings forth a position that, in relation to its analog, is, indeed, distorted and that produces, in the context of romantic concepts of monstrosity, self-begetting extensions of itself. Such a turn in the early decades of the twentieth century has become an observable phenomenon in other literary traditions and has provided much grist for the chorus of critics that have understood modernism as a move toward extremism. It is from this tendency that Fredric Jameson is able to make the claim that modernism in many respects—if not at the overtly political level—provides a model for fascism, or at least an approach to the world that can be considered such, an apolitical "proto-fascism."[1] The elements of such an understanding include the exaltation of the intellectual will, the refusal to recognize the role of historicity in the fabrication of cultural documents, and the tendency to retreat to a radically private, solipsistic understanding in response to an uninviting and alienating public reality. Although the traditional culprits in this enterprise in mainstream criticism have been Eliot, Pound, Yeats, Lewis, and, for some, even Joyce, it is my considered opinion that the most radical manifestation of precisely this type of attitude is to be found in the poetry of Jorge Guillén and Vicente Aleixandre. The subjective models they

1. Jameson, *Fables of Aggression*, 1–23.

develop represent the outer limits of the type of monstrous subjectivity that has been the hallmark of Spanish attitudes throughout its modern literary history. The great difference, of course, is that for perhaps the first time what had consistently been a negative view becomes in these poets an affirmative position. The appeal to force, personal aggressive resolve, so integral to rightist theories and practices, is strongly echoed in attitudes that while indeed apolitical are nevertheless fully consonant with national policies that also preached the "triumph of the will."

Although many consider Guillén a more conventional poet than Aleixandre (Cernuda calls him the "greatest surrealist"),[2] their differences have been overstated. Both Guillén and Aleixandre affirm a vision of the world that challenges bourgeois subjective models by means of the production of well-made, "better" images of a better way to be. Guillén, in fact, specifically designates imagism as the modernist tendency with which he most identifies: "El nombre americano *imagists* podria aplicarse a cuantos escritores de alguna imaginación escribían acá o allá por los años 20" ("The American name *imagists* could be applied to a number of writers with some imagination who were writing here or there during the '20s").[3] During these years, poetry proceeds by means of the production of a different kind of image, not simply a copy of reality but as something that aspires to full immediacy and presence—a "realidad no [. . .] reduplicada en copias sino recreada de manera libérrima" ("reality not [. . .] duplicated in copies but created in the freest manner," 20)—which heralds, in turn, the full presence of being. Aleixandre's poetry may also be read as a progressively more focused summoning into fullness of the same type of alternative reality, an unconventional geography of full being. Whereas in *Cántico* (the 1936 second edition) Guillén assertively presides over his poetic landscapes fabricated by and for the poet through acts of systematic intellectual aggression, Aleixandre must explore an existential order over which his intellectual

---

2. Luis Cernuda, *Prosa completa*, ed. Derek Harris and Luis Maristany (Madrid: Barral, 1975), 429.
3. Jorge Guillén, "Generación," in *El argumento de la obra* (Barcelona: Sinera, 1969), 20.

will, at least initially, is incapable of exerting immediate control. While Guillén aggressively reconstitutes ordinary reality into a better image of full being, Aleixandre engages in an extended struggle to impose his will on a force that seemingly defies such attempts. What seem to be almost spontaneous experiences for Guillén are for Aleixandre protracted engagements to dominate a medium that, nevertheless, progressively affirms the promise of existential plenitude. Like Guillén's, Aleixandre's goal is not so much self-understanding as it is the "monstrous" self-aggrandizement that accompanies the experience of the presence of being. Although their routes may seem quite different, their goal, nevertheless, is to create a private world, a geography of immediacy and fullness, for an elite and privileged consciousness.

I turn first to Guillén and *Cántico*'s first section's initial multi-sectioned poem, "Más allá" ("Beyond"), which serves almost as a manifesto of Guillén's attitude to the mode of being he values and the type of poetic image appropriate to such values. The poem pays homage to two distinct forms of consciousness, both of which are necessary to the creative act, yet only one of which has any real value for the poet. As the title indicates, there are two distinct forms of "otherness," both of which are assigned the same label: "más allá." The "first" realm is empirical reality, which communicates its presence at daybreak as the poet awakens to meet the new day. Yet this "first light" is accompanied by a "second," more aggressive presence as the consciousness affirms an unorthodox interpretation of the meaning of the "outside light" from "beyond." The things that emerge from the light are understood to affirm another purpose, to orient and center the poet's being:

> . . . van presentándose
> Todas las consistencias
> Que al disponerse en cosas
> Me limitan, me centran.[4]

> . . . making their appearance
> All the consistencies

4. Jorge Guillén, *Cántico*, 2nd ed. (Madrid: Cruz y Raya, 1936), 15.

That upon ordering themselves in things
Limit me, center me.

Although it is the accumulation of light particles that produces a temporal image of the day, the light is not the primary medium operating in the poem. It is incapable of effecting the significant transformation that now proceeds under the auspices of a more forceful agent: "mis ojos / Que volverán a ver / Lo extraordinario: todo" ("my eyes / That will see again / The extraordinary: everything," 16). Temporality is suspended by the awakened activity of consciousness that reconstitutes it in an atemporal context. A second "más allá" now asserts itself, for itself:

Todo está concentrado
Por siglos de raíz
Dentro de este minuto,
Eterno y para mi.

Y sobre los instantes
Que pasan de continuo,
Voy salvando el presente:
Eternidad en vilo.
         (16–17)

All is concentrated
For ages entirely
Within this minute,
Eternal and for me.

And above the moments
That continually pass,
I am saving the present:
Eternity suspended.

The "outside" empirical landscape elicits an active response from an intellectual will desirous of affirming its presence against precisely such a visual background:

Ser, nada más. Y basta.
Es la absoluta dicha.
¡Con la esencia en silencio
Tanto se identifica!

¡Al azar de las suertes
Unicas de un tropel
Surgir entre los siglos,
Alzarse con el ser,

Y a la fuerza fundirse
Con la sonoridad
Más tenaz: sí, sí, sí,
La palabra del mar!
        (17–18)

To be, nothing more. And that's enough.
It is absolute bliss.
When being is in silence
So much is recognized.

At random from the unique destinies
Of a throng
To emerge from among the ages,
To rise with being.

And by force to unite
With the most tenacious
Sonority: yes, yes, yes,
The word of the sea!

This "inner" desire to be, the aggressive desire of the intellectual will to affirm an absolute status, transforms the external landscape into a vehicle to express the will to presence:

Todo me comunica,
Vencedor, hecho mundo,
Su brio para ser
De veras real, en triunfo.
        (18)

All communicates to me,
Victorious, made world,
Its daring to be
Truly real, in triumph.

That is to say, nature provides fragmented and empty images, raw material for the activity of self-invention, that achieve plenitude by virtue of their incorporation into a greater unity centered in the consciousness.

Indeed, the second section portrays "este / Ser, avasallador / Universal" ("this / Being, universal / Dominator," 21), the aggressive will-consciousness, which is also a will to form ("vaguedad / Resolviéndose en forma" ["vagueness / Transforming itself into form," 20]). This inner realm is dark, yet at its center there resides "En lo desconocido [. . .] / Un más allá de veras / Misterioso, realísimo" ("In the unknown [. . .] / A beyond truly / Mysterious and most real," 21). Here is a reality that transcends mere representation to embody a principle of artifice unavailable in the sense-dominated "outer realm." Through the assertive activity of this interior otherness the empirically available "más allá" is made to fulfill a more valuable function: to provide the formal building blocks for being, the true and better reality ("realísimo"). The perspectival three-dimensionality of nature is not an end but rather a means to affirm the presence of more significant landscapes. The devaluation of empirical experience is expressed as a violence enacted upon the natural image that is reappropriated to the active medium of consciousness, where form acquires a new shape and meaning, in a plane, that is, a two-dimensional medium.

Such an active principle acknowledges the fusion of the separate functions of will and intellect that, along with the memory (which in *Cántico* has been effectively excised), had formed the basis for all traditional epistemological models before and since the Renaissance. No longer an accumulated record of experiences, the values of being, to which this alternate epistemology responds, require an unencumbered subject with no constraints upon "la energía / De plenitud" ("the energy / Of plenitude," 25). A willed intensification of the understanding redefines the outside medium in order to affirm itself as something completely new.

The poem's final strophes affirm the ascendancy of this alternative principle of image production as the inner principle affirms its dominion over the visual field of creation:

. . . Y con empuje henchido
De afluencias amantes

Se abanica en el sagrado
Presente perdurable

Toda la creación
Que al despertarse un hombre
Lanza la soledad
A un tumulto de acordes.
                (32–33)

. . . And with swelled force
From loving influxes
Fans itself in the sacred
Everlasting present

All of creation,
Which upon awakening a man
Casts off solitude
In a tumult of harmonies.

The awakening is a double one: the poet opens his eyes to a visual do-main that provides the raw materials by which to affirm the "más allá de veras" ("true beyond"). The vocabulary of the final strophes, dominated by aggressive, action-oriented words ("empuje," "se ahinca," "lanza"), suggests that a passive outside principle has been replaced with an active inside principle. The poem has been the account of the poet's meticu-lous valuation of an active principle of consciousness that is also a poetic principle. By the poem's conclusion, inner and outer realities have effec-tively intermingled. Three-dimensional space-reality effectively collaps-es by virtue of its redefinition in terms of the values of being, an inner phenomenon and the true locus of image production. The present los-es its association with temporality as a consequence of a forceful act of consciousness ("con empuje henchido") that reconstitutes an image of the real world in an atemporal setting. Indeed, the "outside" exists only as a necessary pretext for the affirmation of the fullness of being. Images acquire fullness by surrendering their three-dimensionality to become a plane projection on the activate membrane of consciousness where spa-tiality fully collapses.

Poetic expression responds to an existential need to affirm being by means of a landscape appropriated for that purpose. The resultant image is quite different from that typically associated with nineteenth-century realism. The realism of this poetry corresponds not to an objective, observing eye, but to the subjective desire of the poet's eye to seize upon objects that correspond visually to an aesthetic-existential predisposition that covets precisely such an image or landscape. The observed object, however, has status only insofar as it communicates to the poet his own aesthetic-existential agenda. The poetic object's preexisting affinity with the active principle of will-consciousness thus signifies that the distance between subject and object has been greatly diminished from the outset. The poem, in a sense, becomes the process by which the distinction between inner and outer dimensions of the image becomes blurred. The object, in a sense, wills itself as it itself is willed to become part of a more intense and profound landscape that is invariably supplemented by an aggressive principle of consciousness, which also supplies what the object cannot, an affirmation of its own presence in the representation. In formal terms, the effect is a radical oscillation between spatial and plane dimensions, that is, three- and two-dimensional realities. Nearly every poem of the second edition of *Cántico* witnesses the collapse of empirical reality in favor of a "better" image, in which words and images have fused in ecstatic harmony.

The words that appear on the pages of *Cántico* are graphic equivalents of the images from nature that have helped to initiate the creative process; that is, they function as hieroglyphs. The protagonist is never the natural landscape, but rather being, through the landscape. Words do not simply mirror a preexisting image but become the basis for a "better" image that achieves fullness in a plane reality. The most explicit expression of these values is found in "Naturaleza viva" ("Still Life Alive") where the poet ascribes to a plane tabletop the quality of maintaining "Resuelto en una Idea / Su plano: puro, sabio, / Mental para los ojos / Mentales" ("Settled in an Idea / Its plane: pure, wise, / Mental for the eyes / Of the mind," 34). The tabletop that was part of an expansive spatial reality, a "bosque / De nogal" ("forest / Of walnut," 35), has now achieved a higher perfection. Its rings, signs of the presence of time, still refer it to the other reality, but the act of its planing has transformed its essence. It has won a victory over time and by its separation from its original spatial-temporal milieu has become exalted in a new and more intense fullness:

> . . . ¡El nogal
> Confiado a sus nudos
> Y vetas, a su mucho
> Tiempo de potestad
>
> Reconcentrada en este
> Vigor inmóvil, hecho
> Materia de tablero
> Siempre, siempre silvestre!
>   (35)
>
> . . . The walnut tree
> Trusting in its knots
> And grains, in its great
> Time of power
>
> Concentrated in this
> Still vigor, made
> Matter of a tabletop
> Always, always natural!

The unsubtle play on words of the title is very suggestive of Guillén's low valuation of nature and things natural. As the title suggests, the tree acquires greater life by losing its natural form and achieving a plane form. This is, indeed, Guillen's fundamental aesthetic value. The planing of the tree removes it from nature but also from temporality. It acquires, or at least is ascribed, power and autonomy that it could not possess in a spatial-temporal medium. Planing thus signifies a transcending of the flux of time. These qualities are also those associated with the production of poetic images. Not a mere cross-section but rather a dynamic receptacle, the plane represents an intensification of the capacity to produce images. The tabletop's artificed form is a correlative for an alternative epistemology whose goal is an improvement on the natural image.

Spatial perception, which typically characterizes the experience of everyday reality, is also temporal perception since images in space are communicated to the perceiver over a distance. Consciousness, therefore, becomes aware of time through space. The passive consciousness of the empirical model receives images in the tacit awareness that they inscribe themselves temporally. The active will-consciousness, however, imposes itself on these images, collapsing the distinction between itself and the landscape as it banishes the presence of time. In the passive mode of being, nature and time exert power over being, which is unable to establish its full presence in the spatial realm. In the poetry, as an epistemological phenomenon, the spatiality of nature is disrupted in a manner that closely parallels the act of planing glorified in "Naturaleza viva." By excising the spatial element of the images of reality, the active consciousness transcends their temporality. The production of images shifts from space-time to an inner plane, a two-dimensional surface whose highest, and indeed only, value is being, the principal content of the poetry. The poems of *Cántico* that typically celebrate the presence of being represent such experiences by means of an intensified two-dimensional image. The images of empirical reality have no place in poem-making until they are reassembled as a composite image superimposed in planes. The creative will understands the images of raw reality as fragments, building blocks for a better image that contains every partial, perceived image and that has fashioned the parts into a graphically represented whole.

Empirical images are the building blocks of a "better" poetic image whose purpose is to affirm the fullness of being within the plane of artifice. In "El prólogo" ("The Prologue") the poetic process is portrayed as an act of refashioning undesirable, temporally experienced images, characterized as "rodeos" ("detours," 47). Poetry marks the moment when temporal experiences are redefined to become the means, or prologue, to the act of artifice that takes one out of the flux of daily experiences measured by the passage of days: "¡Perezcan / Los días en prólogo! / Buen prólogo: todo, / Todo hacia el Poema" ("May the days in prologue / Perish! / Good prologue: everything, / Everything toward the Poem," 47). "Cima de la delicia" ("Height of Delight") describes a moment so intense that the landscape "Henchido de presencia" ("Filled with presence," 87) acquires the passivity necessary to collapse its spatiality to planeness: "El mundo tiene cándida / Profundidad de espejo" ("The world possesses the innocent / Depth of a mirror," 87). The world has become a mirror for the presence of being, which in empirical reality is rendered invisible by the temporality that provokes the poet's disaffection. The word-image, or hieroglyph, represents the fulfillment of the activity of consciousness. "Perfección del círculo" ("Perfection of the Circle"), a testimonial to the two-dimensional perfection of the circle, concludes by admiring the circle's geometrical form, which possesses the ability to make itself fully present in the act of its representation. Such power contrasts with the difficulty in affirming the same status for being, which requires the excision, by force, of an imperfect spatial-temporal reality. The circle's perfection thus suggests the limits of the poet's aesthetic-existential ideal, which he underscores with the questions that close the poem: "—¿Quién? ¿Dios? ¿El poema? / —Misteriosa-mente . . ." ("—Who? God? The poem? / —Mysteriously . . . ," 89). While Guillén may admire the circle's form, he is incapable of faithfully retracing its trajectory with words. The perfection of the two-dimensional ideal is disrupted by the reality of its closure, which also becomes the closure of the means available to understand such perfection on its own terms. This relegates the poet to an outside position from which he can only babble in ignorance about what he has just experienced. Achieving the circle's perfection would thus require transcending consciousness, the paradoxical antithesis of the desire that has exalted the circle, like a god, as the embodiment of the highest value.

The resolution to this apparent dilemma is to invent an intermediate category, between the natural and abstract, which consists of what the poet can understand, on his terms. The activity of understanding becomes instead the occasion for affirming the principles of understanding themselves but not the specific object appropriated for contemplation.

"Jardín que fue de don Pedro" ("Garden That Belonged to Don Pedro") portrays the poet engaged in the activity of understanding, which provides the opportunity, as the title suggests, for a transfer of ownership, from Don Pedro's artificed landscape to the poet's consciousness. The contemplation of the more perfect nature of the garden is paralleled by the juxtaposition of this image with an even greater perfection, the processes of understanding that "Funden lo vivo y lo puro: / Las salas de este jardín" ("Fuse the living and the pure: / The rooms of this garden," 190). The resultant image, in the membrane of consciousness, exists in an intermediate yet understandable realm. It is not, like the perfection of the circle, pure abstraction. Nor is it alive since, as part of the understanding, it has been dispossessed of its autonomy. It is, effectively, a hieroglyph.

These ideas are more explicitly addressed in Guillén's statement in the Gerardo Diego anthology that poetry should be "poesía bastante pura 'ma non troppo'" ("fairly pure poetry 'ma non troppo'"),[5] an equation that also affirms the basic conditions of knowledge and existence. Poetry must not be understood in absolute terms, for to do so would render it incomprehensible. Absolutely pure or absolutely alive means a poetry that is also absolutely unintelligible. Guillén is not so much concerned with affirming the aliveness of nature as he is the aliveness of being, as compared to the unintelligible purity of being that does not need to understand itself. The not infrequent declarations of his debt to nature, as in "Siempre aguarda mi sangre" ("My Blood Always Waits"), where he declares that "No soy nada sin ti, mundo" ("I am nothing without you, world," 217), which seem to indicate an affirmative attitude, actually measure Guillén's alienation from the fullness of being. Without recourse to the unwanted otherness of external reality, from which he has actively distanced himself, he is literally nothing, impotent to affirm the primordial value, being, from which he is also distanced. Experiential reality has value because it confirms the presence of being, not because

5. Jorge Guillén, in Gerardo Diego, *Poesía española: Antología* (Madrid: Signo, 1931), 344.

of an intrinsic worth. It is "nothing" in exactly the same sense that the poet is "nothing" without the world. Literally nothing has value unless it is affirming and confirming being. Nature, things, and human beings have value only insofar as they provide the opportunities for being to embody itself. Guillén needs the world only insofar as he needs raw images with which to fashion a landscape that he understands corresponds to his desire to know the shape and substance of being. Being demands a landscape, an empty landscape neither pure nor alive.

Of the 125 poems in the second edition of *Cántico*, many represent experiences that take place in nature or rural settings. This does not mean that Guillén has assigned these landscapes a special value. The natural landscape, for example, the rural countryside in "Relieves" ("Reliefs") whose solitary edifices (a castle at the top of a hill and a hermitage) and horizontal landscape provide a striking three-dimensional relief, is primarily a focusing device for the production of the "better image," that is, being. Thus the experience of a relief is superseded by a more significant relief, a product of the poet's understanding that, paradoxically, destroys the natural relief. This destruction is characterized as activities of appropriation ("rendición") and of possession ("Posesión"), which epitomize his aggressive epistemology. At specific moments nature acquires anthropomorphized feminine form, as in the long poem "Salvación de la primavera" ("Salvation of Spring"), to become an embodiment of fragility and subservience. A more direct rendering is developed "El manantial" ("The Source"), which retraces the course of a river to its source, a better image of the river's unwieldy chaos rendered imagistically, in the final strophe, as a young girl:

> Y emerge compacta
> Del río que pudo
> Ser, esbelto y curvo,
> Toda la muchacha.
> (53)

> And there emerges—compact
> From the slim and curved river

> That could have been,
> The whole girl.

Affirmed here is an image, taken from nature, of nature's renunciation of its natural role. Form triumphs over the river's chaos. The girl becomes instead the embodiment of an aesthetic principle, a source of images produced at nature's expense. The physical emergence of the girl from the water marks the final step in a trajectory away from a chaotic nature to a realm of compactness, the better source that affirms itself through this image.

Nature exists to mirror the poet's will-consciousness, not to fulfill a function for itself. Nature, therefore, is never recognized as something of intrinsic value. Nature's elemental function is to provide the raw material for consciousness to fashion a "better" image, to surpass nature. Its principal value is its passivity, availability, and malleability, the ease with which it may be made to assume the forms valued by the understanding. This attitude is carried forward as well in poems set indoors that typically feature an object, ordinary or artistic, through which the poet affirms similar existential states. Perhaps the most well known is the armchair invoked in "Beato sillón" ("Blessed Armchair"), in which the invocation of the massive object within the finite space of the house leads to an unexpected generalization about the world: "El mundo está bien / Hecho" ("The world is well / Made," 195). The poem's brevity does not make clear, however, that Guillén's affirmation is due only minimally to the objective physical presence of the armchair in the room. Although "La casa / Corrobora su presencia" ("The house / corroborates its presence," 195), the chair's massive presence in the limited space of the house provides an even more precise correlative for the presence of being, in the same massive and serene proportions. As with nature, it is not the specific object that is valued but rather the "better" image that emerges from the activity of contemplation. Indeed, the poet's eyes do not "see," since "No pasa / Nada. Los ojos no ven, / Saben" ("Nothing / Happens. The eyes do not see, / They know," 236). The more passive act of observation has long preceded this moment. Not the spontaneous experience of an object but the ecstatic fashioning of an image of being, the true object of exaltation, has refashioned the world once again. As with the natural landscape, this well-made world also affirms itself through objects with no inherent value except as referents for being.

If such affirmative moments almost invariably herald the presence of being, the consciousness of time and death threaten to nullify this capacity. Although the specific references to time are not overabundant, Guillén's awareness of it, and its limitations, is constant. The presence of being witnesses the falling away of time. A moment of plenitude in "La Florida" becomes "Tiempo en presente mío" ("My present time," 231), time's redefinition in the image of being. The excision of temporality, therefore, involves simultaneously acknowledging a more profound mechanism. The unintelligibility of the force and movement of time is overcome by the more forceful activity of being in a timeless present of perfect stillness. More than the artifice of a well-made world, the artificing consciousness affirms its greater perfection in nature, but like time, at the expense of nature, in the creation of a presence that is the poetic image.

In a similar vein, the poems set in cityscapes often express disorientation, confusion, and fatigue, as in "Perdido entre tanta gente" ("Lost among So Many People"). The distaste for such landscapes becomes particularly evident in "Dinero de Dios" ("Money from God") in which the mocking image of an "Hacedor / Supremo" ("Supreme / Maker," 181), a parody of the rationalist idea of a supreme being, wields power through the mass production of the graven image, "el signo / De la Posibilidad" ("the sign / Of Possibility," 181), printed on money that has acquired an absolute value "Hasta convertirse en . . . el Más Allá" ("Until Becoming the . . . Great Beyond/Afterlife," 181). Guillén is contrasting his "better images" produced in a "más allá de veras . . . realísimo" with the mass-produced means of image production in capitalist society that has its own concept of a "más allá." His low opinion of society's values becomes particularly evident in the sarcastic conclusion, "—¡Dioses: gastad!" ("—Gods: spend!" 181), a reference to the fact that under capitalism any mortal can become a god by virtue of the acquisition of sufficient quantities of the images printed on money. The gods define themselves as such through their worship of the supreme maker's graven images, an idolatry that expresses itself in the perverse activity of spending. Such a false economy threatens the privileged status of well-made, superior images.

The only landscapes of unquestioned value are spaces where the bourgeois cityscape does not intrude and which, in turn, are rendered full, still, and plane as their space is appropriated by the productive principle. The collapsing of space is most evident in poems that contemplate works of art. Whether directed toward sculpture or painting, the activity of contemplation also affords the artificing consciousness occasion to express its own values of production. Sculpture holds an attraction not for its massiveness but because it epitomizes movement immobilized. In "Estatua ecuestre" ("Equestrian Statue"), the contemplation of an equestrian statue leads to the understanding that "Tengo en bronce toda el alma" ("My soul is bronze") and that "Permanece el trote aquí, / Entre su arranque y mi mano" ("The trot remains here, / Between its starting point and my hand," 177). The statue is reconstituted as an image held by the hand, a metaphor for the activity of consciousness that has understood a correspondence between the existential ideal and the atemporal, immobile ecstasy of the frozen moment represented in the statue "Inmóvil con todo brío" ("Immobile with full determination," 177). Equally intense sentiments are expressed regarding a group of living horses in "Unos caballos" ("Some Horses"), whose "acción" is a "destino [que] acaba en alma" ("destiny [that] concludes in soul," 237), a grace that expresses itself as an essential form that makes these horses "ya sobrehumanos" ("already superhuman," 237). As living correlatives of an aesthetic-existential ideal, they transcend their own unconscious "acción" to become "alma," embodiments of a higher principle, movement toward full being.

The activity of consciousness that renders the landscape as a well-made world, comparable to a work of art, is only the first step in a process of artifice that leads to the affirmation of the superior image, of being. As described in "Las alamedas" ("The Poplar Grove"), the poet's task is always that of "profundizando paisajes" ("making landscapes more profound," 197), transforming them into something of greater value in which the values of being and art exactly coincide. As expressed in "Lo inmenso del mar" ("The Immensity of the Sea"), the represented image of the sea on a poster embodies the ideal of artifice, "Monótona, lenta, plana" ("Unchanging, atemporal, plane," 198), but also "Ductíl, manejable, mía . . . en vía / De forma por fin humana" ("Flexible, manageable, mine . . . in the process of acquiring / A form at last human," 198). The sea's immensity parallels the force of consciousness in relation to the landscape. As the sea becomes "por fin humana" it becomes as well the vehicle through which the poet expresses his own power to make a given landscape more profound.

Closely related to these landscapes is the female form, whose value is invariably aesthetic, as in "Pasmo de amante" ("Lover's Amazement") which nominally describes the contemplation of feminine beauty. What "stuns" the poet is not the human subject, however, but rather the abstract whiteness of the contemplated object: "Blancura, / Si real, más imaginaria, / Que ante los ojos perdura" ("Whiteness, / If real, more imaginary, / That persists before my eyes," 178). As also expressed in "La blancura," whiteness is an essential aspect of all aesthetic experience as Guillén understands it, a metaphor for the plane of consciousness on which images are inscribed and made profound:

> Recta blancura refrigeradora:
> ¡Qué feliz quien su imagen extendiese,
> Enardecida por los colorines,
> Sobre tu siempre, siempre justa lámina
> Del frío inmóvil bajo el firmamento!
>   (216)

> Straight refrigerating whiteness:
> How happy the one who extends your image,
> Fired by vivid colors,
> Over your always, always just sheet
> Of immobile coldness under the firmament!

Thus in poems such as "Desnudo" ("Nude"), where Guillen speaks of the "Plenitud, sin ambiente, / Del cuerpo femenino" ("Plenitude, without context, / Of the feminine body") that brings him to the experience of an "absoluto Presente" ("absolute Present," 251), the truth is that such experiences have little to do with the female form (such as a real woman, a nude in a painting, or a naked landscape). The fullness associated with the nude exemplifies the "Monotonía justa" ("Measured monotony," 251) of all the poetry. There is essentially one subject, the poet, one object, a landscape in its variant forms, and one value, which is also an economy, of image production: the high valuation of being at reality's expense.

Although Aleixandre shares an ideological agenda quite similar to Guillén's in the sense that the affirmation of the presence of being is always the constant goal, his route to such an affirmation is quite protracted and extends across the entirety of his poetry up to 1936. While Guillén's verses respond to a perception that consciousness has seized upon an object or landscape that responds to the will to the fullness of being, Aleixandre recounts an entire process whereby a dimly glimpsed intuition of the possibility to experience just such a state eventually becomes clear. Also like Guillén, he understands that his goal can be fulfilled only by abandoning the conventional artistic means at his disposal. To affirm a better mode of being he must also embrace a different mode of expression. The preparatory moment to a new value orientation is *Ambito* (*Boundary*, 1924–27),[6] which chronicles Aleixandre's dissatisfaction with the limitations of the given reality while it also subtly undermines and devalues traditional representational and epistemological assumptions. The volume's most persistent image, the reflected light of the moon, epitomizes the limited possibilities of ordinary consciousness as well as the poet's awareness, now as a young adult, of his distance from being. The dissatisfaction is intensified by passive contemplation, the principal consequence of which is the frustrated consciousness of a misspent youth. More than one poem, but notably "Retrato" ("Portrait"), alludes to mas-

6. This and the following poems are from Vicente Aleixandre, *Obras completas* (Madrid: Aguilar, 1968).

turbation as a means of combating the tedium of life, experiences that invariably summon an even greater sense of limitation that "cierra ya el sentido" ("seals the senses," 96). Self-contemplation and self-gratification
are also acts of self-containment, a failure of the will: "El gesto blando
que / mi mano opone al viento" ("The bland gesture / that my hand uses
against the wind," 97).

Images of weakness and impotence abound in *Ambito*, and Aleixandre begins to understand that the shaping forces in his life have been invariably associated with mimetic reproduction and their doubled product:
mirror reflections, simulacra, words translated into images. He begins to
dissociate himself from these agents of existential dilution as he declares
to an imaginary lover: "Lo que yo no quiero / es darte palabras de ensue-
ño, / ni propagar imagen con mis labios" ("What I do not want / is to give
you daydream words, / nor to propagate my image with my lips," 108).
He is looking for an alternative means of representing "love," his better,
fuller self, a new expressive mode, a "Filosofía. Nueva / mirada hacia el
cielo / viejo" ("Philosophy. A new glance toward the old / sky") and hope
for a new "Definición que aguardo / de todo lo disperso" ("Definition that
I await / from everything scattered," 137). An integral aspect of the alienation from empirical values is the devaluation of memory, for memories
as simulacra of past events distance the poet from being by reduplicat-
ing, inflating, and thus devaluing his presence. Indeed, in "Memoria" remembrance is portrayed as a "Valle de ausencias" ("Valley of absences")
that leaves him "sediento" ("thirsty," 168) to experience the presence of
things. The volume concludes with a sense of expectation as "Toda mi
boca se llena / de amor, de fuegos presentes" ("My whole mouth fills /
with love, with present fires," 172).

Pasión de la tierra (*Passion of the Earth*, 1928–29) chronicles Aleixandre's initial experience with an alternative mode of understanding and
the expanded existential possibilities it heralds. In this volume he is concerned more with characterizing and describing the new landscape than
with making conclusions, since the new intuitions about an intensified
existence are overwhelming in every sense. There is a direct correlation

between the prose-poem form and the female creature who populates this realm, the frequent object of address ("ella quedaba desnuda, irisada de acentos, hecha pura prosodia" ["she remained naked, iridescent with accents, made into pure prosody," 181]), which suggests that the poetry is responding to a more powerful will and mode of production that has overturned the earlier artistic-existential premises. A new representational framework emerges as Aleixandre declares conventional understanding inoperative: "Me descrismo y derribo, abro los ojos contra el cielo mojado" ("I explode and destroy, I open my eyes against the liquid sky," 180). Aware from the outset that his relationship with the center of being is a learning process, he tells his female companion: "Tu companía es un abecedario" ("Your company is a reading primer," 179). The old understanding is so many "dibujos ya muy gastados" ("already used up drawings," 179). The principal communicative medium in this realm is a new form of language, "la tos muy ronca [que] escupirá las flores oscuras" ("the very hoarse cough [that] will spit out dark flowers," 180), which requires new means of understanding, "esa puerta" ("that door") that will allow "todos [a besarnos] en la boca" "all of us [to kiss each other] on the mouth," 182), as a special but peculiar form of "love" begins to affirm itself ("qué oscura misión mía de amarte" ["what an obscure mission of mine, loving you," 182]). Aleixandre is attracted to and repelled by an alternative space where "Los amantes se besaban sobre las palabras" ("The lovers kissed beyond words," 182) and where he is able "sentir en el oído la mirada de las cimas de tierra que llegan en volandas" ("to hear in my ear the view from the peaks of land that come through the air," 187). The promise of existential liberation is also a new epistemological burden.

To become a worthy "lover," the poet must overcome this realm's power to overwhelm vision. "Ser de esperanza y lluvia" ("Being of Hope and Rain") acknowledges his willingness to become a prisoner in "ese dulce pozo escondido [. . .] en busca de los dos brazos entreabiertos" ("that sweet hidden well [. . .] in search of the two half-open arms," 187), but also his willful determination to begin to exert an influence over the rush of sounds, images, and language that he cannot understand: "Horizontalmente metido estoy vestido de hojalata para impedir el arroyo clandestino que va a surtir de mi silencio" ("Horizontally situated, I am clothed with tin-plate to impede the clandestine stream that is going to spurt from my silence," 188). This silence remains unknown, uncircumscribable, and thus powerful. The desire becomes "extender mi brazo hasta tocar la delicia" ("to extend my arm until I touch delight"): "Si yo quiero la vida no es para repartirla. Ni para malgastarla. Es solo para tener en orden los labios. Para no mirarme las manos de cera, aunque irrumpa su caudal descifrable" ("If I want life it is not to share it. Nor to waste it. It is only to put my lips in order. In order not to look at my hands of wax, even though their decipherable volume may erupt," 191). As he begins to decipher the strange messages of this medium, he declares that "estoy aquí ya formándome. Cuento uno a uno los centímetros de mi lucha. Por eso me nace una risa del talón que no es humo. Por ti, que no explicas la geografía más profunda" ("I am here forming myself. I count one by one the centimeters of my struggle. This is why there emerges a smile of a smokeless heel. Through you, who do not explain the deepest geography," 192). Understanding the physical terrain of this new geography is a means of acquiring its power, which in turn endows the poet with more substantial form, a new understanding that is a means to the values of full being. Called "pretérita" ("past," 194), the beloved is acknowledged as previous to the poet, a privileged point of origin, a better image by which to orient himself to a primal reality. Becoming her "lover," Aleixandre also becomes her philosopher and translator. Loving means learning to speak the beloved's new language.

Naming and representing the beloved is also a means of self-aggrandizement. A force understood as both a "perla de amor inmensa caída de nosotros" ("immense pearl of love fallen from us") and an aspect of the "infinito universal que está en una garganta palpitando" ("universal infinite that is in a palpitating throat," 195), she is a medium of being but also uncontrollable and destructive, a "rojo callado que [crece] monstruoso hasta venir a un primer plano" ("silent red color that [grows] monstrous until it comes to the fore," 196). Aleixandre must master the epistemological premises underlying his love before he can participate in its liberating energy. The beloved brings a new thesis regarding the possibilities of understanding, which impels the poet to "olvidarse de los límites y buscar a destiempo la forma de las núbiles, el nacimiento de la luz cuando anochece" ("forget the limits and seek at an inopportune moment the form of the nubile ones, the birth of the light when night falls," 199). She is a productive principle that contradicts traditional models that cannot account for a "luz cuando anochece." She brings her own light, independent of traditional representational formulas, and thus heralds herself as a primary apparition, a presence and not a simulacrum or copy. Although Aleixandre is still lamenting his impotence and weakness ("nunca he conseguido ver la forma de vuestros labios" ["I have never gotten to see the form of your lips," 199]), he is also very much aware of his will to penetrate and to capture this medium's power: "Mi brazo es una expedición en silencio" ("My arm is an expedition in silence," 200). In "Del color de la nada" ("About the Color of Nothingness") he takes another step toward understanding the new reality as he describes in physical terms what has been happening epistemologically. He sees "los ojos, salidos, de su esfera [. . .] [que] acabarían brillando como puntos de dolor, con peligro de atravesarse en las gargantas" ("eyes, wandered from their sphere [. . .] [that] would wind up shining like points of pain, with fear of piercing each other in the throats," 204). Like Guillén, Aleixandre is becoming convinced that it is possible to render the presence of a thing, to erase the distance between the word or image that stands for an object. Aleixandre intuits this new type of language in "El crimen o imposible" ("The Crime or the Impossible"): "Yo espío la palabra que circula, la que yo sé un día tomará la forma de corazón. La que precisamente todo ignora que florecerá en mi pecho" ("I watch the word that circulates, the one that I know one day will take the form of a heart. The one that is precisely unaware that it will flower in my bosom," 208–9). He is also aware of the failure of traditional words and images to summon the alternative reality: "el misterio no puede encerrarse en una cáscara de huevo, no puede saberse por más que lo besemos diciendo las palabras expresivas, aquéllas que me han nacido en la frente cuando el sueño" ("the mystery cannot be enclosed in an eggshell, it cannot know itself however much we kiss it while saying expressive words, those that have been born in my forehead during dreams," 209). The concept "word" is acquiring an entirely different meaning as Aleixandre becomes progressively aware of empirical limitations, as in "El mar no es una hoja de papel" ("The Sea Is Not a Sheet of Paper"), a possible allusion to Guillén: "esperad que me quite estos grabados antiguos" ("wait so I can get rid of these old engravings," 210), a rather pointed reference to the requirements of mimetic representation and the necessity to confront "grabados"—the printing process but also the imprinting metaphor that characterizes cognition in empiricist terminology—the presence of absences.

In "El solitario" ("The Solitary One") as Aleixandre searches for "palabras que certificarían mi altura, los frutos que están al alcance de la mano" ("word that would certify my height, the fruits within reach of my hand," 219), he becomes more aware of the nature of his struggle and his power as a "lover." He declares that it is he, and not this "señorita," who is actually in control of the course of his life, metaphorized into a game of solitaire: "yo manejo y pongo en fila [esta señorita] para completar" ("I direct and align [this girl] in order to complete myself," 220). The true locus of the other reality is an inner silence from which emanate new words and images. This brings a new understanding about their production during "ese minuto tránsito que consiste en firmar con agua sobre una cuartilla blanca, aprovechando el instante en que el corazón retrocede" ("that transitory minute that consists in signing one's name with water on a white sheet, taking advantage of the instant in which the heart retreats," 221). But he will not be satisfied with a poetry that "oculta el armazón de huesos" ("hides the framework of bones"). He wants to limit the power of his "muchacha," to transform her "en una bahía limitada, en una respiración con fronteras a la que no le ha de sorprender la luna nueva" ("into a slow-witted bay, into a breath with boundaries that the new moon will not surprise," 222). He wants a source of strength to call upon in order to discover "donde los ojos podrán al cabo presenciar un paisaje caliente, una suave transición que consiste en musitar un nombre en el oído mientras se olvida que el cielo es siempre el mismo" ("where the eyes will be able finally to witness a hot landscape, a soft transition that consists of muttering a name in my ear while it is forgotten that the sky is always the same," 222). His "love" is a means to a better end, a "paisaje caliente" ("hot landscape"), the true source from which this hybrid language and its startling images proceed.

To realize his goal, he must discover the means to unburden himself from "la cruz de la memoria contra el cielo" ("the cross of memory against the sky," 224). The ultimate barrier to unmediated being is memory and the consciousness of temporality. Word, image, poetry, and plenitude are all contained in the same experience, which exists beyond the final empirical barrier. Aleixandre's surrealistic songbird "busca aguas, no espejos" ("looks for waters, not mirrors," 224), presences, not mimetic copies. In "Del engaño y la renuncia" ("Of Deception and Renunciation"), he emphasizes the inner strength available to him, symbolized in his "brazo muy largo" ("very long arm") which is "presto a cazar pájaros incogibles" ("ready to hunt uncatchable birds") and, especially, his "pierna muy larga [. . .] destruyéndome todas las memorias" ("extremely long leg [. . .] destroying all my memories," 226). The epistemological assault continues in "Ansiedad para el día" ("Anxiety for the Day"), where he again makes a value comparison between his empirical eyes, "dos lienzos vacilantes que me ocultaban mi destino" ("two vacillating canvases that were hiding my destiny") and his intuition of an alternative existence, "aquella dulce arena, aquella sola pepita de oro que me cayó de mi silencio una tarde de roca" ("that sweet sand, that one gold nugget that fell to me from my silence one afternoon of rock," 228). By now there is no question of the much higher valuation of the alternative realm even though he still fears "el monstruo sin oído que lleva en lugar de su palabra una tijera breve, la justa para cortar la explicación abierta" ("the unhearing monster that carries instead of its word brief scissors, the right size to cut off an open explanation," 229).

Such is also the vision in "El mundo está bien hecho" ("The World Is Well Made"), alluding to Guillen's poem, in which he contrasts both the positive aspect of the hidden center of being, "la mujer del sombrero enorme" ("the woman with an enormous hat," 233), and the more ominous aspect of the same force that appears as a "gran serpiente larga" ("great long serpent," 234). Both utter what appear to be contradictory appeals: "'Amame para que te enseñe'" ("'Love me so I can teach you'") and the other, "'Muere, muere'" ("'Die, die,'" 234). The contradiction is not to be resolved by choosing, or seeking to avoid, one possibility over the other. Aleixandre must achieve the same understanding as the "ojo divino" ("divine eye," 234), the unique perspective from which this alternative world truly reveals itself as "bien hecho" ("well made") and thus capable of synthesis. At the volume's conclusion, he calls for "un vaso de nata o una afiladísima espada con que yo parta en dos la ceguera de bruma, esta niebla que estoy acariciando como frente" ("a glass of cream or an extremely well-sharpened sword with which I may split in two the blindness of the mist, this fog that I am caressing like a forehead," 237), that is, the raw and virile force necessary to overcome his confusion. He has understood that the knowledge he seeks can be achieved only through radically different means: "toser para conocer la existencia, para amar la forma perpendicular de uno mismo" ("to cough in order to know existence, in order to love the perpendicular form of oneself," 239). He must understand the involuntary manifestations of "existencia" that erupt as irrationally as a cough. To "amar la forma perpendicular" of himself he must also learn to love the involuntary "coughing" that holds the key to the mystery of who he is and can be.

Espadas como labios (*Swords Like Lips*, 1930–31) begins with the awareness that "[es posible] ya [. . .] el horizonte, / ese decir palabras sin sentido / que ruedan como oidos [. . .] entre la luz pisada" ("the horizon [. . .] [is] already [possible], / that saying of words without meaning / that roll around like ears [. . .] in the trampled light," 247). He acknowledges two types of words and images, each responding to a different mode of production. The words "sin sentido" are possible only after the light, the source of empirically produced images, has been trampled, which leaves him at the mercy of an alternative mode of production he cannot understand. This is the posture in "La palabra" ("The Word"), where he portrays consciousness as "un caracol pequeñísimo" ("an extremely small snail") but, nevertheless, "capaz de pronunciar el nombre, / de dar sangre" ("capable of pronouncing the name, / of giving forth blood," 248–49), of retaining his existential integrity in the face of a force that threatens to overwhelm it. He declares

> que mi voz no es la tuya
> y que cuando solloces tu garganta
> sepa distinguir todavía
> mi beso de tu esfuerzo
> por pronunciar los nombres con mi lengua.
>   (249)
> my voice is not yours
> and whenever you sob, may your throat
> still know how to distinguish
> my kiss from your force
> by pronouncing the names with my tongue.

Aleixandre is laying claim to a more willful role in the poetic process, however insignificant in comparison to the power of the new geography. He must confront the "silencio que es carbón" ("silence that is coal," 251), which brings unintelligible words, and, in "Muerte" ("Death"), the vision of a "morir sin horizonte por palabras, / oyendo que nos llaman con los pelos" ("horizonless death through words, / hearing that they call to us fully," 251). "Circuito" postulates the existence of "sirenas vírgenes / que ensartan en sus dedos las gargantas" ("virgin sirens / that string together throats on their fingers," 252), willful counterforces that will control the involuntary production of the throats, followed by the declaration that "Yo no quiero la sangre ni su espejo. [. . .] Por mis venas no nombres, no agonía, / sino cabellos núbiles circulan" ("I do not want the blood or its mirror. [. . .] Through my vein not names, not agony, / but rather nubile hairs circulate," 252). Finding the correct circuit means rejecting conventional epistemology: not "nombres" or "espejos," words or images that impotently mirror each other, but a new circuit connected to a different set of intellectual-existential premises. This brings forth the "ojo profundo que vigila" ("deep eye that watches," 253), a counterforce "para evitar los labios cuando queman" ("in order to avoid the lips when they burn," 253), a new willfulness that allows him to proclaim: "Soy esa tierra alegre que no regatea su reflejo" ("I am that happy earth that does not bargain away its reflection," 257). He is the ultimate ground of the alternative reality: "he dominado el horizonte" ("I have dominated the horizon," 257). Rejuvenated, he becomes "alto como una juventud que no cesa" ("tall as ceaseless youth," 257). The question now becomes "¿Hacia qué cielos o qué suelos van esos ojos no pisados / que tienen como yemas una fecundidad invisible?" ("Toward what skies or what floors go those untrammeled eyes / that have an invisible fecundity like that of yolks?" 257).

Aleixandre continues his exploration in "El vals" ("The Waltz"): "Todo lo que está suficientemente visto / no puede sorprender a nadie" ("Everything that is sufficiently seen / cannot surprise anybody," 261). Learning to see in this new way offers a means to resist the involuntary eruptions from "este hondo silencio" ("this deep silence") of the "garganta que se derrumba sobre los ojos" ("throat that hurls itself on the eyes," 264). It heralds the advent of the fullness of being, "la eternidad" ("eternity"), when "El tiempo [es] sólo una tremenda mano sobre el cabello largo detenida" ("Time [is] only a terrible slow hand laid on long locks," 264). However, it is only his force of will that confirms his presence and importance in this order:

> La verdad, la verdad, la verdad es ésta que digo,
> esa inmensa pistola que yace sobre el camino,
> ese silencio—el mismo—que finalmente queda
> Cuando con una escoba primera aparto los senderos.
>   (270)
> The truth, the truth, the truth is this that I say,
> that immense pistol which lies in the road,
> that silence—the same one—that finally remains
> when with the first broom I separate the paths.

The poetry is progressively becoming the record of a contest of wills, the poet's will or that of the involuntary producer of unintelligible images. Aleixandre finds himself in an adversarial relationship with the otherness that is being, the victim of a "love" whose finality seems inevitably to be the affirmation of one of the parties of this relationship at the other's expense. Aleixandre reacts to this impasse in "Acaba" ("Finish"), which recalls his deficient understanding ("he visto golondrinas de plomo triste anidadas en ojos / y una mejilla rota por una letra" ["I have seen swallows of sad lead nested in eyes / and a cheek broken by a letter," 275]) and which in turn reminds him that he remains distant from "la única desnudez que yo amo" ("the only nakedness that I love"), that is, "mi tos caída como una pieza" ("my cough fallen like a coin," 275). The means of capturing such an evasive prize is the aggressive imposition of will that arises from within, "como un ojo herido / se va a clavar en el azul indefenso" ("as a wounded eye / is going to fix its gaze on the defenseless blue") to "convertirlo todo en un lienzo sin sonido" ("to convert it all into a soundless canvas," 276), to remake his consciousness into "ese rostro que no piensa" ("that face which does not think," 276). This "will to willfulness" is epitomized in the word-command "ACABA" that entitles and concludes the poem, providing substantive evidence of his aggressiveness and desire to place a framework of understanding on the force responsible for an understanding associated with a higher form of truth.

In "Por último" ("Finally"), Aleixandre declares himself among "todo lo que se nombra o sonríe" ("all that names itself or smiles," 277), an entity capable of giving order and names to a realm he earlier thought to be "palabras sin sentido" ("meaningless words," 277). His experience has become "este aprender la dicha" ("this learning of happiness," 283), a search for "lo ardiente o el desierto" ("the inflamed or the desert"), the absolute limits of existential possibility. He has also learned that these involuntarily produced images must be understood as means to greater truths and thus a better image of reality. "Madre, madre" ("Mother, Mother") acknowledges precisely this. The "mother" is the transformed image of the beloved that has assumed various shapes throughout the poetry ("Madre, madre, está herida, esta mano tocada, / madre, en un pozo abierto en el pecho o extravío" ["Mother, mother, this wound, this touched hand, / mother, in an open well in the heart or deviation," 258]). Here, however, the female figure becomes a self-conscious evocation of Aleixandre's intuitions about the realm she populates. He sees this "mother" as "espejo mío silente" ("my silent mirror," 285), which now responds to his will. The images emanating from her are now understood not as reflections but as embodiments of the poet himself. Likewise, in "Palabras" ("Words") words become the agents by which the image of a "muchacha casi desnuda" ("almost naked girl," 287), a familiar symbol of the alternate realm, becomes "manchad[a] de espuma delicada" ("stained with delicate foam," 287). The conventional understanding offered by words ("palabra que se pierde como arena" ["a word that gets lost like sand," 287]) simply does not compare to "Este pasar despacio sin sonido, / esperando el gemido de lo oscuro" ("This slow and soundless passage, / hoping for the cry of the darkness") or to the "marmól de carne soberana" ("marble of sovereign flesh," 288), the intuited presence of full being, which begins to loom as a greater possibility. Indeed, in "Río" ("River") he proclaims the death of his empirical consciousness, which heralds his entrance to the unknown underworld of being: "Así la muerte es flotar sobre un recuerdo no vida" ("Thus death is to float over a memory not life," 295). As recounted in "Suicidio" ("Suicide"), his persistent impasse has been "saliendo del fondo de sus ojos" ("leaving the bottom of your eyes," 301), his separation from direct and present images in order to partake of reality at a distance. As with Guillén, where the idea of an interior plane of image production is prominent, Aleixandre is affirming a representational model for which empirical theories cannot account. The desire is not to reproduce the image at a distance but rather to encounter it at its origin, to make a hieroglyphic image that effectively functions as the "thing itself."

Aleixandre understands that he can impose meaning by intellectual force or continue to be tormented. The special words and images that he encounters remain unsatisfying because he has yet to grasp that their means of production is also the means to a full existence. Being, not representation, is the ultimate goal, "responder con mi propio reflejo a las ya luces extinguidas" ("to respond with my own reflection to the already extinguished lights," 304). The old representational system is characterized in "Con todo respeto" ("With All Respect") as "esta limitación sobre la que apoyar la cabeza / para oír la mejor música, la de los planetas distantes" ("this limitation on which to rest my head / to listen to the best music, that of the distant planets," 306). Only through the intellectual will can the poet penetrate this alternative reality: "Con mis puños de cristal lúcido quiero ignorar las luces, / quiero ignorar tu nombre, oh belleza diminuta" ("With my fists of lucid crystal I want to be ignorant of the lights, / I want to be unaware of your name, oh diminutive beauty," 309). The new intuition of a "diminutive beauty" is a geography where words are not signs but presences, "lingotes de carne que no pueden envolverse con nada" ("ingots of flesh that cannot become enmeshed with anything," 310). Likewise, in this realm "no sirve cerrar los ojos" ("it is useless to close your eyes," 310) since the reality of images is also a carnal, existential one that responds to the throat, the involuntary center of production.

La destrucción o el amor (Destruction or Love, 1932–33) intensifies the struggle to achieve direct knowledge of the alternative reality and thus of the fullness of being. In "La selva y el mar" ("The Jungle and the Sea") Aleixandre expresses, in much more willful terms, his growing desire "Mirar esos ojos que sólo de noche fulgen" ("To see those eyes that only shine at night," 323), to understand the productive principle of the alternate reality. His own understanding, characterized here as "el pequeño escorpión [. . .] con sus pinzas" ("the small scorpion [. . .] with its pincers") wants "oprimir un instante la vida" ("to oppress life for a moment"), defined as "la menguada presencia de un cuerpo de hombre que jamás podrá ser confundido con una selva" ("the diminished presence of the body of a man that can never be confused with a jungle," 324). Desire is equated with exercising the will to summon the full and unconfused presence of his "cuerpo de hombre," full being. Aware of his continued distance from "ese mundo reducido o sangre mínima" ("that reduced world or minimal blood," 326), he is equally aware of his will, which "busca la forma de poner el corazón en la lengua" ("seeks a means of putting the heart in the tongue," 329), which seeks to unify his understanding. Such a presentiment of unity is expressed in "Unidad en ella" ("Unity in Her"), which again features a female figure, a "rostro amado donde contemplo el mundo" ("beloved face where I contemplate the world"), being, "la región donde nada se olvida" ("the region where nothing is forgotten," 331). Such an experience, called "love," is also "destruction," as the volume's title underscores, in the same sense that it is the antithesis of ordinary experience. The declaration that nothing "podrá destruir la unidad de este mundo" ("nothing will be able to destroy the unity of this world," 332) is an affirmation that such a world is not a separate and distinct reality, that his alienation from being has had an epistemological origin.

Affirming the fullness of being means understanding the premises under which such fullness is possible. These intuitions become intensified in subsequent sections, as in "Mañana no viviré" ("Tomorrow I Won't Live") where Aleixandre affirms to his beloved, whom he now summons to him, that "besándote tu humedad no es pensamiento" ("kissing your dampness is not thought," 346). He understands it as a different type of intellectual experience and says that the beloved is "amorosa insistencia en este aire que es mío" ("amorous insistence in this air that is mine," 346). Their association is a contest of wills within a landscape of being that he now understands is all his. In "Ven, ven tú" ("Come, Come") he also senses a domain "donde las palabras se murmuran como a un oído" ("where words whisper as to an ear"), a unifying principle under which "ni los peces innumerables que pueblan otros cielos / son más que lentísimas aguas de una pupila remota" ("not even the innumerable fish that populate other skies / are more than the slowest waters of a remote pupil," 347). Eye and ear, as newly defined, now work in concert as the poet senses that "Esta oreja próxima escucha mis palabras" ("This nearby ear listens to my words," 348) and as "el mundo rechazado" ("the rejected world"), conventional understanding, "se retira como un mar que muge sin destino" ("retreats like a sea that moos without a destiny," 348). A "better" destiny looms as a consequence of "esa dureza juvenil" ("that youthful hardness"), the aggressive will now able "iluminar en redondo el paisaje vencido" ("to illuminate all around the defeated landscape," 349).

Aleixandre becomes more explicit in his characterization of the alternative realm, as in "Paisaje," a reference to the existential geography acquiring added definition. As he draws closer, he is also able to speak to, and for, the otherness that defines full being: "no existes y existes, / Te llamas vivo ser" ("you do not exist and you exist, / You are called living being," 351). The domain of being becomes "Pájaro, nube o dedo que escribe sin memoria" ("Bird, cloud or finger that writes without memory") and "mirada que en tierra finge un río" ("a gaze that on earth simulates a river," 352). In "A ti, viva" ("To You, Living One"), he again expresses his desire to know his beloved ("Mirar tu cuerpo sin más luz que la tuya" ["To look at your body with no more light than your own," 355]) but, more importantly, his growing conviction that she is also the source of a more profound mode of understanding. This is consciously articulated in "Quiero saber" ("I Want to Know"), whose title emphasizes that the process of epistemological adjustment facilitating these new insights is inseparable from the goal itself. Thus when he tells his beloved that he wants to know "el secreto de tu existencia" ("the secret of your existence," 358) he is referring to his own. There is no separation between the experience of plentiful being and the epistemological premises of the alternate geography. Or more explicitly, "el mundo todo es uno, la ribera y el párpado" ("The world is all one, the shore and the eyelid," 358).

The truth does not lie in specific words or images the poet may happen to perceive but in the higher principle responsible for their presence, "una música indefinible, / nacida en el rincón donde las palabras no se tocan, / donde el sonido no puede acariciarse" ("an undefinable music, / born in the corner where words do not touch each other, / where sound cannot be caressed," 372). There is no longer a separation among words, images, and their "unintelligible" origin: "Todo es sangre o amor o latido o existencia, / todo soy yo que siento como el mundo se calla / y como así me duelen el sollozo o la tierra" ("Everything is blood or love or heartbeat or existence, / everything am I who feels how the world grows quiet / and how the sob or the earth gives me pain," 373). The goal becomes to summon this "amorosa presencia de un día que sé existe" ("amorous presence of a day that I know exists," 384), to make the absent fully present. With each poem, his hope grows: "Yo sé quien ama y vive, quien muere y gira y vuela. / Sé que lunas se extinguen, renacen, viven, lloran. / Sé que dos cuerpos aman, dos almas se confunden" ("I know who loves and lives, who dies and turns and flies. / I know that moons extinguish themselves, are reborn, live, cry. / I know that two bodies love, two souls are mingled," 386). And further, in "Sobre la misma tierra" ("On the Same Earth") "que la noche y el día no son lo negro o lo blanco, / sino la boca misma que duerme entre las rocas" ("that night and day are not the blackness or the whiteness, / but rather the very mouth that sleeps among the rocks," 389). The two realities are inextricably intertwined. The desire for existential presence is to know an "inmensa mano que oprime un mundo alterno" ("immense hand that oppresses an alternative world," 390), which brings the necessity "Matar la limpia superficie sobre la cual golpeamos, / [. . .] superficie que copia un cielo estremecido" ("To kill the clean surface on which we pound, / [. . .] a surface that copies a trembling sky," 391), conventional understanding. As he further proclaims in "Soy el destino" ("I Am Destiny"): "renuncio a ese espejo que dondequiera las montañas ofrecen, / pelada roca donde se refleja mi frente / cruzada por unos pájaros cuyo sentido ignoro" ("I renounce that mirror which the mountains offer anywhere, / sheared rock where my face is reflected / traversed by some birds whose meaning I do not know," 395). The values of mimesis cede to the experience of himself in the fullness of being:

> Soy el destino que convoca a todos los que aman,
> mar único al que vendrán todos los radios amantes
> que buscan a su centro, rizados por el círculo
> que gira como la rosa rumorosa y total.
> (396)

I am the destiny that convokes all who love,
only sea to which come all the lovers, like spokes
that search for their center, rippling around the circle
that turns like the murmuring and total rose.

The geography of presence, "el oscuro chorro [que] pasa indescifrable / como un río que desprecia el paisaje" ("the dark stream [that] passes undecipherable / like a river that despises the landscape," 399), prefers "una lengua no de hombre" ("a language not of man," 400). "La luna es una ausencia" ("The Moon Is an Absence") looks back to the moon, the embodiment of the inadequacies of ordinary consciousness, and to the "otro lado donde el vacío es luna" ("the other side where the emptiness is moon," 402), where absence and emptiness dominate. In "Quiero pisar" ("I Want to Step") Aleixandre reaffirms his will to know a different medium, "esa garganta o guijo fría al pie desnudo" ("that throat or gravel cold to the naked foot," 403) and to confront the "pupila lentísima que casi no se mueve" ("slowest of pupils that almost does not move"), that "yo casi no veo, pero que sé que escucho; / aquel punto invisible adonde una tos o un pecho que aún respira, / llega como la sombra de los brazos ausentes" ("I almost do not see, but certainly hear; / that invisible point where a cough or a breast that still breathes, / arrives like the shadow of absent arms," 405). The desire to confront "un amor que destruye" ("a love that destroys," 406) is to know a loving presence capable of destroying all absent images that distance him from full being. The proximity to such a destructive encounter signals in "Cobra" the transformation of Aleixandre's willful consciousness, now a phallic cobra, that is "todo ojos" ("all eyes," 407) and to whom he beseeches, "ama todo despacio. [. . .] Ama el fondo con sangre donde brilla / el carbunclo logrado" ("love everything slowly. [. . .] Love the bottom with blood where there shines / the attained carbuncle," 408). This leads to yet another image of the will-consciousness in "El escarabajo" ("The Scarab"), the image of the plodding, durable, and virtually indestructible scarab, an apt metaphor for the poet's strength in the face of the alternative reality's destructive power. The scarab's arrival also signals that it "por fin llega al verbo también" ("at last arrives as well at the verb," 411).

The long-sought understanding has finally been achieved, and he is able now to descend "a unos brazos que un diminuto mundo oscuro crean" ("to some arms that create a diminutive dark world," 412) and to the triumphal declaration in "Cuerpo de piedra" ("Body of Stone") that "Ya no quema el fuego que en las ingles / aquel remoto mar dejó al marcharse" ("No longer burns the fire which that remote sea left behind in my groin / when it retreated," 414). Indeed, the poet has now made contact with a much greater source of power.

In the final section, Aleixandre examines even more closely his relationship to the beloved at the center of being, who is now understood to possess "ojos que no giran" ("eyes that do not turn") and a "corazón constante como una nuez vencida" ("heart constant like a defeated walnut," 417). He beseeches her to reveal her full presence: "Vive, vive, despierta, ama, corazón, ser, despierta como tierra a la lluvia naciente, / como lo verde nuevo que crece entre la carne" ("Live, live, awaken, love, heart, being, awaken like the land to an incipient rain, / like the new green that grows in the flesh," 418). "La noche" ("The Night") describes "el viaje de un ser quien se siente arrastrado / a la final desembocadura en que a nadie se conoce" ("the jouney of a being who feels dragged / to the final river's mouth in which no one is recognized," 422). This climactic moment, which resists precise description, is recounted in "Se querían" ("They Were Loving") where the male-female, conscious-unconscious, willful-involuntary aspects of Aleixandre's struggle achieve a brief unity: "mar o tierra, navío, lecho, pluma, cristal, / metal, música, labio, silencio, vegetal, / mundo, quietud, su forma. Se querían, sabedlo" ("sea or earth, ship, bed, pen, windowpane, / metal, music, lip, silence, vegetable, / world, stillness, its form. They were loving, know it," 425). The quest has been one of knowing, the affirmation of being: "la luz [. . .] como el corazón [. . .] / que pide no ser ya el ni su reflejo, sino el rio feliz, / lo que transcurre sin la memoria azul, / camino de los mares que entre todos se funden / y son lo amado y lo que ama, y lo que goza y sufre" ("the light [. . .] like the heart [. . .] / that asks to be neither it or its reflection, but rather the happy river, / that which moves along without the blue memory, / av-

enue of the seas that are fused together / and that are the beloved and that
which loves, and that which delights and suffers," 426).

Aleixandre has portrayed an existential quest in amorous terms. Lover and beloved are aspects of the same phenomenon, willful, aggressive
self-understanding via

> El amor como lo que rueda,
> como el universo sereno,
> como la mente excelsa,
> el corazón conjugado, la sangre que circula,
> el luminoso destello que en la noche crepita
> y pasa por la lengua oscura, que ahora entiende.
>
> (427)
>
> Love like that which rolls along,
> like the serene universe,
> like the exalted mind,
> the conjugated heart, the blood that circulates,
> the luminous gleam that in the night crackles
> and passes through the dark tongue, which now understands.

Love is self-affirmation that has required the destruction of the intellectual premises that had prevented the poet from achieving a privileged
understanding. The bourgeois subject is destroyed to bring into being
"lo que no vive, / lo que es el beso indestructible [. . .] mientras la luz
dorada está dentro de los párpados" ("that which does not live, / that
which is the indestructible kiss [. . .] while the golden light is inside the
eyelids," 428), an absolute value. In the concluding poem, "La Muerte"
("Death"), being brings an invocation of "death":

> Mátame como si un puñal, un sol dorado o lúcido,
> una mirada buida de un inviolable ojo,
> un brazo prepotente en que la desnudez fuese el frío,
> un relámpago que buscase mi pecho o su destino.
>
> (433)
>
> Kill me as if a dagger, a gilded or lucid sun,
> a pointed glance of an inviolable eye,
> a strong arm in which nakedness were the cold,
> a lightning flash that searched for my breast or its destiny.

The death of the bourgeois self has given birth to a new mode of being, which becomes the principal theme of the final pre–Civil War volume, *Mundo a solas (World Alone, 1934–36)*.

When Aleixandre declares in "No existe el hombre" ("Man Does Not Exist") that "el hombre no existe. / Nunca ha existido, nunca" ("man does not exist. He has never existed, never," 442), he is referring again to bourgeois definitions of subjectivity incapable of expressing the "better" truth he has experienced. The true embodiment of the nature of existence is found in the "árbol [que] jamás duerme" ("tree [that] never sleeps"), which is "verde siempre como los duros ojos" ("always green like the hard eyes") and about which it can never be said that it "quiera ser otra cosa" ("may want to be another thing," 443). The tree symbolizes the existential state to which Aleixandre's intuitions have led him: "un árbol es sabio, y plantado domina" ("a tree is wise, and planted it dominates," 443). The poetry has been, in a sense, the history of the planting of the tree of the full being that "vive y puede pero no clama nunca, / ni a los hombres mortales arroja nunca su sombra" ("lives and is able but that never clamors, / nor to mortal men does it ever extend its shade," 444). The mortals are those necessarily lesser beings trapped in ordinary reality who must continue to experience and to think via "esos ojos que te duelen, / en esa frente pura encerrada en sus muros" ("those eyes that throb, / in that pure face enclosed in its walls," 445). This lies in contrast, in "Bajo la tierra" ("Below the Earth"), to the geography of full being: "Debajo de la tierra hay, más honda, la roca, / la desnuda, la purísima roca donde sólo podrían vivir seres humanos" ("Below the earth there is, deeper, the rock, / the naked, the purest rock where only human beings can live," 450). The center of being is solid, massive, silent, immobile: a frozen, statuesque, pristine realm from which a new definition of his humanity has emerged. In "Humano ardor" ("Human Ardor") he affirms to his beloved that "Besarte es pronunciarte" ("To kiss you is to pronounce you," 451). He has seen her "pasar arrebatando la realidad constante" ("pass taking away the constant reality," 451) and now understands that her "labios" ("lips"), her presence, "eran, no una palabra,

/ sino su sueño mismo, / su imperioso mandato que castiga con beso" ("were, not a word, / but your dream itself, / your imperious command that punishes with a kiss," 451–52). This love that is also death has redefined his humanity: "Morir, morir es tener en los brazos un cuerpo / del que nunca salir se podrá como hombre" ("To die, to die is to have in your arms a body / from which one will never be able to escape as a man," 452). At the center of being, conventional definitions of subjectivity and manhood are superseded by one that uses words not to define or describe but to be "su sueño mismo."

The eventual separation from the experience of existential fullness does not change Aleixandre's opinion of its value, only of his capacity to summon the "otra tierra invisible" ("other invisible land," 460). He persists in affirming that "yo te sentí, yo te vi, yo te adiviné" ("I felt you, I saw you, I foretold you," 460). The beloved, full being's creature, is, finally, "mínima" ("minimal," 465), the most fitting word to describe an experience in which he has penetrated to the "Profundidad sin noche donde la vida es vida" ("Depths without night where life is life," 470) in order to aggrandize his understanding as "un ojo inyectado en la furia / de presenciar los límites de la tierra pequeña" ("an eye injected into the fury / of witnessing the limits of the small earth," 473). The final poem, "Los cielos" ("The Heavens") offers what may be read as a last will, in the aftermath of his death in and after love: "buscad la vida acaso como brillo inestable, / oscuridad profunda para un único pecho" ("look for life perhaps like an unstable brilliance, / a profound darkness for a unique breast," 478). These sentiments express in large part this poetry's principal theme, which has been a search for a "brillo inestable" capable of being understood only by "un único pecho" whose guiding values have been "los fuegos inhumanos" ("the inhuman fires," 479), the slow but methodical transcendence of ordinary human consciousness and subjectivity. Like Guillén's, Aleixandre's poetry is dedicated to the fabrication of private landscapes of will, "better images" that have brought forth "geographies of presence," that is, fundamental positions regarding the question of being: that it is knowable and representable on their terms.

CHAPTER 5

Absence and Experience in the Poetry of Luis Cernuda and Rafael Alberti

In sharp contrast to Guillén and Aleixandre's "geographies of presence" that proclaim these poets' aggressive capacities to affirm the fullness of being, the poetry of Luis Cernuda and Rafael Alberti recounts their distance and absence from an existential center, the consequence of life experiences that defeat attempts to contend with the intellectual-psychic locales that Guillén and Aleixandre are able to summon and affirm at will. Cernuda and Alberti recount shaping experiences that move them in a contrary direction to such private visions and that bring them to affirm a much more public and confrontational posture that also asserts a much different subjective model, one that in many aspects resembles what Johanna Drucker has characterized as the predominant subjective posture of modernism premised around an open-ended "structural model." Such a model is "never complete, whole, or intact: it is split from the very outset between self/other, conscious/unconscious and makes use of representation in the continual mediation according to which it seeks its own definition."[1] Alberti's experiences take him progressively away from his early privileged world and into the "street," where his art becomes rededicated—as is the case with a

1. Drucker, *Theorizing Modernism,* 110.

number of European writers at this time—to political commitment and the vision of a new and different public world. Although Cernuda also flirted with political activism briefly, his public commitment, perhaps even more daring than Alberti's, is ultimately to a truthful image of himself, the open acknowledgment of his homosexuality—at a time when it remained, especially in Spain, a form of love and being that "dare not speak its name"—and the creation of a misanthropic public persona for which the "Spanish tradition" up until this time had no equivalent model. If these poets begin from essentially the same existential starting point as Guillén and Aleixandre, experience requires that they move past such egocentric, "monstrous" postures in order to ratify a model for being that upholds a structural model of subjectivity, subjective positions that demand their poetry acknowledge a much wider and, indeed, open-ended sphere.

Cernuda's rejection of conventionality and his desire to affirm an alternate mode of existence is particularly intense, an attitude evident throughout his life. Indeed, Cernuda's later poetry is laced with diatribes against many of his contemporaries, mostly for propagating what he considers false or trivializing images about his friends and himself, in his own case an alleged discipleship to Guillén that he found quite difficult to dispel.[2] Cernuda's most severe judgments are, in fact, leveled against Guillén, whose poetry he considers expresses "un concepto burgués de la vida y que en ella la imagen del poeta no trasciende al hombre sino a una forma histórica y transitoria del hombre, que es el burgués" ("a bourgeois conception of life in which the image of the poet does not transcend the man but rather an historical and transitory form of man, which is the bourgeois").[3] The term "imagen del poeta" is a decisive concept for Cernuda, underscoring that his work is to a significant degree about the fabrication of an alternative image, a modern myth, about the role of the poet in the contemporary world. Cernuda's introduction

2. See Derek Harris, ed., *Perfil del aire* (London: Tamesis, 1971), 45–78; Agustín Delgado, *La poética de Luis Cernuda* (Madrid: Editora Nacional, 1975), 67–75.
3. Cernuda, *Prosa completa*, 432; all prose quotations are from this volume.

to the 1936 first edition of *La realidad y el deseo*, "Palabras ante una lectura" ("Words before a Reading"), makes clear his understanding that his poetry will likely not appeal to a middle-class audience incapable of understanding the "experiencias fragmentarias" ("fragmentary experiences"), the individual poems "que nos [permiten] suponer el pensamiento completo del poeta" ("that allow us to imagine the complete thinking of the poet," 871). His essay echoes the poetry, which champions an "imagen del poeta" understood as a higher calling.[4]

Cernuda ascribes responsibility for his becoming the special poet he claims to be to a larger-than-life force against which he must struggle, a "daimonic power," which parallels at an invisible level his struggle against bourgeois society:

> La sociedad moderna, a diferencia de aquellas que la precedieron, ha decidido prescindir del elemento misterioso inseparable de la vida. [. . .] Pero el poeta no puede proceder así y debe contar en la vida con esa zona de sombra y de niebla que flota en torno de los cuerpos humanos. Ella constituye el refugio de un poder indefinido y vasto que maneja nuestros destinos [. . .] un poder demóniaco, o mejor dicho, daimónico, que actúa sobre los hombres. [. . .] Ese poder [. . .] está estrechamente unido a mis creencias poéticas. (874)

> Modern society, unlike those which preceded it, has decided to do without the inseparable mysterious element of life. [. . .] But the poet cannot operate that way and must rely, in life, on this zone of shadow and mist that floats around human bodies. This constitutes the refuge of a vast and indefinite power that runs our destinies [. . .] a demonic power, or better said, daimonic, that acts upon men. [. . .] This power [. . .] is closely tied to my poetic beliefs.]

Cernuda's experience with this daimonic power describes the process through which he becomes a poet, doomed to lament "la pérdida y la destrucción de la hermosura" ("the loss and destruction of beauty," 875), to understand the circumstantial nature of all images of reality while at the same time being irresistibly attracted to them. As "esa oscura fuerza

4. See also Octavio Paz, "La palabra edificante," *Papeles de Son Armadans* 36 (1964): 41–82.

daimónica que rige el mundo" ("that obscure daimonic force that rules the world," 875), daimonic power exists in a dark realm beyond images but communicates to mortals by imagistic means, compared to the biblical "fuego en la zarza ardiente que vio Moises" ("fire in the burning bush that Moses saw," 876), the brightest of divine images. This is not a contradiction but an affirmation of the working premise of *La realidad y el deseo*: some images are better than others; no image is an end unto itself. The bourgeois understands life as a matter of affirming and accepting the images of ordinary reality as the exclusive ground of existence. Cernuda confronts poetry and the task of image-making as both a distrustful iconoclast and one invariably enamored of better images he knows to be indices of a superior reality.

This is certainly true of *Primeras poesías (First Poems)*,[5] a much reworked version, possibly as late as 1935, primarily of his rather poorly received first book, *Perfil del aire (Profile of the Air*, 1927), and other uncollected poems of the same period. This retrospective anthology does not faithfully capture the essence of the early poetry, which was written before the intuition of a daimonic force in his life. *Primeras poesías* reinterprets the past in terms of the later existential equation, "la realidad y el deseo." Cernuda's "pensamiento poético" begins with the adolescent's victimization by traditional subjective models of understanding and image-making. The initial poems recount representative moments in the development of the adolescent as he becomes aware of desire as a decisive force in his life and of his calling as a poet. The initial poem is dominated by the landscape contemplated from the open window of the adolescent's room, which functions almost as a photographic lens that also re-creates the conditions of empirical cognition. The daylight images from the window confirm a passive and submissive consciousness absent and distant from the world indolently contemplated:

> Tan sólo un arbol turba
> la distancia que duerme:

5. The following poems are from this section of *La realidad y el deseo*, ed. Miguel J. Flys (Madrid: Castalia, 1982).

así el fervor alerta
la indolencia presente.
(73)

Only a tree disturbs
The distance that sleeps:
Thus the ardor makes alert
The present indolence.

With the advent of the night, however, the window plays a different role:

En su paz la ventana
restituye a diario
las estrellas, el aire
y el que estaba soñando.
(74)

In its peace the window
restores daily
The stars, the air,
And the one who was dreaming.

In the darkness and in the absence of the visual spectacle of the landscape, a more profound activity continues under more favorable conditions. The images of visible reality are perceived from the outset as simply one possible source of understanding. Thus although he seems to establish his artistic origin in *La realidad y el deseo* in an apparently classical empiricism in which sensory experiences form the sole and passive basis for cognition, for knowledge, and thus for desire, Cernuda is actually overturning empiricism, if imperfectly, which is already intuited as a hindrance.[6] The young dreamer must wait until dark to resume this more useful activity in the absence of empirical images. Such impotence lies in contrast to the strength of Guillén in the face of the landscape that invariably affirms his will to being and the activity of consciousness.

Nevertheless, the adolescent wants to bring his dream to the world, to affirm its presence in the world and thus to erase the distance, and dif-

6. See also J. M. Aguirre, "*Primeras poesías* de Luis Cernuda," in *Luis Cernuda*, ed. Derek Harris (Madrid: Taurus, 1977), 225–27.

ference, between the two domains. Cernuda describes such an experience in poem V as "el acorde total" ("total harmony," 78). Although it resembles the experience of the fullness of being recounted in Guillén's *Cántico*, the *acorde* experience in *La realidad y el deseo* is confined to this poem only, which serves as the record of a prehistory beyond which Cernuda must move to affirm the "imagen del poeta" that distinguishes him from his contemporaries. The *acorde* is recounted much later in the prose poetry of *Ocnos*, described as an "unidad de sentimiento y conciencia; ser, existir, puramente y sin confusión" ("unity of feeling and consciousness; being, existing, purely and without confusion," 104), a state in which "la vida se intensifica y, llena de si misma, toma un punto más allá del cual no llegaría sin romperse" ("life intensifies, full of itself, reaches a point beyond which it would break," 103). While the *acorde* is a very positive existential experience, it has almost nothing to do with *La realidad y el deseo* despite the importance ascribed to it by Cernuda's critics.[7] The *acorde* that "nunca [. . .] se produce de por sí" ("never [. . .] is generated by itself," 103) lies beyond the poet's power to will or summon it and thus differs exceedingly from the willed experience of full being in Guillén and Aleixandre.

Poem V, however, also underscores the emptiness of the adolescent's life. The sky that he addresses provides the mirror image of his own existential nullity, "nuestra nada divina" ("our divine nothingness," 78), as empty as it is vast and "divine." Poem VI describes the corollary moment to the *acorde*. The adolescent is again in his room but is now aware of his solitude, and of time. The fullness of the earlier timeless moment now becomes a

> [. . .] Tibio vacío,
> ingrávida somnolencia [que]
> retiene aquí mi presencia,
> toda moroso albedrío,
> en este salón tan frío
> (78)

7. See Philip Silver, "*Et in Arcadia Ego*": A Study of the Poetry of Luis Cernuda (London: Tamesis, 1965), 30–50, 57–62; Derek Harris, *Luis Cernuda: A Study of the Poetry* (London: Tamesis, 1973), 23, 98.

[. . .] Tepid void,
weightless somnolence [that]
retains my presence here,
all sluggish will,
in this room so cold,
realm of the tyrant time.

The awareness of the destructiveness of time brings the youth to an understanding of the unsuitability of continued adherence to the limiting existential possibilities of ordinary existence. Such an awareness spurs Cernuda to a new way of thinking and to the first of a number of manifestos regarding the question of being:

Existo bien lo sé
porque le transparenta
el mundo a mis sentidos
su amorosa presencia

Mas no quiero estos muros,
aire infiel a sí mismo,
ni esas ramas que cantan
en el aire dormido.

Quiero como horizonte
para mi muda gloria
tus brazos, que ciñendo
mi vida la deshojan.

Vivo un solo deseo,
un afán claro, unánime;
afán de amor y olvido.

(79)

I exist and well I know,
because the world
makes transparent to my senses
its amorous presence.

But I don't want these walls,
air unfaithful to itself,
or those branches that sing
in the sleeping air.

I want as a horizon
for my mute glory
your arms, which girding
my life strip away its leaves.

I live a single desire,
a clear, unanimous zeal;
a desire for love and oblivion.

Love, the intuited goal of existence, is much different from that affirmed by Guillén and Aleixandre since it cannot be willfully summoned. Cernuda makes his existential presence contingent on the presence of another desiring body, the antithesis of the solitary *acorde* experience. From the outset, Cernuda defines himself as an absence unable to validate his existence by means of his will alone. The love experience becomes the means to forget his ordinary understanding, which is that he is the sum total of the remembered images of visual reality.

The adolescent's rejection of the bourgeois formula of existence is accompanied by a growing distrust of ordinary images as well as the products of impotent dreaming, which brings him to his first intuitions about poetry understood in terms of his experience of "better images," as in poem X, which recounts allegorically such a discovery via the appearance of an angel looking for "Un soneto [. . .] / perdido entre sus plumas." ("A sonnet [. . .] / lost among its feathers."). As he describes it:

La palabra esperada
ilumina los ámbitos;
un nuevo amor resurge
al sentido postrado.
(82)

The hoped-for word
illumines the boundaries;
A new love revives
The prostrate senses.

At this point, poetry offers something of an outlet, a substitute for love's absence and a means by which to avoid indolent dreaming ("Olvidados los sueños / los aires se los llevan" ["Dreams forgotten / the breezes take them away," 82]). Poetry, however, brings the corollary awareness that it is also susceptible to temporal laws. An almost inevitable consequence is a growing narcissism, recounted in poem XIII. Bereft of meaningful experiences, the youth becomes a "Narciso enamorado" ("enamored Narcissus," 84). He returns to his room to continue dreaming as before but with a growing sense of desperation:

> Levanta entre las hojas,
> mi aurora futura;
> no dejes que me anegue
> el sueño entre sus plumas.
>
> (86)

> Arise from among the leaves,
> you, my future dawn;
> don't let the dream
> overwhelm me in its feathers.

The existential accord proclaimed earlier now becomes the realization that "alma y vida son ajenas" ("soul and life are alien," 90), an estrangement from full being complemented by an equal failure to embrace the vocation of poet, symbolized in the blank paper: "Tu juventud nula, en pena / de un blanco papel vacío" ("Your youth nil, grieving / over an empty sheet of white paper," 92). In this section's final poem set in a garden, existential emptiness defines the adolescent who understands quite clearly that "En vano / resplandece el destino. / Junto a las aguas quietas / sueño y pienso que vivo" ("In vain / shines destiny. / Next to the quiet waters / I dream and think that I am alive," 92). The setting embodies a domesticated space where he can dream and think but little else. The garden setting is ultimately no different from others that have brought him to compromise his earlier intuitions of a higher reality.

In "Historial de un libro" ("Record of a Book," 1958), a commentary on the making of *La realidad y el deseo*, Cernuda holds no fond memories for the compositions of the second section: "mucha parte viva y esencial en mi no hallaba expresión en dichos poemas" ("a large living and essential part of me did not find expression in those poems," 905). *Eglo-*

ga, elegía, oda (*Eclogue, Elegy, Ode,* 1927–28) intensifies the contradictions of the earlier thoughts and dreams. The insufficiency of his existential equation becomes explicit in "Egloga," whose protagonist is an idyllic landscape, notable among its beautiful objects being a rose, the embodiment of adolescence that

> [. . .] asume una presencia pura
> irguiéndose en la rama tan altiva,
> o equívoca se sume
> entre la fronda oscura,
> adolescente, esbelta, fugitiva.
> (99)

> [. . .] assumes a pure presence
> swelling pridefully on the haughty branch,
> or equivocally it sinks
> among the dark fronds,
> adolescent, svelte, fleeing.

Like the youth, these roses dilute their value as they also come under the influence of the narcissistic "agua tan serena, / gozando de sí misma en su hermosura" ("water so serene, / enjoying itself in its beauty," 100), which offers only a vague approximation of the intensity of the sky: "sólo copia del cielo / algún rumbo, algún vuelo / que vibrando no burla tan ingrata / plenitud sin porfía" ("only copies from the sky / some direction or flight / that vibrating does not deceive such ungrateful / plenitude without persistence," 29). The poem effectively retraces the trajectory of *Primeras poesías*, concluding that such "presence" is actually "Nula felicidad; monotonía" ("Null happiness, monotony," 100).

That nullity is embodied in "Elegía" in the self-contemplative form of a naked youth, yet again in his familiar indoor setting, another "pura presencia" who offers to a mirror "su estéril indolencia / con un claro, cruel escalofrío" ("his sterile indolence / with a clear, cruel shiver," 104). The adolescent's "Soledad amorosa" ("amorous Solitude," 105), indeed, expresses itself as masturbation: "Melancólica pausa. En triste nieve / el ardor soberano se deshace" ("Melancholy pause. In sad snow / the supreme ardor comes undone," 105). The faint image that lingers as "una lejana / forma dormida [. . .] ausente y vana / entre la sorda soledad del mundo" ("a far-off / sleeping form [. . .] absent and unreal / among the deaf solitude of the world," 105) provides the basis for "Oda" and the emergence "vivo, bello y divino [de] / un joven dios" ("alive, beautiful and divine [of] a young god," 106), the fulfillment of this dream's impotent promise. This god, a "contorno tibiamente pleno" ("tepidly full contour," 107) that in every way resembles the youthful body in "Elegía," cedes his presence to an "eco suyo [. . .] / el hombre que ninguna nube cela" ("echo of himself [. . .] / the man that no cloud watches," 107). This "man," a self-sufficient being who "sólo fía / en sí mismo ese orgullo tan altivo" ("only trusts / in himself that arrogant pride") is, for all his swagger, but a self-conscious echo of an echo whose reason for being is to justify a loveless existence. The virile young man, however, has nothing to do in this empty paradise except to pursue his "extraña imagen" ("strange image," 109), to dilute further whatever essence he may have originally possessed.

The indefensibleness of such an impotent existence occasions the tortured *Un río, un amor* (*A River, A Love*, 1929), whose title makes explicit reference to the solitary form of "love" of past experiences. A similar form of subject-centered love that for Guillén and Aleixandre is a means to expanded consciousness and creativity is for Cernuda conclusive proof of his impotence and failure. Adolescence has been an unrequited wait for a "tierna imagen ajena" that has failed to materialize. *Un río, un amor* represents the first attempt to establish the primacy of desire by rejecting the self-absorbed impotent "innocence" into which he had drifted and by embracing his adult calling, to become a poet. As Cernuda recalls in "Historial," his definitive commitment to poetry comes after 1927 as a gradual realization that "el trabajo poético era razón principal, si no única, de mi existencia" ("poetry was the principal, if not sole, reason for my existence," 903). *Un río, un amor* is best read as an extended palinode, a chagrined and bitter renunciation of a failed way of life.[8]

8. See Harris, *Luis Cernuda*, 33–36.

In the initial poem, "Remordimiento en traje de noche" ("Remorse in Evening Dress"), there emerges an "hombre gris [. . .] un cuerpo vacío" ("gray man [. . .] an empty body," 115), a new protagonist but not essentially different from the earlier empty "presences." A number of poems examine "ligeros paisajes dormidos en el aire" ("light landscapes asleep in the air," 116), called "el sur" ("the south"; and elsewhere "el oeste" ["the west"], "Nevada," "Durango," and "Virginia," among others), desolate embodiments of an absent existence that now bring remorse: "El sur es un desierto que llora mientras canta, / [. . .] hacia el mar encamina sus deseos amargos / abriendo un eco débil que vive lentamente" ("The south is a desert that cries while it sings, / [. . .] toward the sea it directs its bitter desires / opening a weak echo that lives slowly," 116). The vacuousness of the adolescent experience is further underscored in "Nevada," where "el estado de Nevada" ("the state of Nevada") becomes synonymous with an impotence that has yielded "amor inconstante" ("inconstant love," 120), "nieve dormida / sobre otra nieve, allá en Nevada" ("slow sleeping / on top of other snow, there in Nevada," 120), reminiscent of the "triste nieve" of "Elegía." Left alone "Gritando locamente" ("Shouting wildly"), he obsesses over the tormenting consciousness that his earlier hopes for existential presence has left him instead with "La presencia del frío" ("The presence of the cold," 121) and the painful truth about love: "ningún cuerpo viene ciegamente soñando" ("no body comes blindly dreaming," 121). This culminates in the condemnation of the adolescent experience itself in "Durango." Recalling the open window of *Primeras poesías*, Cernuda sees "Por la ventana abierta" ("Through the open window") that "muestra el destino su silencio" ("destiny shows its silence," 126). The adolescent has had no destiny. His only accomplishment is the making of "Durango postrado, / con hambre, miedo, / frío, / pues sus bellos guerreros sólo dieron, / raza estéril en flor, tristeza, lágrimas" ("Durango prostrate, / with hunger, fear, cold, / whose beautiful warriors only produced, / a sterile race in blossom, sadness, tears," 126). He has waited too long, and alone.

The message of the concluding poems, beginning with "La canción

del oeste" ("Song of the West"), is the need to move beyond disappoint-
ment, to relegate the false images that live in "the west," if not to oblivion, at least to their proper place. He must turn away from such images to
avoid repeating the errors of adolescence that "como cualquier monarca / aguarda que las torres maduren hasta frutos podridos" ("like any
monarch / waits for the towers to ripen into rotten fruits," 139). To re-
claim the lost promise of youth he must renew the potential of "los deseos cortados a raiz / antes de dar su flor, / su flor grande como un niño"
("desires cut at the root / before yielding their flower, / their flower big
as a child," 140). When he returns to the image of the adolescent's window in the final poem, what was in the early poetry the symbol of ordinary understanding becomes here a "Ventana huérfana con cabellos ha-
bituales" ("Orphaned window with habitual hair," 140), to look inwardly
upon an

> atroz paisaje entre cristal de roca [. . .]
> penetrando en los huesos basta hallar la carne,
> sin saber que en el fondo no bay fondo,
> no hay nada, sino un grito,
> un grito, otro deseo
> sobre una trampa de adormideras crueles.
> (140)

> atrocious landscape among rock crystal [. . .]
> penetrating into the bones until it finds the flesh
> without knowing that at the bottom there is no bottom,
> there is nothing, only a scream,
> a scream, another desire
> Above a trap door of cruel poppies.

Although desire has become central in his thinking, nevertheless it remains little more than an empty concept, the painful acknowledgment
of the poet's absence and distance from a better vision.

By 1931, the date of Los placeres prohibidos (The Prohibited Pleasures),
Cernuda has become aware of the "poder daimónico." At this earlier
date, however, it is understood, in "Carta a Lafcadio Wluiki" ("Letter
to Lafcadio Wluiki"), in more positive terms as a force that "va rigien-

do nuestras vidas" ("is governing our lives," 1095) and, in a piece of the same year "Escuela de los adolescentes" ("School for Adolescents"), that "tiene siempre un sutil afinidad más o menos exacta, con nuestro espiritu" ("always that a subtle affinity more or less exact, with our spirit" 1236). The darker, irresistible, and more irrational aspect of this force, which becomes prominent in "Palabras ante una lectura" four years later, has yet to manifest itself. This is because daimonic power, Cernuda's belief in the agency of an outside presence that will validate his dreams, first manifests itself as an invocation rather than as part of a narration of a lived experience. In "La escuela de los adolescentes," a narrator who seems very much like a mouthpiece for Cernuda himself relates to his listener-pupil that it has been necessary for him "creer en una presencia, presencia que nosotros mismos evocamos de la nada con el poder taumatúrgico del arnor, y que surge, al fin, radiante y arnenazadora, ante nuestros ojos cegados" ("to believe in a presence, a presence that we ourselves call up from nothingness with the wondrous power of love, and that emerges, finally, radiant and threatening, before our blinded eyes," 1237). If in Un río, un amor Cernuda flounders in darkness to complain about the adolescent's hesitation to affirm love, Los placeres prohibidos allows him to rewrite this chapter in his life and to affirm the "pleasures" that he had prohibited to himself.

The separate introductory poem, "Diré cómo nacisteis" ("I Will Tell How You Were Born"), typically interpreted as a diatribe against society,[9] is also a critique of the adolescent experience. While the "regimen caído" ("fallen regime") may certainly allude to the fall of Alfonso XIII, the poem just as surely refers to the "reyes sin corona" ("kings without a crown") and the impotent "monarca" of Un río, un amor, the adolescent "king" who has also fallen. The "placeres prohibidos" offer the promise of a new "fulgor [que] puede destruir vuestro mundo" ("radiance [that] can destroy your world," 147), the inner and outer dimensions of his experience, self-inflicted and society-inflicted, that have kept him from be-

9. José María Capote Benot, El surrealismo en la poesía de Luis Cernuda (Sevilla: Universidad de Sevilla, 1976), 147–48; Harris, Luis Cernuda, 46–47.

ing free. Freedom, simply put, is the capacity to love, to affirm a calling beyond the loveless solipsism of adolescence. This new faith in finding a beloved becomes the repository of all value, the means to forget "esta existencia mezquina" ("this miserable existence," 151): "Tú justificas mi existencia. / Si no te conozco, no he vivido; / si muero sin conocerte, no muero, porque no he vivido" ("You justify my existence. / If I do not know you, I haven't lived; / if I die without knowing you, I do not die, because I haven't lived," 151).

As the poems progress, Cernuda becomes better able to use the image of love and to distance himself from the earlier egocentric ideal. In "El mirlo, la gaviota" ("The Blackbird, the Seagull"), he is able, finally, to reformulate his relationship to adolescence, and as a consequence the poem becomes the occasion for a much stronger amorous profession:

> Creo en el mundo,
> creo en ti que no conozco aún,
> creo en mi mismo;
> porque algún día yo seré todas las cosas que amo:
> el aire, el agua, las plantas, el adolescente.
> (159)

> I believe in the world,
> I believe in you whom I still do not know,
> I believe in myself;
> Because one day I will be all the things I love:
> The air, the water, the plants, the adolescent.

By supplementing this new faith Cernuda is able, in "Como leve sonido" ("As a Light Sound"), to equate "todo aquello que de cerca o de lejos / me roza, me besa, me hiere" ("all that from near or far / rubs me, kisses me, wounds me," 160) with the image of love:

> tu presencia está conmigo fuera y dentro,
> es mi vida misma y no es mi vida,
> así como una hoja y otra hoja
> son la apariencia del viento que las lleva.
> (160)

> your presence is with me outside and in,
> it is my life, and it is not my life,

just as one leaf and another leaf
are the outward sign of the wind that carries them.

This leads in turn to Cernuda's even greater commitment to poetry, which in "Te quiero" ("I Love You") is equated with the various means, all inadequate, that he has employed to say the words "I love you." The ultimate conclusion is that even the "terribles palabras" ("terrible words"), the surrealistic discourse of Un río, un amor and the present volume, have proven insufficient to express such sentiments:

> así no me basta;
> más allá de la vida,
> quiero decírtelo con la muerte;
> más allá del amor,
> quiero decírtelo con el olvido.
>
> (161)

> that way is not enough;
> beyond life,
> I want to say it to you with death;
> beyond love,
> I want to say it to you with obvlivion.

However inadequate his professions and intuitions, they are the only means to maintain his newfound faith. At the volume's conclusion, however, Cernuda finds himself once again with himself, alone and waiting for the time when a real-life beloved's "propia presencia / haga inútil este triste trabajo / de ser yo solo el amor y su imagen" ("own presence / will make useless this sad work / of being by myself alone love and its image," 162).

Donde habite el olvido (Where Oblivion Dwells, 1932–33) recounts the memory of the love experience for which Cernuda had been preparing himself. If Los placeres prohibidos blindly invokes an unknown intuition of love, Donde habite el olvido represents the blinded account of an all-consuming love whose memory now haunts him. "Olvido," a realm where it might be possible to forget his pain, becomes the only place

> donde el amor, ángel terrible,
> no esconda como acero

en mi pecho su ala,
sonriendo lleno de gracia aérea mientras crece el tormento
(168)
where love, terrible angel,
will not conceal like steel
in my breast his wing,
smiling full of airy grace while the torment increases

and "donde termine este afán que exige un dueño a imagen suya, / som-
etiendo a otra vida su vida, / sin más horizonte que otros ojos frente a frente" ("where will end this desire that demands a master in its own image, / surrendering its life to another life, / with no more horizon than
other eyes face to face," 168). Only in its wake does the demonic nature
of his desire—to possess "el fondo del mismo amor que ningún hombre
ha visto [. . .] un dios en mis días / para crear mi vida a su imagen" ("the
ground of love itself that no man has seen [. . .] a god in my days / to create my life in his image," 169)—begin to express itself more fully.

Besides characterizing his erotic experience as a personal defeat,
Cernuda's identification with fallen angels also marks a decisive step
in the torturous process of his becoming a poet. Even though he may
cast himself as "un ángel que arrojan / de aquel edén nativo" ("an angel
that they throw out / from that native paradise," 174), condemned now
to walk the earth like an "errabundo mendigo, recordando, deseando; /
recordando, deseando" ("wandering beggar, / remembering, desiring, /
remembering, desiring," 175), his remembrances are impotent only in
the context of his experience with and his attempt to possess the absolute, "en lo más poderoso descansando, / mano en la mano, frente en
la frente" ("resting in the most powerful thing, / hand in hand, face to
face," 175). Cernuda's failure in love is also cast in terms of a secular version of "original sin." His penance, however, is to become a poet, to see
and remember the fragmentary images that remind him of an irremedia-
ble distance from love and the fullness of being. If this is a fall, into mortality and even nihilism (the belief in "la muerte de todo [. . .] como tus
ojos, como tus deseos, como tu amor" ["the death of everything [. . .]
like your eyes, like your desires, like your love," 181]), the "impotent"
creature who emerges is, like his counterpart in the biblical myth, some-

thing of a devil whose present is grounded in memories of his experience of "aquel cuerpo de ángel que el amor levantara" ("that body of an angel that love raised," 177) and of the limitation of "mis ojos en el mundo, / dueños de todo por cualquier instante" ("my eyes in the world, / masters of everything for whatever moment," 178).

Cernuda emerges from these memories with a new understanding of the daimonic force he had earlier intuited and of his own intermediate status, as a medium, a special mortal with whom daimons, the gods' messengers, make contact. The pagan concept of an irrational, amoral force affecting mortals for good or ill, but usually for ill,[10] is an apt metaphor for the experience that he has survived. Cernuda's failure in love, however, is again attributable to his failure to affirm an adequate medium in which to express his expectations. The ultimate consequence is his estrangement from love's divine image and the embittered acknowledgment that "El amor no tiene esta o aquella forma, / no puede detenerse en criatura alguna" ("Love does not have this or that form, / it cannot be contained in any creature," 182). Although he may now be conscious of his new status, that he shares the same space as other residents of the earth and that

> [la tierra queda] con el deseo,
> con este deseo que aparenta ser mio y ni siquiera es mío,
> sino el deseo de todos,
> malvados, inocentes,
> enamorados o canallas,
> (183)

> [the earth remains] with desire,
> with this desire that seems to be mine and is not even mine,
> but räther the desire of everybody,
> villains, innocents,
> lovers or riffraff,

his recognition of the likeness of his image to that of others is only partial and short-lived. Cernuda does not fall so far or lose so much as those

---

10. See C. Christopher Soufas, "Cernuda and Daimonic Power," *Hispania* 66 (1983): 167–75.

in whose midst he now recognizes himself. Along with a sense of loss, maturity brings the awareness that poetry has become his definitive vocation. If poetry cannot equal the absolute experience he strived to possess in the culminating moment of his youth, it nevertheless affords the opportunity, in the aftermath of his amorous failure, to affirm his own mythic "imagen del poeta," the open-ended search for himself and for a destiny always guided by desire.

In contrast to his earlier poetry, which invoked ideals yet to be experienced, *Invocaciones a las gracias del mundo* (*Invocations to the Graces of the World*, 1934–35; known later simply as *Invocaciones*) continues, from a calmer, melancholic, yet more universal perspective, the remembrances and experiences of *Donde habite el olvido*. This posture becomes evident in "A un muchacho andaluz" ("To an Andalusian Boy") which invokes his now spent youth in the image of an adolescent that emerges as "un resto de memoria [que] / levantaba tu imagen como recuerdo único" ("a remnant of memory [that] / raised your memory like a unique remembrance," 188). Unlike the "dioses crucificados, / tristes dioses que insultan / esa tierra ardorosa que te hizo y deshace" ("crucified gods, / sad gods that insult / that ardent earth that made you and unmakes you," 188), this "muchacho que [surgió] / al caer de la luz" ("boy that [emerged] / on falling from the light," 187) fulfills a different role in Cernuda's system of values. The antithesis of "los ateridos fantasmas que habitan nuestro mundo" ("the numb phantoms that inhabit our world," 188), the adolescent offers an image worthy of veneration. Inspired by the memory and example of the godlike adolescent, Cernuda is also poised to accept the burden of creating his own superior being and mythic poetic protagonist, the better image of himself. The memory of the adolescent, therefore, fulfills an almost religious function, as a "forma primera, [. . .] fuerza inconsciente de su propia hermosura" ("first form, [. . .] a force unconscious of its own beauty," 187).

If the strength of the adolescent is his unconsciousness and independence of inferior forms of love, then his undoing is his heightened expectations as a lover, for whom only an absolute experience will suffice. The desire to know being is to be conscious of something that consciousness paradoxically destroys. Consciousness means consciousness of one's mortality and ultimate insignificance in the context of a universe of images destined, like the eyes that gaze upon them, to disappear. His absence from being, however, further confirms his intuition of a transcendent force ("ese impulso que guía / un cuerpo hacia otro cuerpo" ["that impulse that guides / one body to another body," 193]), not entirely unsympathetic to the plight of certain "better" mortals who have attempted demonic feats. This daimonic force becomes the metaphor in adulthood for Cernuda's contact with a better reality, a divine medium that confers a temporary "divinity" on the poet who, in the making of an image, is able to produce an immortal version of an object of beauty, like its contemplator, threatened with destruction.[11] Among such objects, of course, is Cemuda's own adult figure, whose full presence in being is impossible to affirm. It should be clear at this point that Cernuda's vision, while sharing Guillén's and Aleixandre's belief in the poet's capacity to fashion a superior image of the world, is altogether different.

At every opportunity, Cernuda is suggesting the superiority of his values, however difficult to endure, which seem even more divine when compared to the contemporary scene surveyed in "La gloria del poeta" ("The Glory of the Poet"). Cemuda addresses a "Demonio hermano mio, mi semejante" ("Devil my brother, my fellow man," 196), the idealized image of himself as poet, which he has accepted except for one detail, "el flamígero puñal codiciado" ("fiery coveted dagger of the poet," 199), the final deformation of his "pecho sonoro y vibrante" ("sonorous and vibrant breast") that only death will be able to "hacer resonar la melodía prometida" ("make the promised melody ring," 199). Such a consciousness is fully lacking in his fellow men with their "interminables palabras" ("endless words," 197) and their "marmóreos preceptos / sobre lo útil, lo normal y lo hermoso" ("marmoreal precepts / on the useful, the normal and the beautiful," 198), false images by which they enable themselves to

11. See Harris, *Luis Cernuda*, 66–67.

"dictar la ley al mundo, acotar el amor, dar canon a la belleza inexpresable" ("dictate the law to the world, limit love, canonize inexpressible beauty," 198). The fate of these better images, therefore, lies ultimately in the hands of others. The culminating image—the young sailor ("cifra de todo cuerpo bello" ["sum of every beautiful body," 206]) of "El joven marino" ("The Young Sailor") who reenacts in mythic terms the final moment of youth in his reunion in death with the sea, "el único ser de la creación digno de ti" ("only being of creation worthy of you," 206)—reenacts the moment of conferral of the "flamígero puñal del poeta." At the moment of declaring it lost forever, Cernuda is nevertheless revaluing youth. The sailor's exemplary death will continue to guide his values in maturity that, although conditioned on the remembrance of loss, are nevertheless superior in every way to a bourgeois existence.

It is clearly inadequate to characterize Cernuda's early poetry in terms of the loss of innocence or the fall from an edenic state. Finally forced to acknowledge his place among the phantoms of the world, Cernuda falls, into time and adult society. But as he underscores in "Palabras ante una lectura," his type of poetry requires "un estado de espíritu juvenil, y hasta no es raro que el poder de la juventud lo prolongue la poesía en el poeta más allá del tiempo asignado para aquella" ("a state of youthful spirit, to the point that it is not odd that poetry may prolong the power of youth beyond the time assigned to it," 873). This is precisely the phenomenon in the first edition of La realidad y el deseo. Cernuda's definition of himself, his subjectivity, is necessarily ongoing and open-ended. It is shaped in, and as, a structure whose foundation stone is the memory of youth. The role of memory in Cernuda is perhaps the sharpest contradistinction to Guillén and Aleixandre. His experiences are not, to recall a verse from Guillén "completo para un dios" ("complete for a god") yet his existence is hardly at the same level of his fellow human beings. His disdain for the bourgeoisie is precisely because they defined themselves in terms of their completeness. Even though life proceeds under unfavorable conditions, Cernuda has discovered his own means to produce the "better images" that will sustain him.

At the same time that Aleixandre and Guillén are affirming discreet, private spaces where being can be willed into conformity with one's vision of it, Cernuda painfully and publicly acknowledges the limits of "sueños creados con mi pensamiento" ("dreams created by my thought," 208). The first edition of *La realidad y el deseo* represents as well Cernuda's growing, and ultimately total, commitment to the vocation of poet premised on a structure of existence that is continually affirming an open-ended subjective position.

From the outset, Rafael Alberti's poetry is distanced from the landscapes of ordinary reality, mediums through which to represent his absence and estrangement from being. An acute awareness of separation from his human center dominates the poetry, and his poetic landscapes parallel the inner dimension of that alienation. Despite an apparent exuberance, sentiments of impotence permeate his first major work, *Marinero en tierra* (*Sailor on Land*, 1924). The poems recount the experiences of a landlocked "sailor" who recounts his relationship with the sea from the perspective of absence and loss: "El mar. La mar. / El mar. ¡Sólo la mar!" ("The sea. The sea. / The sea. Only the sea!" 59).[12] The bifurcation of the sea into masculine and feminine aspects (as alluded to by the articles *el* and *la*) is also an acknowledgment of the division of reality into an empirical-visual realm, "la mar," and a domain, "el mar," where empirical rules do not apply. The experience of "el mar," associated with the fullness of being, is never a real possibility. The question the sailor asks of his father "¿Por qué me desenterraste / del mar?" ("Why did you unearth me / from the sea?") is the same as asking why he has come into consciousness, why he would want to partake of a destiny that diminishes him and makes him a "marinerito en tierra."

The *marinero*'s insignificance in the landlocked medium only intensifies feelings of absence from a vital center embodied in the sea-that-is-being. This progressive sense of impotence is expressed by the loss of imaginative vision. The images of ordinary experience, which tempt him

12. This and the following quotations are from *Poesía* (1924–1967) (Madrid: Aguilar, 1972).

to accept them as finalities, have collectively become "Una ciudad marinera / [que] quiere a tu casa arribar" ("A marine city / [that] wants to put
into port at your house," 82). He comes to realize that a more valuable
medium has been exchanged for one of lesser value, "una mar muerta,
/ [que] la empujó un mal viento" ("a dead sea, / [that] a bad wind pro-
pelled," 87), and that in the act of producing his poetic images he is also
effectively emptying himself.

By the next major volume, El alba del alhelí (Dawn of the Wallflower,
1925–26), his dilemma has intensified. His proposal in the "Prólogo" is
for an exchange:

> Todo lo que por ti vi
> —la estrella sobre el aprisco,
> el carro estival del heno
> y el alba del albelí—,
> si me miras, para ti.
>   (149)

> All that I saw through you
> —the star over the sheepfold,
> the summer hay wagon,
> and the dawn of the wallflower—,
> if you look at me, for you.

Alberti calls on an otherness that has not been experienced satisfactori-
ly to reveal itself more fully. Yet he has progressively less to exchange for
this hoped-for encounter. As symbolized in the "alhelí," the rose, and
the carnation, the emergence of the decentering influence of sexual desire makes it more difficult to assemble sufficient existential "capital" to
maintain even this tenuous position. His poetic surrogates continue to
voice his existential concerns: "¿Cómo vivir sin dinero? / —¡Vendedor, /
que se muere mi alba en flor!" ("How to live without money? / —¡Seller,
/ my flowering dawn is dying!"; 154). Another character, in "El pescador
sin dinero" ("The Fisherman without Money"), is berated by an accus-
ing voice that tells him, "Ya te lo has tirado todo. / Y ya no tienes amigo"
("You've thrown it all away. / And you have no friend," 165), seconded by

the fisherman's own lament: "¡Oh campo mío en la mar, / ya no te po-
dré comprar, / que me quedé sin dinero!" ("Oh my field in the sea, / I
won't be able to buy you / since I am penniless!" 166). Given the context
of these statements, these characters present strong evidence of a dete-
riorating existential position. These figures are accompanied by further
losses, abandonment in "La novia" ("The Bride") in which the bride is
left "sin mi amante, / yéndome a casar" ("without my lover, / on the way
to get married," 168), a pattern repeated in a number of variant forms.
Desire is progressively overwhelmed by a more powerful medium that
keeps love always at a distance. Equally ominous is that the poet's weak-
ening position is also specifically represented as a loss of vision at the
hands of irresistible destructive forces ("Vinieron, vida, vinieron / los negros quebrantahuesos / y me sacaron los ojos. / [. . .] Y no veía" ["They
came, life / the black ospreys came / and they scratched out my eyes /
[. . .] And I did not see," 196]), that suggest impotence and further estrangement from self.

The deterioration of vision is accompanied by a new awareness of
sound that occupies a different domain. New personae, the prisoner of
"El prisionero" ("The Prisoner") and the foreigner of "El extranjero"
("The Foreigner"), embody alienated roles and herald a much greater
dependence on a medium that expresses itself in sound:

> —Oído, mi blando oído,
> ¿qué sientes tu contra el muro?
> —La voz del mar, el zumbido
> de este calabozo oscuro.
> (199)

> —Ear, my bland ear,
> What do you hear against the wall?
> —The voice of the sea, the buzz
> of this dark prison.

This intuition about the unconventional language of "el mar" leads in "El
extranjero" to the conclusion that "Mi lengua natal, ¿de qué / me sirve en
tierras extrañas?" ("My native language, what / good does it do me in

foreign lands?" 200). A new sound-dominated medium relentlessly imposes itself and its foreign language. Succeeding poems recount further undermining of vision. "Torre de Iznajar" ("Iznajar Tower") represents a prisoner content to remain in his prison ("Prisionero en esta torre, / prisionero quedaría" ["A prisoner in this tower, / a prisoner I would remain," 206]) since it has "Cuatro ventanas al viento" ("Four windows to the wind," 206), objective means of verifying his presence there. The poem, nevertheless, recounts the unexplained disappearance of these windows and the subsequent realization of the prisoner's effective effacement: "—¿Quién llora al Oeste, amiga? / —Yo, que voy muerta a tu entierro" ("—Who cries to the West wind, friend? / —I, who go dead to your funeral," 207). The reliance on vision has resulted in the failure to be able to continue to situate himself in his geography: "Mis ojos, mis dos amores, / se me han caído a la fuente. / Ya para mí estará ausente / la estrella de los albores" ("My eyes, my two loves, / have fallen into the fountain. / And for me will be missing / the star of the dawn," 208). All that remains, as he phrases it in his burlesque self-portrait "El tonto de Rafael" ("Silly Rafael") is "el cretino eco fiel" ("the faithful cretinous echo"), the absent, irrational remnant of an estrangement from desire that leaves him a "Tonto llovido del cielo / del limbo, sin un ochavo" ("Fool rained from the sky / of limbo, without a dime," 214). In more dramatic terms toward the volume's end, Alberti recounts the wind of irrational forces overwhelming the subjective will. Turning to one of his most trustworthy consorts, the "sirenilla marinera" ("little sailor siren"), now grown, who speaks with a "Voz de mujer" ("Voice of a woman"), the poet asks her a question that is its own answer: "¿quién querrá hacerme a mí ver / que estoy viviendo engañado / no creyéndote mentira?" ("who will want to make me see / that I am living deceived / by not believing you to be a lie?" 230). He must definitively abandon the "seascape" geography in which the early poetry was grounded and from which he is by now fully estranged.

Cal y canto (1926–27) is even more suggestive of the growing existential impasse recounted in El alba del alhelí. The sound-centered medium progressively overwhelms his efforts to maintain conscious dominion over himself. In "Busca" ("Search"), for example, he asks his "can decapitado" ("decapitated dog") a reference to his diminished psychosexual energy: "¿Por dónde tú, si ardiendo en la marea / va, vengador, mi can decapitado?" ("Where do you travel, if you go burning in the tide, / avenger, my decapitated dog," 241). In "Amaranta," the "Rubios, pulidos senos de Amaranta, / por una lengua de lebrel limados" ("Golden, polished breasts of Amaranta, / smoothed over by the tongue of a greyhound," 243) become conduits that direct attention to a new productive locus "por el canal que asciende a tu garganta" ("through the canal that ascends to your throat," 243). Amaranta becomes an attractive-destructive force that imprisons the greyhound "como un ascua impura, / entre Amaranta y su amador" ("like an impure coal, / between Amaranta and her lover," 243), the poet himself.

The destructive process continues in "El arquero y la sirena" ("The Archer and the Siren") as a siren "atenta al hilo y no a la puntería" ("attentive to the bowstring and not to the aim") embodies an idea of visual representation that is now "En diez espejos rota" ("Into ten mirrors broken," 248). This is followed in "Oso de mar y tierra" ("Bear of Sea and Land") with a new landscape, a

Bar en los puertos y en las interiores
ciudades navegadas de tranvías,
tras la nereida azul que en los licores
cuenta al oido y canta al marinero
coplas del mar y de sus valles frías.
(250)

Bar in the ports and in the interior
cities navigates by trolley cars,
beyond the blue Nereid that in the liquors
tells stories to the ear and sings to the sailor
verses from the sea and its cold valleys.

As the earlier paradise of the sea "Rompe, hirviendo, el Edén, hecha océano" ("Bursts, boiling, Eden, become ocean," 251), Alberti portrays his attempt to forestall the collapse of his old representational structure with a new protagonist dependent on an artificial medium: "Dios desciende al mar en hidroplano" ("God descends to the sea in a hydroplane," 251). The implausibility of such means is underscored in the "Sueño de las tres sirenas" ("Dream of the Three Sirens") in which, among other human inventions, the hydroplane appears again in a sterile "redondo vuelo" ("circular flight," 252). Alberti is confronted by the image of an empty identity, from which his artistic evasions cannot save him, the narcissistic sailor of "Narciso": "Narciso, tú, la insignia en el sombrero, / del club alpino, *sportman*, retratado / en el fijo cristal del camisero" ("Narcissus, you, the insignia on your hat, / of the alpine club, *sportman*, portrayed / in the fixed crystal of your outfitter," 254). Another in the succession of unprofitable exchanges brings him to what amounts to a sterile bourgeois existence and further loss of imaginative power.

"Romeo y Julieta" recounts continued deterioration of the poet's existential position as he loses his "Precipitada rosa" ("Cast-down rose," 262), the remains of his psychosexual energy, that is replaced by a "rosa mecánica." The poem "Romance que perdió el barco" ("Ballad That Lost the Boat") marks the end of the sailor as a character in the poetry while it underscores the inseparability in Alberti of medium and content. The demise of the sailor, who also embodied a specific aesthetic mode, heralds as well the demise of the sustaining existential structure. As Alberti surveys his wrecked Paradise ("¡Ni mar, ni buque, ni nada!" ["No sea, or boat, or anything!"; 268]), "ángeles albañiles" ("bricklaying angels") have already descended to begin a new mode of production that he cannot resist:

—Angeles, ¿qué estáis haciendo?
Derribada en tres mi frente,
mina de yeso, su sangre
sorben los cubos celestes,
y arriba, arriba y arriba,
ya en los columpios del siete,
los angeles albañiles
encalan astros y hoteles.
(268–69)

—Angels, what are you building?
My face has crumbled in three,
a mine of plaster, the celestial cubes
suck up its blood,
and up, up and up,
already in the swings of seventh heaven,
the bricklaying angels
whitewash stars and hotels.

The angels' medium is the same "puño de cal [que] paralizaba / mi lengua, pies y manos" ("fist of lime [that] paralyzed / my tongue, feet, and hands," 272), the by-product of an incapacitated will. *Cal y canto (Resistance)* marks the appearance of a sound-dominated medium, not song but the uncontrollable utterances that erupt from the throat. As the aesthetic paradigm shifts from eye to ear, the throat becomes the primary means by which the poet continues to communicate with his inner geography. The empty echoes resisted in *El alba del alhelí* now become all-inclusive. In "Soledad tercera" ("Third Solitude"), Alberti in the role of "joven caminante" ("young traveler") continues to flounder. This tribute to Gongora is a stylization of what has just befallen him, a youth who "vio, música segura, / volar y, estrella pura, / diluirse en la lira, perezoso" ("lazily saw, sure music, / fly and, pure star, / become watered down in the Lyre," 275).

"Madrigal al billete del tranvía" ("Madrigal of the Trolley Car Ticket") envisions a "flor nueva" ("new flower"), the streetcar ticket (in sharp contrast to the natural flowers that earlier symbolized Alberti's psychosexual energy). As the guarantor of the ride, the ticket becomes yet another impotent symbol of his failure to encounter his existential center. The ticket's ascribed attributes—"no arde en ti la rosa ni en ti priva / el finado clavel" ("in you the rose does not burn nor in you does / the dead carnation deprive," 283), an idealized destination where he will be free of desire and its "giratorio idioma de los faros, los vientos, detenidos" ("gyrating language of the lighthouse beacons, the winds, stopped," 283)—are clearly wishful thinking. Subsequent landscapes along this journey invoke other confining, desolate locales in the sad geography he now inhabits. "Venus en ascensor" ("Venus in an Elevator") allegorizes the trajectory of his lifeless desire embodied in a mannequin Venus, a "niña, de madera / y de alambre" ("girl, of wood / and wire," 287), as it traverses the various levels of the poet's psychic department store in an elevator that passes a "Despacho de poesías" ("Poetry office") and a level where "Se perfila el sonido" ("Sound shows its profile," 287), exactly the phenomenon fast becoming Alberti's almost exclusive means of understating. The ascent produces no change in Venus, only an inventory of the store's dubious contents. The next section, "A Miss X, enterrada en el viento del oeste" ("To Miss X, Buried in the West Wind"), repeats the previous sentiments but in a much more diffuse medium. If Venus the niña travels by elevator in a well-defined poetic inscape, the lost and "buried" "Miss X niña" (299), of the same essence, has disappeared. The only traces of her are vague memories of her superficial milieu ("El barman, ¡oh, qué triste!" "The barman, oh how sad!") that quickly fade: "Ya nadie piensa en ti" ("No one thinks of you," 299). Miss X thus provides the perfect counterpart to Narcissus and his false way of life.

"Platko" was inspired by newspaper headlines and photographs of a Hungarian soccer goalkeeper who, in the national championship match between Barcelona and San Sebastian played on May 20, 1928, demonstrated exceptional courage in defense of the goal, for which he received a bloody head wound. The poem, however, is only nominally about this soccer player. It equates the photograph and story of the bleeding goalie with the means by which Alberti has become informed about the state of his "defense" of his own inner space. "Platko lejano" ("Far-off Platko") bears only a superficial resemblance to the heroic goalie. Platko/Alberti represents the final trace of the poet's resistance, which persists only in its resonance in the memory:

> ¡Oh Platko, Platko, Platko,
> tú, tan lejos de Hungría!
> ¿Qué mar hubiera sido capaz de no llorarte?
> Nadie, nadie se olvida,
> no, nadie, nadie, nadie.
> (303)

Oh Platko, Platko, Platko,
you, so far from Hungary!
What sea would not have been capable of weeping for you?
Nobody, nobody forgets,
no, nobody, nobody, nobody.

It is as nobody, an existential nullity, that Alberti concludes, in "Carta abierta" ("Open Letter"), a fragment at that, to proclaim that "mi alma [. . .] bate el record continuo de la ausencia" ("my soul [. . .] bats the extended record for absence," 308). He is constituted as an absence, having arrived at end of the streetcar line at the center of the *absence* of being: "tú, desde tu rosa, / desde tu centro inmóvil, sin billete, / muda la lengua, riges rey de todo. [. . .] / Y es que el mundo es un album de postales" ("you, from your rose, / from your immobile center, without a ticket, / your tongue mute, you rule as the king of everything. [. . .] And the world is an album of postcards," 308). His capitulation to overwhelming forces seems complete:

Vi los telefonemas que llovían,
plumas de angel azul desde los cielos.
Las orquestas seráficas del aire
guardó el auricular en mis oídos.
(308)

I saw the telephone calls that rained,
feathers of blue angel, from the skies.
The telephone receiver held
the seraphic orchestras to my ears.

His demise seems, almost sarcastically, complete: "¿Quién eres tú, de acero, rayo y plomo? / —Un relámpago más, la nueva vida" ("Who are you, made of steel, thunderbolt and lead? / One flash more, the new life," 309).

In the context of the earlier poetry, *Sobre los angeles* (*Concerning the Angels*, 1927–28) is simply a continuing exploration of an absent existence that expresses itself in language relayed by "carteros [que] no creen en las sirenas" ("postmen [that] do not believe in the sirens," 308), that is, by angels. These angels, however, are perhaps the full antithesis of biblical angels. Like the "ángel muerto, vigía" ("dead angel, lookout," 317) lamented in the initial poem, they are dead remains, the by-products of an untenable poetic-existential mode that nevertheless, somewhat as conventional angels, herald a new mode of expression. The Dantesque prologue "Entrada" ("Entrance") announces his entrance to a hellish realm where, "muerta en mi la esperanza" ("dead all hope in me") he languishes hoping to encounter "ese pórtico verde" ("that green portico," 318), a means of escape. Evicted from his earlier residence, as the title "Desahucio" ("Eviction") indicates, the angels ("ángeles malos, crueles, / quieren de nuevo alquilarla" ["bad, cruel angels / want to rent it again," 321]) begin to assault him. The first, in "Angel desconocido" ("Unknown Angel") presents the poet a familiar image, of himself, dressed in the fashionable clothes of his alienation, as depicted earlier in "Narciso," tormented because

> Zapatos son mis sandalias.
> Mi túnica, pantalones
> y chaqueta inglesa.
> Dime quien soy.
>   (322)

> Shoes are my sandals.
> My tunic, pants
> and English jacket.
> Tell me who I am.

It suggests that his present emptiness is a consequence of acts committed against his earlier essence: "Yo te arrojé de mi cuerpo, / yo, con un carbon ardiendo" ("I hurled you from my body, / I, with a burning coal," 322), a likely reference to desire overwhelmed, heat that generated no light, that destroyed the old geography ("Llevaba una ciudad dentro. / La perdió" ["He carried a city within him. / He lost it," 325]) and that left him "Sin ojos, sin voz, sin sombra" ("Without eyes, without a voice, without a shadow," 325), at the will of a "fría luz en silencio / de una oculta ventana" ("cold light in silence / of a hidden window," 327), the haunting "angelic" images that now emerge, involuntarily. A momentary insight, however, occurs in "El angel bueno" in which a "good angel" reveals one of the causes of his downfall: the desire to maintain a fixed position, to remain his static self forever. The angel's words recreate his willful pride: "¡Oh anhelo, fijo mármol, / fija luz, fijas aguas / movibles de mi alma!" ("Oh longing, fixed marble, / fixed light, fixed movable waters / of my soul!"; 328). His sin has been to make the mapping of his private geography an exclusive end, which now culminates in the presence of these angels. With each new angel, however, Alberti begins to understand more. In "El angel desengañado" ("The Undeceived Angel"), he receives what amounts to an invitation ("ven a mi país" ["come to my country," 332]) to a new understanding: "Te esperan ciudades, / sin vivos ni muertos, para coronarte" ("Cities await you, / without living or dead people, to crown you," 332).

Exerting a much more intense and direct effect on Alberti in the second section, much more hellish than the first, the angels force him to relive the process by which his "voz y los albedríos" ("voice and the wills," 342) have been defeated. "Engaño" ("Deception") summarizes the conditions of his self-estrangement and self-deception:

Alguien detrás, a tu espalda,
tapándote los ojos con palabras.
Detrás de ti, sin cuerpo,
sin alma.
Ahumada voz de sueño
cortado.
        (344)

Somebody behind, at your back,
covering your eyes with words.
Behind you, bodyless,
without a soul.
Smoked voice of
interrupted dream.

These "palabras, vidrios falsos" ("words, false glasses") have effaced his earlier identity, ascribed, in "El ángel ángel" ("The Angel Angel") to the presence of "el mar" ("Y el mar fue y le dio un nombre" ["And the sea was and it gave him a name," 343]). Alberti senses in "El ángel del misterio" ("The Angel of Mystery") that "en las almenas grita, muerto, alguien / que yo toqué, dormido en un espejo" ("In the battlements shouts, dead, someone / who I touched, asleep in a mirror," 350), the remains of his earlier self now attempting to communicate to him in "Ecos del alma hundida en un sueño moribundo" ("Echoes of the soul sunken in a moribund dream," 351). The "ángeles mudos" ("mute angels") who want to but cannot ask the question "¿Cómo tú por aquí y en otra parte?" ("How can you be here and in another place?"; 352), and are paralleled by "Hombres, mujeres, mudos, [que] querrían ver claro" ("Men, women, silent, [who] would want to see clearly"), suggest a deeper penetration that in "Alma en pena" ("Soul in Torment") is expressed even more forcefully: "te conozco aunque ataques diluido en el viento" ("I know you even though you attack diluted in the wind," 353). This brings him in "El ángel avaro" ("The Greedy Angel") to the objective image of his bankrupt self:

> Ese hombre está muerto
> y no lo sabe.
> Quiere asaltar la banca,
> robar nubes, estrellas, cometas de oro,
> comprar lo más difícil: el cielo.
> Y ese hombre está muerto.
>   (355)
> That man is dead
> and he doesn't know it.
> He wants to assault the bank,
> rob clouds, stars, golden comets,
> buy the most difficult thing: the sky. And that man is dead.

This lowest point, however, immediately follows in "Los ángeles sonámbulos" ("The Sleep-Walking Angels") by another revelation, the objective image of the expressive medium into which he has fallen, characterized politically as a rebellion against "un rey en tinieblas" ("a king in darkness," 355), the earlier self from which he has descended. It has been a rebellion of both eye and ear, the "ojos invisibles de las alcobas" ("invisible eyes of the bedrooms," 355), the tormented vision, including the angels, that overwhelmed his "pupilas muertas" ("dead pupils") yet "también los oídos invisibles de las alcobas" ("also the invisible ears of the bedrooms"), which "se agrandan contra el pecho" ("aggrandize themselves against the breast") and which "bajan a la garganta" ("descend to the throat," 356) to expose this "king" that the poet can no longer be: "Un rey es un erizo sin secreto" ("A king is a hedgehog without a secret," 356). Alberti has thus come full circle, to the utter defeat of his earlier self but also to the threshold of a new existential-artistic paradigm.

The final section marks another step, backward, in the circular progression that leads, finally, to the preconscious paradise from which he emerged. The "Tres recuerdos del cielo" ("Three Memories of the Sky") are approximations of an imagined existential prehistory ("Todo anterior al cuerpo, al nombre y al tiempo" ["Everything before the body, the word and time," 359]). The first memory offers an ideal vision in which it is possible to "[mirarse] sin verse" ("[look at yourself] without seeing yourself," 359) in a medium of presence that underscores the inadequacy of the conscious human vision irremediably distanced from, and thus incapable of representing, the full existence (pure vision unconscious of itself) from which he emerged. The second remembrance corresponds to a slightly later time, yet before the emergence of the king alluded to earlier, "Cuando tú abriste en la frente sin corona. [. . .] Cuando tú, al mirarme en la nada, / inventaste la primera palabra" ("When you opened in the crownless face. [. . .] When you, on looking at me in nothingness, / invented the first word," 360). In the "Tercer recuerdo" ("Third Memory") these mediums wed to produce an offspring, "nuestra luna primera" ("our first moon," 361), consciousness, at a sharp remove from the unmediated presence of being. Alberti is now able to understand the rest of the story: "que el mar verdadero era un muchacho que saltaba desnudo, / invitándome a un plato de estrellas y a un reposo de algas" ("that the true sea was a boy who jumped naked, / inviting me to a plate of stars and to a repose of algae," 361). He had been sated, put to sleep by his extended love affair with his youthful self. This image lies at the heart of his crisis. As he begins to realize that it is possible to affirm "que más de una ventana puede abrir con su eco otra voz, si es buena" ("that more than one window can open with another voice its echo, if it is good," 363), he also begins to associate responsibility for his "descenso de la vía lactea a las gargantas terrestres" ("descent from the Milky Way to the terrestrial throats," 365) with the word niño, his earlier self, and the judgment that "Para ir al infierno no hace falta cambiar de sitio ni postura" ("To go to hell it is not necessary to change place or position," 366).

Alberti is now able to explore a hitherto unknown existential geography, as in "Expedición" ("Expedition") and "Los ángeles colegiales" ("The School Angels"), where he also confronts necessary truths about himself. In "Novela" ("Novel"), he recounts the death of "un monarca" (368), his youthful self who refused to cede to a new and more mature regime, whose passing is fittingly called "un suicida lento de noviembre / [que] había olvidado en mi estancia. / Era la última voluntad de un monarca" ("a slow November suicide / [that] I had forgotten in my room. It was the last will of a monarch," 368). "Invitación al arpa" ("Invitation to the Harp") affirms renewed existential and aesthetic energy: "Una voz desde el olvido mueve el agua dormida de los pianos" ("A voice from forgetfulness moves the sleeping water of the pianos," 370). In what will become the hallmark of his poetry from this point forward, Alberti raises his voice, his public voice, to ask that he be heard ("Oidme. [. . .] Oidme aún. Más todavía [. . .] porque siempre hay un último posterior a la caída de los páramos" ["Hear me. [. . .] Hear me more. Still more [. . .] because there is always a last thing after the fall of the wastelands"], 372). He calls for "un poco de distancia: / la mínima para comprender un sueño" ("a little bit of distance: / the minimum to understand a dream," 374), which leads to a willingness to accept his "fall" in affirmative terms: "una rosa es más rosa habitada por las orugas / que sobre la nieve marchita de esta luna de quince años" ("a rose is more a rose inhabited by the caterpillars / than over the withered snow of this fifteen-year-old moon," 377). The present, a public present, is finally preferable to the private geography that he has endured to enter upon it, in all its non-angelic ugliness. It leaves Alberti, like the "ángel superviviente" ("surviving angel") wounded and wingless but with a voice.

Sermones y moradas (*Sermons and Dwellings*, 1929–30) recounts the emergence of this new poetic voice that continues to uses the irrational language of *Sobre los ángeles* but in a worldly context. The self-critical fall from a false paradise of prolonged youth reverses the focus of the poetry. Rather than to write for himself, Alberti begins to examine his mistaken assumptions in a more public fashion. He feels compelled to tell others, to give sermons, amounting to palinodes, about a disastrous existence: "En frío, voy a revelaros lo que es un sótano por dentro" ("Coldly, I am going to reveal to you the meaning of a basement from the inside," 383). What needs to be emphasized at this point is that the solipsistic existence he is now abandoning resembled quite closely the very existential ideals that dominate the poetry of Guillén and Aleixandre. He leaves behind his private geography for the public world of men, women, and politics, which he now claims to have known "desde el primer día que la luz se dio cuenta de su inutilidad en el mundo" ("from the first day that the light became aware of its uselessness in the world," 386). This is also the subject of "Adios a las luces perdidas" ("Goodbye to the Lost Lights") in which he remembers that "le dieron la vida los espejos que recogen el frío de esos ojos que se deshacen" ("the mirrors that gather the cold of those eyes that come undone gave him life") and asks for "olvido y láigrimas para las luces que se creen ya perdidas definitivamente" ("forgetfulness and tears for the lights that believe themselves definitively lost," 390). "Se han ido" ("They've Gone") continues his self-criticism as he recalls that his crisis has been inspired by "las hojas" ("the leaves"), perhaps a reference to the pages on which he had written his earlier poetry that he now declares "derrotadas por un abuso de querer ser eternas" ("defeated by an abuse of wanting to be eternal," 390), a refusal to grow that he finally recognizes has happened in spite of himself. Clinging to his earlier paradise had denied him the experience of a wider medium, the world itself: "Tenías tú que vivir más de una media vida sin conocer las voces que ya llegan pasadas por el mundo" ("You had to live more than half a life without knowing the voices that already come, passed on by the world," 391). The conclusion is a positive one: "Hace ya treinta años que ni leo los periódicos: mañana hará buen tiempo" ("It's been thirty years since I have read the newspapers: tomorrow the weather will be good," 391). And also that "Yo anduve toda una noche con los ojos cerrados [. . .] Ya a mi no me hace falta para nada comprobar la redondez de la Tierra" ("I wandered a whole night with my eyes closed [. . .] I no longer have any need to verify the roundness of the Earth," 393). Much like Cernuda, Alberti is now poised to leave behind his youth to affirm an adult role. What remains, however, is to fill this void.

Alberti's growing up is also a growing away from the poet he has been. His earlier repertoire of protagonists becomes in *Yo soy un tonto y lo que he visto me ha hecho dos tontos* (*I Am One Fool and What I Have Seen Has Made Me Two Fools*, also 1929) the occasion to bid farewell to the "tonto" he has been as a consequence of "lo que he visto," a self-critical reference via Calderón to his "tragic" life that now seems comic or perhaps absurd. This volume's nominal protagonists are the movie stars of the early cinema (Charlie Chaplin, Harold Lloyd, Buster Keaton, and others). In keeping with the physical geography of his earlier landscapes, they offer a delicious set of phantom images with which to construct a nonmoving picture. Instead of sailors or sirens, he chooses slapstick comedians to embody the poetic content and to continue his prolonged act of self-criticism. That Alberti can no longer take seriously the poet he has been culminates in "Charles Bower, inventor," where, in effect, Alberti-Bower, the "Difunto inventor" ("Dead inventor") who Alberti once was, signs his own poem, something of a last will and testament.

The poem begins with a lament by Bower-Alberti (a minor light in comparison with the other stars, an exaggerated absence, a persona who fails to play the part) over "La defunción ante mi chaleco de los más poéticos bosques" ("the demise before my jacket of the most poetic forests," 431), the private geography clearly understood as "la creación de un fantasma" ("the creation of a phantom," 432). The poem concludes with the signature and new title "Charles Bower. / Difunto inventor" (432). The act of signing his name marks the precise moment when Bower gives up his identity completely to another force, which completes his self-critique. An entire production dedicated to reading and writing "mi nombre" is declared dead. In this context, his growing commitment to politics and to becoming a "poeta en la calle" ("poet in the street") is an almost logical next step.

Indeed, there is evidence in his first serious attempt at "poetry in the street," "Con los zapatos puestos tengo que morir" ("I Must Die with My Shoes On," 1930), also called the "Elegía cívica" ("Civic Elegy"), that there is an effort to link the political poetry to the earlier writing. The political poetry becomes a "voz pública" ("public voice") that has emerged from his private voices and interior geography in order to move him "into the street." "Elegía cívica" is a political poem by virtue of Alberti's including it under this genre. Yet it could have easily been placed in *Sermones y moradas* and, indeed, makes more sense in terms of its being understood as a poem in which Alberti is groping to find the voice that will shortly make him a public poet "in the street." Judith Nantell considers this to be a flawed political poem because Alberti "forgoes investigating the causes of the social disorder in favor of listing, with surrealist rhetoric and hermetically private images, aspects of his own malaise."[13] This seems precisely the point, to establish the ground for a poetry in the street because it intently focuses on "his own malaise."

Thus when Alberti calls out to an Aurelio and declares "que tus ojos de asco los hemos visto derramarse sobre una muchedumbre de ranas en cualquier plaza pública" ("that we have seen your eyes of loathing spill out on a multitude of frogs in any public plaza"),[14] the remark can be taken to refer to "the street" or, more aptly, to the phenomenon of "his own malaise." A "multitude of frogs" (Lorca often uses croaking

13. Judith Nantell, *Rafael Alberti's Poetry of the Thirties: The Poet's Public Voice* (Athens: University of Georgia Press, 1986), 128.

14. Rafael Alberti, *El poeta en la calle* (Madrid: Aguilar, 1978), 22.

frogs to refer to the involuntary production of sound-voice-language) is an apt metaphor to characterize the cacophony of inner voices, the "surrealistic rhetoric" that informs the poetry from *Cal y canto* onward. None of the images of "Elegía cívica" is "hermetically private," especially the most often cited verse: "Oíd el alba de las manos arriba" ("Listen to the dawn of the raised hands," 23), which seems to suggest that Alberti is throwing in his lot with the clenched-fist salute of international communism. The verb *oír*, however, alludes not simply to the fact of his political conversion but also to the process. Unlike French poet Louis Aragon, who rejects surrealism to "return to reality," Alberti is suggesting in this image an aesthetic closely associated with the processes of hearing that has led him to a new strength that has brought him to the threshold of political affirmation.

Poeta en la calle makes self-conscious use of references that in an earlier context are negative in order to suggest, to himself if nobody else, both the distance he has come and the growth he has achieved. In "Un fantasma recorre Europa" ("A Phantom Crosses Europe") he uses the phantom, earlier the symbol of the absent content of the youthful self under the spell of phantom images (recall Cernuda's reference to the "fantasmas con quienes muero a solas"), to refer to something altogether different: "Un fantasma recorre Europa, el mundo. / Nosotros le llamamos camarada" ("A phantom crosses Europe, the world. / We call him comrade," 30). From the false phantoms of his earlier life emerges its antithesis, the embodiment of comradeship. As "La familia" proclaims, the public poetry brings Alberti to a new sense of belonging:

Hace falta estar ciego,
tener como metidas en los ojos raspaduras de vidrio,
cal viva,
arena hirviendo,
para no ver la luz que salta en nuestros actos,
que ilumina por dentro nuestra lengua,
nuestra diaria palabra.
(55)

It is necessary to be blind,
to have placed glass filings in your eyes,
quicklime,
boiling sand,
in order not to see the light that leaps into our acts,
that from within illumines our tongue,
our daily word.

Like Cernuda, Alberti has left behind the private self in order to engage a public reality.

CHAPTER 6

Subjective Fragmentation in the Theater of
Federico García Lorca

Things fall apart; the center cannot hold.

YEATS, "THE SECOND COMING"

Although Federico García Lorca's writing develops outlooks similar
to Cernuda's and Alberti's in relation to the question of existence—
that being expresses itself diffusely and in a pattern that the conscious will is incapable of substantially influencing—Lorca's vision
is ultimately more somber, and tragic. In sharp contrast to Cernuda,
whose ardent belief in the transforming power of desire allows him
to affirm a viable, indeed, mythic image of himself as a poet and as
a homosexual, Lorca portrays the progressive incapacity—for himself as well as for his poetic and dramatic characters—to establish
a viable ground for the type of affirmations that accompany the mature art of his colleagues. Early in his career and in a fashion that resembles Cernuda's "daimonic power," Lorca evokes his experience
of an inspirational force quite colorfully in "Teoría y juego del Duende" ("Theory and Game of the Duende"). As with Cernuda's "zarza ardiente," Lorca characterizes the experience of contact with a
folkloric "duende" as "una comunicación con Dios por medio de los

cinco sentidos" ("a communication with God by means of the five senses"),[1] a metaphor for his encounters with a force that breathes into the
vacant spaces of the human soul: "¿Dónde está el duende? Por el arco
vacío entra un aire mental que sopla con insistencia sobre las cabezas de
los muertos, en busca de nuevos paisajes y acentos ignorados" ("Where
is the duende? Through an empty arch enters a mental air that blows with
insistence over the heads of the dead, in search of new landscapes and
unknown accents," 3:1109). Lorca's understanding of this hidden force,
nevertheless, differs significantly from the creative-destructive equations
of Cernuda and Aleixandre. What in Aleixandre becomes a celebration of
the aggrandizement of the human will in order to affirm his presence in
being becomes in Lorca the recognition of his impotence to establish hegemony over the landscapes it encounters. Lorca's work should be read,
therefore, as the record of absence from being but also as an extended
process that outlines the fragmentation of subjectivity, a consequence of
the paralysis of the imaginative vision by destructive forces.

     The early poetry presages this negative potential and alludes to a
growing existential discord. In *Primeras canciones* (*First Songs*, 1922) Lorca
mythologizes his dilemma in "Adán" ("Adam"), which retells the biblical story of the creation of man. As the poem begins, God has just taken
Adam's rib in order to create Eve, to whom Adam remains indifferent.
He dreams instead of "un niño que se acerca galopando / por el doble
latir de su mejilla" ("a child that comes galloping / through the double beating of his cheek," 1:264), the vital embodiment of his existential and creative potential. In this double pulse, however, there is another
"Adán oscuro" ("dark Adam") who dreams a sterile dream, "neutra luna
de piedra sin semilla / donde el niño de luz se irá quemando" ("neutral
moon of stone without seed / where the child of light will slowly be consumed," 1:264). Lorca's version of the myth portrays an Adam tragically
incapable of realizing his designs because of a self-destructive ambiva-

     1. All quotations are from Federico García Lorca, *Obras completas*, ed. Arturo del Hoyo,
3 vols. (Madrid: Aguilar, 1986), 3:1102.

lence that nullifies his will to creativity. This idea is repeated decisively in "Canción" ("Song"), where the poet sees "dos palomas oscuras" ("two dark doves"), the sun and the moon, symbols of imaginative discord. As aspects of the same desire for existential fullness, they nevertheless compete against each other and bring instead estrangement from being. In the final verses, the poet penetrates the shadows in order to see "dos palomas desnudas" ("two naked doves") but also to proclaim that "la una era la otra / y las dos eran ninguna" ("one was the other / and the two were neither," 1:267).

Canciones (Songs, 1921–24) expands on this impasse, notably in "Canción de jinete (1860)" ("Rider's Song [1860]") as a dead rider's horse continues to carry him forward, even though no one—rider, horse, or narrator—can answer the question "¿Dónde llevas tu jinete muerto?" ("Where do you take your dead rider?" 1:307). The reply is voiced in another poem of the same title as the suggestion of the horse's continued, if useless, resistance to the destructive force, its persistence in the darkness, cedes to resignation. The rider laments here that "yo nunca llegaré a Córdoba" ("I will never get to Córdoba," 1:313). Acknowledging the primacy of a destructive force which sees him but which he cannot see, he recognizes that he will not achieve his goal. The possibility of simply being, of finding a place to "vivir sin verme" ("live without seeing myself," 1:389), progressively cedes to the terrible image of the self emptied of its content, a never-ending cycle in which existential autonomy is undermined and fragmented with every new and false image of the self.

The awareness of this impasse becomes particularly acute in the multi-sectioned uncollected "Suite de los espejos" ("Suite of the Mirrors"), whose initial segment, "Símbolo" ("Symbol"), presents a Christ as the embodiment of a noble but doomed way of life:

Cristo
tenía un espejo
en cada mano.
Multiplicaba
su propio espectro.
Proyectaba su corazón

en las miradas
negras.
(1:625)

Christ
had a mirror
in each hand.
He multiplied
his own specter.
He projected his heart
into the dark
gazes.

In effect, Christ's activity is Lorca's and affirms the price he continues to pay for representing his existential absence in a destructive, fragmenting medium, the "miradas negras" of others. This religious statement is actually a poetics that reflects Lorca's growing consciousness of artistic premises that have led to a dead end. Like this Christ, Lorca finds it exceedingly difficult to represent his heart to others. These ideas are complemented by the segment entitled "Los ojos" ("The Eyes"), in which the eyes are understood to contain "infinitos senderos" ("infinite paths," 1:633), infinite possibilities for diverting the human will: "Las pupilas no tienen / horizontes. / Nos perdemos en ellas / como en la selva virgen" ("The pupils do not have / horizons. / We get lost in them / as in the virgin wood," 1:633).

The gypsy protagonists of *Romancero gitano* (*Gypsy Ballads*, 1924–27) represent something of an interlude in which Lorca is better able to marshal the fragmenting dialectic that forms the dynamic of his art, affording him a certain dramatic distance from these forces and where he begins to objectify his attitudes toward an audience—appropriately labeled "aquella gente" ("those people," 1:397). In "Preciosa y el aire" ("Preciosa and the Air"), an uncomprehending public that has no framework for understanding Preciosa's story of her fear of desire does not free her of her burden but does provide a respite from her inner drama of resistance. Preciosa's storytelling objectifies an existential dilemma and makes it the occasion for art.

"La casada infiel" ("The Unfaithful Wife"), which recounts an erotic experience, is also in this vein. Like Preciosa, the Gypsy narrator fails to recount an experience of plenitude, "el mejor de los caminos" ("the best road," 1:407), which he initially believes to be a sexual encounter with a virginal woman. Rather, he uncovers what proves to be his own manipulation by a married woman, fully tainting the experience. The "casada infiel" is the real protagonist and becomes the Gypsy's continuing obsession. His plenitude actually belongs to the adulterous wife and as a consequence elicits an attempt to redefine and devalue the experience by consigning it to the category of prostitute and client: "Me porté como quien soy. / Como gitano legítimo. / La regalé un costurero / grande de raso pajizo" ("I conducted myself like the person I am. / Like a legitimate gypsy. / I gave her a large sewing box / of fine straw," 1:407). Yet the Gypsy who "no quise enamorarme" ("refused to fall in love," 1:407) has by now become obsessed with the false circumstances under which he advertised his glorious moment. Recalling it for others, he exposes his loss of control and manliness, becoming instead a slave to conventional conduct that further diminishes his stature. This, in effect, is the theme of virtually every poem of the volume.

"Romance de la Guardia Civil española" ("Romance of the Spanish Civil Guard") marks the culmination of these themes, offering the fullest physical and visual portrayal of the destructive inspirational force consuming the poet and his proxy-protagonists. The narrator equates the Gypsies' destruction with his own person: "¡Oh ciudad de los gitanos! / ¡Quién te vio y no te recuerda? / Que te busquen en mi frente. / Juego de luna y arena" ("Oh city of the gypsies! / Who that saw you does not remember you? / Let them look for you in my face. / Play of moon and sand," 1:430). Here the idea of dramatic distance all but disappears as an equivalent destruction is visited on both Gypsies and narrator, who represents them from a vantage point "donde joven y desnuda / la imaginación se quema" ("where young and naked / the imagination is consumed," 1:429). The destruction of the Gypsy "city" acknowledges the tenuousness of Lorca's attempts to ameliorate the destructive effects of a force unknowable despite the images assigned to it here. The volume concludes with three "romances históricos" ("historical ballads"), further acknowledgments of the loss of creative will and a return to a more intimate personal history, culminating in a story of incest in "Thamar y Amnón." The poem concludes with a final impotent gesture as King David, the father of this ill-fated family, "con unas tijeras / cortó las cuerdas del arpa" ("with some scissors / cut the strings of the harp," 1:442).

Such is Lorca's vulnerable state as he undertakes his most ambitious project, *Poeta en Nueva York* (*Poet in New York*, 1929–30), a continuation of his imaginative collapse, this time in a real city where he portrays himself "Tropezando con mi rostro distinto de cada día" ("Colliding with my different face every day," 1:471). The imaginative consequences are much more serious since it becomes all but impossible to dissociate his person from the poetry, to establish an aesthetic distance between himself and the New York landscape. In "Paisaje de la multitud que vomita" ("Landscape of the Vomiting Multitude"), the "ciudad entera se agolpó en las barandillas del embarcadero" ("whole city hit the railings of the wharf") to vomit and to embody physically the uncontrolled flood of images of the self that has overwhelmed the poet's imagination, the "mirada [. . .] mía [que] / fue mía, pero ya no es mía" ("my gaze [. . .] [that] / used to be mine, but is no longer mine," 1:474). Rather than to represent specific happenings that occur during his stay in New York, these poems make physical use of landscapes that, although they suggest a temporal narrative, actually chronicle Lorca's failure to establish his presence in the New York landscape:

> ¿Qué voy a hacer? ¿Ordenar los paisajes?
> ¿Ordenar los amores que luego son fotografías,
> que luego son pedazos de madera
> y bocanadas de sangre?
>   (1:518–19)

> What am I going to do? Put the landscapes in order?
> Arrange loves that later become photographs,
> and after that pieces of wood
> and mouthfuls of blood?

The poems have become like photographic double exposures, the physical landscapes providing merely the visual backdrops for the poet's progressive subjective fragmentation. The multitudes of New York embody official society's repressive "miradas negras" that thwart "la voluntad de la Tierra" ("will of the Earth," 1:527), making his self-estrangement complete. As the concluding "Son de negros en Cuba" ("*Son* of Negroes in Cuba") emphasizes, *Poeta en Nueva York* is not the unified expression of one voice but of multiple contradictory voices, an almost self-mocking, parodic exposition of Lorca's failure to coordinate voices and landscapes. This is also poignantly illustrated later, in the final poem of *Diván del Tamarít*, "Casida de las palomas oscuras" ("*Casida* of the Dark Doves"), which is a literal transcription of "Canción" of *Primeras canciones* in which antithetical forces fragment and nullify each other: "Por las ramas del laurel / vi dos palomas desnudas. La una era la otra / y las dos eran ninguna" ("In the branches of the laurel tree / I saw two naked doves. One was the other / and the two were neither," 1:598). Subjective fragmentation is also a prominent feature of Lorca's mature theater, which begins in earnest with the experimental plays El público *(The Public)* and Así que pasen cinco años *(As Soon as Five Years Pass)*.

Partly the consequence of the long delay in their critical scrutiny, the experimental plays have not been considered integral to the development of Lorca's mature theater. Rather than a departure, however, the experimental theater emerges as a logical progression of the tragic intuition of the destructive, fragmenting force so conspicuous in the poetry. These plays intensify the implications of such a vision, allowing Lorca to bridge a rather formidable gap between his private world and the public-commercial demands that force him to make compromises with that understanding. The focus in the experimental plays is to trace the trajectory of desire that moves Lorca in a daring new direction. These works witness a significant expansion of his theatrical agenda that makes no concessions to the "horizon of expectations" of the theater-going public. Quite simply, the audience must either accept their premises or refuse to participate altogether.

Critical opinion has insisted that *Así que pasen cinco años* is physically set in the dream, or reverie, of the Joven (Youth), considered the play's protagonist, and a cast of supporting characters generally thought to reflect some aspect of his experience or life choices that he has not embraced, for example, the sexual inclinations, respectively underdeveloped and excessive, of Amigo 1 and Amigo 2. My view recognizes a structural protagonist, that is, a fully developed human consciousness that features all relevant subject positions yet that also includes an offstage character that critics have not acknowledged, the mature adult who houses the dream and who has imagined the Joven. Beginning with a conversation between the Joven and the Viejo (Old Man), the dream moves ambivalently in two directions. It shifts toward the past and the time of youth, embodied in the Joven, who aggressively persists in the dreamer's imagination. Yet it also advances toward present and future embodied in the Viejo, who, in the pattern of the old men of earlier plays such as *La zapatera prodigiosa* and *Don Perlimplín*, presages the advent of a more conventional existence. An offstage presence and not the Joven's projections, therefore, provides script and scenario for a dream representation produced by desire. The Joven is not a self-referential icon but rather the unmediated projection of a living presence, a "photographic" trace in a one-to-one relationship with his dreaming referent. Accompanied by the Viejo and others who attempt to sway him in a specific direction, the Joven embodies but one of the play's competing crosscurrents of desire. He is the most prominent effect, but not the cause, in someone else's dream.

Alternating its focus between the Joven's amorous dilemma and the more philosophical question of time, the play evinces as well frequent temporal and spatial shifts. The initial dialog between the Viejo and the Joven moves immediately toward the past, the true ground of the Joven's personality and the explanation for his compulsion to postpone gratification. The Viejo advocates a different course by proposing what seems to be an unorthodox possibility: "hay que recordar hacia mañana" ("it is necessary to remember toward tomorrow," 2:501). While it is impossible to remember a phenomenon yet to be experienced, these words make perfect, and conventional, sense if the Joven is understood to belong to a larger continuum extending beyond the time of youth. "Remember toward tomorrow" is an exhortation to adopt a more appropriate role in a scenario relentlessly undermining and fragmenting this earlier identity. A more authoritative protagonist whose mission can no longer be postponed thus intensifies the focus on issues left unresolved from the earlier theater—perhaps best symbolized in Perlimplín's "hermoso adolescente" ("beautiful adolescent," 2:496), the very image of resistance to a conventional destiny. The relationship between the Viejo and the Joven thus reveals a hidden struggle to compel the Joven to resolve an impasse.

The Viejo believes that such a pathway lies in the Joven's marriage to the Novia (Bride), which requires that he adapt his image of her. The Viejo considers the five-year postponement of marriage plans in a positive light, a prelude to remembering the future and the affirmation of a more appropriate image of the Novia. To accept her more mature image, the Joven must abandon his established frame of temporal reference strongly resistive of change. The Joven fully understands that the Viejo is attempting by this to dislodge him from a secure site that the Joven has defined in relation to a much younger, pre-sexual Novia: "Ud. quiere apartarme de ella" ("You want to separate me from her," 2:503). Their positions become clearer in the subsequent discussion about the Novia's physical appearance. Both acknowledge that things change more slowly in the present context, an unconventional realm of dream space "sin distancia debajo de la frente" ("without distance beneath the forehead," 2:505). This is why the Joven prefers "lo de adentro aunque también cambie" ("the inside stuff even though it also changes," 2:506), for it is here where the image of the Joven has resisted mature formulation. Resistance, in fact, constitutes the Joven's very essence. When at this moment the Mecanógrafa (Typist) appears, prompting the Joven to ask her "¿Terminaste de escribir las cartas?" ("Did you finish writing the letters?" 2:507), she confesses both her love for him and a strong desire to abandon his employ. The Viejo considers her to be dangerous since as guardian of the written medium through which the Joven continues to express his ambivalence, the Mecanógrafa is serving to prolong his resistance to a more mature Novia. The Novia has been a pretext for the Joven to postpone indefinitely the demands of a conventional destiny that he now must confront. She exists in multiple aspects that embody both the Joven's unfocused "amor sin objeto" ("love without an object") and the more mature face of desire that has emerged over the course of five years. By the time the Joven is ready to declare himself, the scenario has changed decisively. The Novia's reality exceeds his ability to imagine her, and she finds him unsuitable. Emptied of all illusions associated with the Novia's image, the Joven feels forsaken: "se me olvidan hasta las letras" ("even the letters forget me," 2:549). His loss thus reveals, and also parodies, the more imposing requirements of this relationship: to remember who he is by awakening from this dream.

At precisely this point the Joven looks to the "other woman" in his life, "la mujer que me quiere" ("the woman who loves me," 2:558), the Mecanógrafa. Earlier the submissive conduit and transcriber of the Joven's thoughts, the Mecanógrafa now acquires all of the aggressive traits displayed by the Novia. The Novia and the Mecanógrafa embody, respectively, the decisive image of the Joven's life and his impotent epistemological means of closure regarding this issue. As such they also parody empirical cognition and mimesis premised on the easy interchangeability of visual and verbal signs. In *Así que pasen cinco años*, images overwhelm and words fail the Joven. The Joven's reliance on a bourgeois model of consciousness in a realm premised on a different set of assumptions makes it impossible for him to stabilize either his scene or the medium of signification embodied in the Novia and the Mecanógrafa. The Joven persists in understanding his scene as an autonomous finality, yet the signs of his immediate milieu do not display the characteristics of conventional referentiality. They refer instead toward the dreaming entity in and through whom the Joven's drama transpires.

This becomes more explicit at the beginning of act 3, which offers a significant meta-dramatic assessment of central issues in the evolution of Lorca's theater. As the stage directions indicate, the physical setting is self-consciously evocative, in a symbolic sense, of the play's psychic scenario:

> Bosque. Grandes troncos. En el centro, un teatro rodeado de cortinas barrocas con el telón echado. Una escalerilla une el tabladillo con el escenario. Al levantarse el telón cruzan entre los troncos dos figuras vestidas de negro, con las caras blancas de yeso y las manos también blancas. Suena una música lejana. Sale el Arlequín. Viste de negro y verde. Lleva dos caretas, una en cada mano y ocultas tras la espalda. Acciona de modo plástico, como un bailarín. (2:560)

> A forest. Large trunks. In the center, a theater surrounded by baroque curtains with the stage curtain lowered. A small stairway unites the small stage with the larger stage. As the curtain rises two figures dressed in black cross among the trunks, their faces as well as their hands white with plaster. A far-away music sounds. The Harlequin enters. He is dressed in black and green. He carries two masks hidden behind his back, one in each hand. He moves in an evocative fashion, as would a ballet dancer.

The forest is evocative of a paradoxical "deeper" level within the dream landscape that exists "sin distancia debajo de la frente." At this level, where form itself is threatened with dissolution and destruction by unconscious forces, emerges a clearing where the issues inherent in this unorthodox representational medium expose their conflicting and contradictory dimensions. The principal actor in this open-air theater is the Arlequín, accompanied by a Muchacha (Girl) dressed in a black Greek tunic and later by a guffawing Payaso (Clown) costumed in sequins. The Arlequín begins by offering observations about three distinct modes of understanding, that is, three different alternate configurations that in fact disrupt standard epistemology. In the first, "el sueño va sobre el tiempo / flotando como un velero" ("the dream goes on above time / floating like a weathervane," 2:560). When the dream state dominates time, empirical understanding, premised on time's orderly progression, is rendered effectively inoperative. This arrangement is unproductive since "nadie puede abrir semillas / en el corazón del sueño" ("nobody can open seeds / in the heart of the dream," 2:560). Nevertheless, as the association with the weathervane underscores, the salient characteristic of the functioning of signs in the dream state is their indexicality. The dream of desire moves in a constant, yet uncomprehended, direction. The second possibility, in which "el tiempo va sobre el sueño" ("time goes on above the dream," 2:561), corresponds to the dominion of time in an empirical context. This mode is also unsatisfying since desire's dream is overwhelmed by the consciousness of time's destruction as "ayer y mañana comen / oscuras flores de duelo" ("yesterday and tomorrow eat / dark flowers of grief," 2:561). Although the debilitating effects of this mode of consciousness are articulated by the Joven's growing awareness that "no me pertenezco" ("I don't belong to myself," 2:509), its most succinct articulation is offered in the Old Man's invocation to "recordar hacia mañana," an implicit demand that the past be surpassed or forgotten.

The final possibility, and the one upon which the play turns, is an epistemological and representational framework recognizing that "sobre la misma columna, / abrazados sueño y tiempo, / cruza el gemido del niño, / la lengua rota del viejo" ("upon the same column, / dream and time embraced, / intersect the cry of the child, / the broken tongue of the old man," 2:561). The largely atemporal-spatial values of the dream state and the temporal-directional movement (past-present-future) inherent in realist models combine to create a hybrid mode of representation in which the visual-verbal building blocks of empirico-mimetic discourse become indexical points of reference for the primary agency, the directing authority of desire. That is to say, desire reveals its presence and authority along a temporal continuum rather than in a point or moment, in a direction and not in self-referential visual-verbal signs. The characters, including the Joven, are secondary aspects of a larger scene provided by both the dream and time. Unifying the play's diverse stories and scenes is desire's fuller manifestation and revelation while resisting an arbitrary point of closure. Thus, for example, the Niño's story is not separate from the Joven's but a fragment of an ongoing narration. Although corresponding to different moments in the dream saga, both are similar in their resistance to the closure that circumstances, of an empirical nature, attempt to impose. The dead child resists the closure that death imposes just as the Joven resists a conventional image of love. While resistance explains the Joven's conduct, it also explains the workings of desire, which supersedes the Joven's resistance with its own more authoritative dimension.

Interspliced with the Arlequín's pronouncements is a second movement, the laments of the Muchacha, who, in a fashion that closely parallels Joven's dilemma, finds herself in a state of psychic disarray at the loss of her bridegroom. Yet her lamentations are exposed by the Arlequín as so much facade when he imitates the voice of her bridegroom, only to have her reply no thank you (2:565), again a response that fully reduplicates the significant events in the Joven's story. Although she professes a desire to encounter her lover at a deeper level, expressed here as the depths of the ocean, the Arlequín does not allow her the consolation of this obviously false illusion. When he laughingly confronts her, she is forced to admit the truth, ending her presence in the scene in the manner in which she entered, lamenting her loss. The girl, therefore, reenacts the Arlequín's speech outlining the unconventional directions for theater that emerge from the confrontation of empirical and dream realms.

The ultimate consequence of this hybrid order is a complete theatricalization and fragmentation of character, the awareness that instead of being an autonomous personality-consciousness one occupies a role, or rather roles, as the Payaso also underscores later in this scene when he is asked to reveal his destination:

A representar.
Un niño pequeño
que quiere cambiar
en flores de acero
su trozo de pan.
    (2:566)

To represent.
A small child

who wants to change
his bit of bread
into flowers of steel.

Rather than to a point in space and time, the Payaso returns to an ongoing role, that of the dead child, who, ironically, symbolizes resistance to just this type of subjective displacement and fragmentation. Rather than to become substantial temporal/spatial subjects, these characters function as directions in a hybrid dream/time medium. Recalling the forced marriages of Lorca's earlier plays, this juxtaposition of realities creates an unstable scene yet one in which there is a continual exchange of identities, or masks, all moving in an inexorable direction but not to a point of closure. Directionality, a continuum of movement through an unconventional space/time, strongly underlies the content of this play. The visual-verbal signs from which audiences traditionally produce meaning acquire in the dreamed time scenario an indexical dimension that serves to situate the play's locus offstage with a referent not physically part of the scene. The Arlequín describes the dream state unhindered by time in terms of pure indexicality: "El sueño va sobre el tiempo / flotando como un velero" ("The dream goes above time / floating like a weathervane"). The weathervane is the index of the invisible force that moves it, the trace of its presence that indicates the direction of its referent. Pure indexicality, however, is also directionless floating. In the play, therefore, dream and time affiliate to provide a more orderly sense of direction that nevertheless strongly resists closure, "sobre la misma columna." The character-masks on stage refer, and defer, to a directing force whose strategy is neither definitive closure nor surrealistic chaos.

Directionality progressively becomes a dominant theme as the play moves toward a climax. When the Mecanógrafa asks, in a song,

¿Dónde vas, amor mío,
amor mío,
con el aire en un vaso
y el mar en un vidrio?
(3:572)

Where are you going, my love,
my love,
with air in a bottle
and the sea in a glass?

the Joven answers with an exact repetition of these words, which underscores both his estrangement from desire and his displacement from the
protagonist's role. He has had the task of containing a force as vast as the
sea in a medium likened to a fragile glass. Therefore, not only is he rejected by the Novia but he is abandoned by his "amor mío," the force that
has sustained him. In a parody of the Novia's earlier forsaking, the Mecanógrafa's subsequent rejection scorns the very trajectory of the Joven's
existence as she utters the phrase that is itself an index of his ambivalent
progression through time under untenable epistemological premises:
"Así que pasen cinco años" (2:581). Love remains always at a distance,
measured in time. The fundamental contradiction of the Joven's life is
more succinctly addressed in the final tableau, where he asks the Criado (Butler): "¿Se encuentra bien una veleta girando como el viento quiere?" ("Is a weathervane all right when it turns in the direction that the
wind moves it?" 2:584), to which the Criado replies that the better question should be, "¿Se encuentra bien el viento?" ("Is the wind all right?"
2:585). That is to say, the index of the wind, the weathervane, is merely the visible symptom of a more authoritative invisible agent directing
its movement. This also describes the dynamic in the play, in which the
visible entities progressively lose autonomous self-referentiality in order
to indicate the direction of the offstage center from which they are projected.

Así que pasen cinco años thus depicts a convergence of fragmented realities where the effects of causes originating outside the Joven's visible
scene are more fully acknowledged. The Joven, however, is the victim of
another aspect prominent in the representational equation: an account
of phenomena that understands everything, including the unconscious,
as being subject to temporal laws. The Youth resists change in a medium
that is undergoing its own inexorable temporal transformation. Indeed,

the dream is ultimately a response to the challenge of yet another un-represented force, the public demands of consciousness, the audience in front of whom the Joven must wear his masks. The agents of his destruction, the three Jugadores (Gamblers), *señoritos* quite similar to himself invited for a game of cards, arise from the remnants of the Joven's dream in order to fulfill the logical consequences of an inexorable process.

The means of the Joven's assassination again exemplifies the unorthodox nature of the representation. Rather than the Joven's being physically assaulted by the Jugadores, the Jugador 1 shoots an arrow from a noiseless gun into the illuminated image of the ace of hearts, at which point the Joven "se lleva las manos al corazòn" ("brings his hands to his heart," 2:594). The act of assassination underscores again that the primary content of the play is the tracing of a trajectory, a direction that has proceeded through various mediums in a constant evolution. Emblematic of indexicality, the arrow, like the weathervane, signals the final moment of the epistemological displacement that has undermined autonomous self-referentiality in this play. Consistent with the emphasis on the direction and evolution of desire, the Joven's death does not definitively conclude a story, only his centrality in an ongoing scenario. His fate is succinctly suggested in the question, interrupted by echoes, he asks as he is dying: "¿No hay [. . .]? [. . .] ¿Ningún hombre aquí?" ("Is there [. . .]? [. . .] No one here?" 2:595–96). Two successive echoes answer with the word "aquí." The repetition of "aquí" underscores the fundamental paradox of this play. No longer present but neither definitively absent, the Joven comes to embody subjective fragmentation. He will occupy a different space or plane in an existential and theatrical equation in which "aquí" is a constant variable. The Joven's resistance to the imperative of desire fails to stabilize an inexorable movement that, ironically, not even his death can halt.

El público is also about the ruinous contradictions of desire, revealed in yet another dream scenario that exposes the theatrical and existential shortcomings of the Director, discredited as a consequence of his decision to use an adolescent boy in the role of Juliet in his production of

Shakespeare's *Romeo and Juliet*. In comparison to *Así que pasen cinco años*, *El público* is decidedly more ambiguous, indeed, fragmented. The audience cannot be certain if the action is consequent to the failure of the Director's production or if the initial tableaus precede the act of theater that brings him to ruin. It is even uncertain if the Director's production has been staged or if it exists simply as a vivid premonitory dream. Whatever the true circumstances, the Director is violently dispossessed of his authority over a play that outrages its contemporary audience, ironically, because of its faithfulness to Elizabethan conventions. The Director's production is further displaced by an extra-dramatic scrutiny of the causes, private and public, for its failure, which largely constitutes the play's content.

When at the outset the Director declares that "he perdido toda mi fortuna" ("I have lost all my fortune," 2:599), he is referring to his bankrupt imagination that has nothing tangible to offer a private audience, the Caballos Blancos (White Horses), symbols of the fragmented imaginative energy that he can no longer summon. Since the Director is without "financing," the horses abandon him to their successors, the Tres Hombres (Three Men), a second audience whose physical resemblance to the Director suggests that, as in *Así que pasen cinco años*, the Director is only the nominal protagonist, the public-professional aspect of a more complex and contradictory personality whose dream brings together an entire group of players. As the Director confronts his loss of authority in what appears to be a conventional "teatro al aire libre" ("open air theater") he becomes the unwitting herald of an underground playhouse called the "teatro bajo la arena" ("theater beneath the sand"). Here he eventually discovers that his real motivation for the production is to reveal "el perfil de una fuerza oculta cuando ya el público no tuviera más remedio que atender, lleno de espíritu y subyugado por la acción" ("the profile of a hidden force when the public has no choice except to pay full attention, full of spirit and overpowered by the action," 2:665). The stage is not an autonomous finality but an open-ended medium, or tunnel, for the fuller materialization of this hidden force in public contexts.

The Director further confesses that "yo hice el túnel para apoderarme de los trajes" ("I made the tunnel in order to take possession of the masks," 2:665), stage characters instilled with the consciousness that they are not self-referential ends in themselves but rather the visible effects of an offstage authority that extends, like a tunnel, into the imaginations of the theater audience. Also more pronounced than in *Así que pasen cinco años* is the dysfunction of conventional visual-verbal signification. As emphasized by the use of a folding screen to effect character transformations that are conspicuously incomplete, the full visual representation of a character or character aspect is not revealed in one autonomous, self-referring space but by means of a series of incomplete hybrid images that extend across multiple planes. As the Director is forced to confront troubling aspects of his personal life instrumental in his casting decisions, the play uncovers the fragments of a personal and professional reality revealed along a directional axis that exposes again the error of wearing an unchanging public mask in this medium beyond empirical consciousness.

The Director's casting for *Romeo and Juliet*, a literal imitation of a stage convention in Shakespeare's time, becomes an intolerable social/sexual transgression because the audience brings its own more authoritative Shakespeare scenario to the theater. The "open air" and underground theaters are similar, however, in that both audiences displace the Director as stage authority. Indeed, *El público* becomes a confluence of competing performance texts: the Director's exact imitation of Shakespeare; the "open air" audience's version of Shakespeare; the private audience, in the theater beneath the sand, that reveals the workings of the hidden force at the further expense of the Director's authority; and, finally, the Director's personal drama, as inseparable from these audiences as are the competing versions of *Romeo and Juliet*. These simultaneously projected scenarios, which do not follow a cause-and-effect progression, correlate well with the Arlequín's description in *Así que pasen cinco años* of one of the possible modes of the dream state in which time is completely supplanted by effectively unmediated images: "El sueño va sobre el tiempo / flotando como un velero" ("The dream goes above time / floating like a weathervane"). The Director fails to establish himself in either the medium dominated by convention or the underground theater governed by an "abominable" force.

The final gasp of the Director's imagination witnesses the horses' invention of a neologism—"blenamiboá," a reversal of the syllables of *abominable*—which succinctly characterizes the content of the play. Theater is constituted in El público as a reverse direction, movement through the unmediated and fragmented indexical domain of the theater beneath the sand. As an open-ended tunnel rather than an enclosed space, the stage functions as a medium through which antagonistic offstage forces intervene to discredit those who continue to cling to the illusion of stage autonomy. The Director becomes the physical pretext upon which competing realities—expressed here as competing audiences—sustain themselves. El público is, ironically, the truest name for Shakespeare's *Romeo and Juliet*. The only version of this play that the Director can legitimately bring to the stage is a performance text reformulated in the imaginations of generations of audiences. The Director was not the exclusive stage authority for this production. As a consequence, the public audience engenders a private audience of unrelenting critics, in the theater beneath the sand, to expose his failure to assert his stage authority.

The Director's reply to the Hombre 1's assertion that "Romeo puede ser un grano de sal y Julieta puede ser un mapa" ("Romeo can be a grain of salt and Juliet can be a map") is that while private interpretations of these characters are possible, "nunca dejarán de ser Romeo y Julieta" ("there will never stop being Romeo and Juliet," 2:602). They are an inseparable part of the public imagination. As a consequence, his own attempt to reinterpret these characters, which features Juliet's role played by "un muchacho de quince" ("a boy of fifteen," 2:657), becomes immediately transparent. As the Estudiante 4 later explains: "Por eso ha estallado la revolución. El Director de escena abrió los escotillones y la gente pudo ver cómo el veneno de las venas falsas había causado la muerte verdadera de muchos niños. No son las formas disfrazadas las que levantan la vida, sino el cabello de barómetro que tienen detrás" ("This is why the revolution has broken out. The stage director opened the trap doors and the people could see how the venom of the false veins had caused the true death of many children. It is not the disguised forms that bring forth life, but rather the barometric hair that lies behind," 2:653). Rather than becoming an innovative force, the Director succeeds only in exposing his own fragmented and ambivalent sexual identity, which he is forced to confront, strongly resisting, in the theater beneath the sand. A deeper truth awaits him, "un final ocasionado por el miedo" ("an ending occasioned by fear," 2:605), the destructive consequences of an abiding fear of the audience and the truth of himself.

In the underground as in the "open air," an audience challenges the Director's authority to dominate the scene. Indeed, in the second tableau, subtitled "Ruina romana" ("Roman Ruin"), the Director is compelled to become an actor in a representation that further exposes his shortcomings. Two characters named Cascabeles (Bells) and Pámpanos (Vine Shoots), aspects or more honest visual projections, respectively, of the Director and the Hombre 1,[2] emerge from the folding screen in order to reveal deeper truths about their counterparts. Their dialog, a series of hypothetical propositions each followed by a logical response, underscores both the pretextual nature of their discourse and the incapacity of their utterances to stabilize their relationship, or even to establish their prominence, in a scene identified as a ruin. One of the more telling examples is the following:

> Cascabeles: ¿Si yo me convirtiera en caca?
> Pámpanos: Yo me conviertiría en mosca.
> (2:611)

> Bells: And if I were to transform into excrement?
> Vine Shoots: I would transform into a fly.

Here a squalid medium determines the nature of the creature appropriate to such a scenario, which evinces both the mutual dependence and the self-destructive animosity of the parties as the consequence of an un-

2. Rafael Martínez Nadal, El público: amor, teatro y caballos en la obra de Federico García Lorca (Oxford: Dolphin Book, 1970), 48.

wanted pairing. The culminating invocation is of "un cuchillo afilado durante cuatro largas primaveras" ("a knife sharpened during four long springs," 2:613), evocative of the latent violence inherent in the impasse of finding oneself matched in a relationship against one's will.

Indeed, the ruins become a visual correlative for ambivalence toward the other, as is further underscored by the entrance of the Emperador to proclaim the authority of the "one": "Uno es uno y siempre uno. He degollado más de cuarenta muchachos que no lo quisieron decir" ("One is one and always one. I have slit the throats of more than forty boys that refused to say it," 2:618). The Emperor, who champions resistance to the physical expression of homoeroticism, like the ruins over which he presides, cannot impose his authority over the scene. "Oneness" is an untenable position, the consequence of a refusal to acknowledge the truth about oneself and the nature of desire. As the scene concludes, the Emperor is embraced by Pámpanos, which occasions the commentary at the beginning of the third tableau. The Hombre 3 declares: "Debieron morir los dos. No he presenciado nunca un festín más sangriento" ("Those two must have died. I have never witnessed a bloodier feast," 2:621). Others offer different and contradictory opinions:

> Hombre 1: Dos leones. Dos semidioses.
> Hombre 2: Dos semidioses, si no tuvieran ano.
> (2:621)
> Man 1: Two lions. Two demigods.
> Man 2: Two demigods, if they did not have an anus.

While there is the recognition of the validity, and even the potential superiority, of homosexual love, there is the equal appreciation that the inescapable necessity to express this love by physical means—that is, by means of two rather than one—negates its positive potential: "El ano es el castigo del hombre. El ano es el fracaso del hombre, es su vergüenza y su muerte. Los dos tenían ano y ninguno de los dos podía luchar con la belleza pura de los mármoles que brillaban conservando deseos íntimos defendidos por una superficie intachable" ("The anus is the punishment of man. The anus is the failure of man, it is his shame and his death. The two had an anus and neither of them could fight with the pure beauty of the marble that was shining and conserving intimate desires defended by a perfect surface," 2:622).

The Emperor is ultimately the most prominent embodiment of the ambivalence that has authorized the ruin over which he presides. The creative search for the "one" inevitably summons an "other" and thus inexorable movement toward ruin and subjective fragmentation: "El Emperador que bebe nuestra sangre está en la ruina" ("The Emperor who drinks our blood is in the ruins," 2:623). The Hombre 1, the character most sympathetic to homosexual love, wants to murder the Emperor and bring back his head to the Director. The Director agrees that this would make an excellent present, not for him but for Elena, the muse who has inspired his earlier theater. Like so many others, this exchange simply rephrases the conditions that have led to the Director's theatrical and existential crisis. Ambivalence to the authority of the hidden force has brought him to ruin. When the Hombre 1 reminds him that "la cabeza del Emperador quema los cuerpos de todas las mujeres" ("the head of the Emperor burns the bodies of all the women," 2:625), that his ideal is universally impractical, the Director abandons Elena as well—"No, no la llames. Yo me convertiré en lo que tú desees" ("Don't call her. I will transform into what you want," 2:627)—thereby reenacting the very abdication of authority that has brought him to the theater beneath the sand.

As an altercation between the Hombre 2 and the Hombre 3 causes them to depart the scene, a more profound dimension of the theater beneath the sand reveals itself in Juliet, who arises from her coffin to complain: "A mí no me importan las discusiones sobre el amor ni el teatro. Yo lo que quiero es amar" ("I don't care about discussions of love or the theater. What I want is to love," 2:628). Righteously indignant at developments undertaken in her name, she lashes out: "Son cuatro muchachos los que me han querido poner un falito de barro y estaban decididos a pintarme un bigote de tinta" ("four boys who have wanted to give me a little clay phallus and were intent on painting an ink moustache on me," 2:632), a reference to the Hombres and the Director, who have appropriated her form while concealing the passion that motivates it. This Juliet is not the character from Shakespeare's original or the Juliet of the Director's version. Shakespeare's Juliet has been appropriated by contemporary theater audiences, who have bound and gagged her and have forced her to sit with the audience. The Director's Juliet is equally distasteful to her, however, for that Juliet, ironically, is simply another means to disguise her true potential.

Tied neither to any public audience nor to the Director, she is searching for an appropriate medium to invigorate with the form of love she has to offer. Her principal suitors here are the horses who had earlier abandoned the Director. They now proclaim the "true" theater, the "teatro bajo la arena" ("theater beneath the sand," 2:636) at the core of which is Juliet's form, the first visual expression of such a potentially rejuvenating force. Juliet's energizing presence allows the Hombre 1 to affirm that "Yo no tengo máscara" ("I don't have a mask," 2:637) while it also elicits the Director's continuing resistance and the opposite avowal that "No hay más que máscara" ("There is nothing except the mask," 2:638). Juliet proclaims that she cannot be domesticated, diverted, or used for a lesser purpose: "No soy yo una esclava para que me hinquen punzones de ámbar en los senos, ni un oráculo para los que tiemblan de amor a la salida de las ciudades. Todo mi sueño ha sido con el olor de la higuera y la cintura del que corta las espigas. ¡Nadie a través de mí! ¡Yo a través de vosotros!" ("I am not a slave so that they can thrust burins of amber into my breasts, nor an oracle for those who tremble with love as they exit the city. My whole dream has been with the smell of the fig tree and the waist of the one who cuts the ears of wheat. Nobody through me! I through you!" 2:636). From the depths of the theater beneath the sand, therefore, Juliet heralds the advent of an inspirational force more authoritative than the conventional imaginative energy embodied in the horses.

Similar to the Joven's situation in *Así que pasen cinco años*, the Director's imaginative bankruptcy is a direct consequence of an unrecognized resistance to the hidden force. Although a much more palatable expression of the "abominable" forces impinging upon him, Juliet's demand for greater authority only inspires further conflict between the Director and the Hombre 1. When the Director rebukes the Hombre 1 for embracing him in the company of others, the Hombre 1's response is to proclaim his love "delante de los otros porque abomino de la máscara y porque ya he conseguido arrancártela" ("in front of the others because I hate the mask and because I have already succeeded in taking it from you," 2:639) and thus to press the Director to confront his insincerity with himself. Juliet's hopeful emergence from her coffin, however, is short-lived. As she returns to await a more propitious moment, three new character-masks appear to echo in parodic fashion the Hombre 1's mourning of another lost opportunity.

By the fifth tableau, the contradictions of the Director's resistance to the truth become manifest as the scene returns, not to the coffin from which Juliet arose, but to the sepulcher at the site of the Director's ill-fated production. Interspliced with critical commentary from the Estudiantes is the slow, and sometimes comically ironic, agony of the Desnudo Rojo (Red Nude), the Hombre 1 in perhaps his truest aspect, now in the role of martyr for the sake of the Director's production. The Estudiantes characterize the Director's production as revolutionary: "barrió la cabeza del profesor de retórica" ("he swept away the head of the professor of rhetoric," 2:650), a break with the old rules of stage-centered playmaking. The Director's casting decision attempted to transform the script into something quite different by means of a manipulation of the scenario. It effected, however, an equally "revolutionary" intervention. An angry mob finds the Director in Juliet's coffin, which is where the Director failed to embrace Juliet's promise of a revitalized inspiration. As the Estudiantes continue to debate whether or not Romeo and Juliet need to be "necesariamente un hombre y una mujer para que la escena del sepulcro se produzca de manera viva y desgarradora" ("necessarily a man and a woman for the sepulcher scene to be represented in a living and heart-wrenching manner," 2:653), the scene switches abruptly

230 THE THEATER OF FEDERICO GARCÍA LORCA

to the Desnudo Rojo, who is now finally acknowledged as an essential aspect of the Director's production. The Desnudo Rojo's sacrifice, clearly a parody of Christ's crucifixion, represents the literal, physical costs of the failed production. Under the nominal authority of someone less convinced than the Hombre 1/Desnudo Rojo of the validity of this undertaking, the courage to bring such a production before an audience demands physical sacrifice as much as the expenditure of imaginative "capital." Although the Estudiantes strongly insist that "[u]n espectador no debe formar nunca parte del drama" ("a spectator should never form part of the drama," 2:657), the audience's violent interruption of the representation becomes a final visual confirmation that stage authority resides elsewhere.

With the death of the Hombre 1/Desnudo Rojo, the final tableau turns to a dialog between the Director and a new character, the Prestidigitador (Magician), who offers yet another perspective on the demise of the Director's production. In his discussions with the Hombre 1, the Director had tacitly advocated a position recognizing theater as a trade-off between the naked truth—an impossible set of truths—and lesser or disguised truths that are nevertheless theatrically viable. The Director suggests to the Prestidigitador that his intention, via Shakespeare, was to make a statement about the universality of love no matter what the physical constitution of the partners, in order to express "lo que pasa todos los días en todas las grandes ciudades y en los campos por medio de un ejemplo que, admitido por todos a pesar de su originalidad, ocurrió sólo una vez. Pude haber elegido el Edipo o el Otelo. En cambio, si hubiera levantado el telón con la verdad original, se hubieran manchado de sangre las butacas desde las primeras escenas" ("what happens every day in the big cities and in the country by means of an example that, admitted by everybody in spite of its originality, occurred only once. I could have chosen Oedipus or Othello. On the other hand, if I had raised the curtain with the original truth, the seats of the theater would have been drenched in blood from the first scenes," 2:664).

Since the Director admits that his production was a compromise from the outset, the Prestidigitador criticizes him for not having chosen a more appropriate play, such as *A Midsummer Night's Dream*, to introduce the idea that "el amor es pura casualidad" ("love is pure chance," 2:664), especially given the fact that Juliet's counterpart in that play, Titania, falls in love with a donkey. This would likely have spared the Director the violence that brought him to the theater beneath the sand. Now assuming a posture reminiscent of the Hombre 1, the Director vigorously defends the project and the inherent worth of the theater beneath the sand, the most significant aspect of which has been the opening of the tunnel between public and private domains: "Yo hice el húnel para apoderarme de los trajes y, a través de ellos, haber ense-o el perfil de una fuerza oculta cuando ya el público no tuviera más remedio que atender, lleno de espíritu y subyugado por la acción" ("I made the tunnel in order to take control of the masks and, by means of them, to reveal the profile of a hidden force when the public had no other choice than to pay full attention, full of spirit and overwhelmed by the action," 2:665). The tunnel is animated by desire, now understood as a transcendent force, the creative-destructive potential of which the Director is now able to acknowledge:

> si Romeo y Julieta agonizan y mueren para despertar sonriendo cuando cae el telón, mis personajes, en cambio, queman la cortina y mueren de verdad a presencia de los espectadores. Los caballos, el mar, el ejérccito de las hierbas lo han impedido. Pero algún día, cuando se quemen todos los teatros, se encontrarán en los sofas, detrás de los espejos y dentro de las copas de cartón dorado, la reunión de nuestros muertos encerrados allí por el público. (2:666)

> if Romeo and Juliet agonize and die in order to awaken smiling when the curtain falls, my characters, on the other hand, burn the curtain and die for real in the presence of the spectators. The horses, the sea, the army of grasses have prevented it. But some day, when all the theaters are burned, there will be found in the sofas, behind the mirrors and inside the goblets of gold cardboard, the reunion of our dead shut up there by the public.

Indeed, the only character to survive this spectacle is the Prestidigitador, an apparent master of disguise and stage effects. Nevertheless, there emerges a much deeper appreciation of the relationships involved in the act of theater. Lorca's challenge in the aftermath of this exploration of the fuller geography of theater is to marshal these fragmented forces—the Hombre 1's commitment to the authority of the script of desire, the Director's will to represent such a commitment on stage, the Prestidigitador's advocacy of a subversive expediency in the furtherance of these goals—in an attempt to achieve greater concert with the inexorable presence and direction provided by the hidden force.

It is the interplay of precisely these elements that also informs Lorca's commercial theater of the 1930s, the most notable among these being *La casa de Bernarda Alba (The House of Bernarda Alba)*. A provocative array of posthumously collected working ideas and partially completed scripts—which include *Los sueños de mi prima Aurelia (The Dreams of My Cousin Aurelia)*, *La destrucción de Sodoma (The Destruction of Sodom)* and *La bola negra (Drama epéntico) (The Black Ball [Epentic Drama])*—testify to the continuing intensity of Lorca's dramatic imagination at the untimely end of his life. The most fully developed of these works in progress is the *Comedia sin título (Play without a Title; also known as El sueño de la vida [The Dream of Life])* drafted along with *La casa de Bernarda Alba* during the first half of 1936. Characterizing commercial theater in *Comedia sin título* as an entertaining "juego de palabras [. . .] un panorama donde se vea una casa en la que nada ocurre" ("word game [. . .] a panorama where one sees a house in which nothing happens," 2:1069), the principal character, the Autor, offers his audience instead a much different space, "un pequeño rincón de realidad" ("a small corner of reality," 2:1069), a metatheatrical reality intended to reveal a more profound set of stage relationships. This is also a succinct description of the most significant dimension of *La casa de Bernarda Alba*, whose *advertencia*—both a warning and a declaration of intentions from behind the stage—alludes to the nature of the theatrical experience about to unfold: "El poeta advierte que estos tres actos tienen la intención de un documental fotográfico" ("The poet warns that these three acts have the intention of a photographic documentary," 2:973). Rather than the return to a more conventional theater that many critics have suggested it is, *La casa de Bernarda Alba*, in fact, represents a forceful restatement of the principal issues of the experimental plays—the extended dialectic on subjective fragmentation—in his commercial theater.

The specific words of the *advertencia* also invoke the dramatic structure of the slightly earlier *Doña Rosita, la soltera* (*Doña Rosita, the Spinster*), three effectively discrete acts separated by vast periods of time, culminating in a climactic white-on-black photographic moment. The largely black-on-white images of *La casa de Bernarda Alba* extend and strengthen the association with photography. Resolving to keep her own "pequeño rincón" and its occupants from public view for an extended period, Bernarda admonishes her daughters to conduct themselves as if the house's doors and windows were physically sealed with brick and mortar. The only authorized exception to this directive, the brief opening of the shutters of one window late at night, allows her oldest daughter, Angustias, to converse with her fiancé, Pepe el Romano. Bernarda's imaginative and physical reordering of her house demonstrates striking affinities with the principal features of a camera. The mechanism of the camera obscura is a modern metaphor for the mechanisms of human perception and cognition, given the capacity of photography to render, and to document, instantaneously upon a blank surface the received materials of sense perceptions. Similarly, the special configuration of the stage is a concrete, physical means for Lorca to allude to the truest agents of this representation—not the activity within the house itself but the intrusions upon this activity from two distinct points beyond its visible range, in the form of the disrupting effects of Pepe el Romano and the most authoritative witness to the trajectory implied by those effects, the spectator in the theater audience. The house's status as a completely enclosed space makes further problematic the conventional "four walls" of the arch proscenium stage since, in effect, it leaves spectators little choice but to consider themselves physically present in the house. If the spectator's imagination is called upon in *Doña Rosita, la soltera* to "house" disparate temporal moments, in Bernarda Alba's house it acquires an additional and more intimate role as a revelatory medium that, in the manner of a photographic negative, cannot but document the relentless degradation and fragmentation of this privileged space by forces that never assume visual form.

Critics have noted an intimate correspondence between Bernarda's house and the town, yet more recently they have also begun to consider the spectator's role in relation to these inner and outer spaces. Nina M. Scott suggests that "the viewer becomes as much a prisoner of the house as the five daughters," while C. Brian Morris equates the house with "the space that encloses the reader or spectator together with the characters on stage."[3] While there is merit in these views, it does not necessarily follow that the spectator's visual perspective parallels that of the daughters. Rather, the audience shares more in common with the servants, especially La Poncia—clearly a more perceptive observer than are Bernarda or the daughters—who more fully comprehends the danger threatening the house, which she characterizes as "una cosa muy grande" ("something very big," 2:1031). If she ever did, Bernarda, in her new role as mistress of her house, does not now consider the servants part of her extended family, but simply paid help to whom she is not obliged to listen. Like La Poncia, the spectator quickly understands that Bernarda's unwillingness to acknowledge a hidden agenda within the house compromises her authority.

That the play has been frequently discussed as a return to greater realism is also a partial consequence of the *advertencia*'s explicit invocation of photography. While recognizing that Bernarda's household is not at all typical of Spanish social reality and, if anything, is an extreme case, Andrew A. Anderson nevertheless classifies the play as a work of realism because it is "ordered upon a basis of contrasting blacks and whites, which is precisely what a photograph from the period would offer."[4] This

3. Nina M. Scott, "Sight and Insight in *La casa de Bernarda Alba*," *Revista de estudios hispánicos* 10 (1976): 298; C. Brian Morris, "The 'Austere Abode': Lorca's *La casa de Bernarda Alba*," *Anales de la literatura española contemporánea* 11 (1986): 129.

4. Andrew A. Anderson, "The Strategy of García Lorca's Dramatic Composition, 1930–36," *Romance Quarterly* 33 (1986): 221.

opinion, however, overlooks the significance of photography to modernist aesthetics. The surrealists were especially fascinated with photography because, as Rosalind Krauss has demonstrated, they considered the photograph to transcend mimesis altogether, indeed, to be the visual equivalent of automatic writing. Photography is not iconic representation in the conventional sense but rather "an imprint or transfer off the real [. . .] a photochemically processed trace causally connected to that thing in the world to which it refers in a manner parallel to that of fingerprints or footprints. [. . .] The photograph is thus generically distinct from painting or sculpture or drawing. [. . .] [D]rawings and paintings are icons, while photographs are indexes."[5]

Photography is understood to establish an immediate, point-to-point relationship with a real object. Rather than as copying or reproducing an object, artists "from the period" typically considered the photograph to be the indexical trace of an actual presence. In this context, the *advertencia*'s declaration of a photographic intention is actually a subtle repudiation of mimesis: a warning to the spectator—not unlike the many warnings that Bernarda receives from other characters—that a hidden force, unacknowledged, indeed, unacknowledgeable in empirical terms, is also at work here. It is through these other indexical manifestations on and off the stage that Lorca alludes throughout the play to a presence that surpasses and subsequently invalidates Bernarda's limited, if common-sense, mode of understanding.

The *advertencia* is also a subtle restatement of mature formula for the act of theater, "three acts" that unite as a play only as a consequence of the participation of three factors: author, director, spectator. Bernarda herself approaches the task of consolidating her authority over her household as if she were a stage director. Her comments after the mourners leave could easily express a director's thoughts after a performance: "¡Andar a vuestras casas a criticar todo lo que habéis visto!" ("Run to your houses to criticize everything you have seen!" 2:984). Her house becomes center stage for a peculiar yet exemplary representation,

5. Krauss, "The Photographic Conditions of Surrealism," 26.

the content of which is her authority. The viability of this production, however, is premised on a repudiation of conventional theater tenets. Bernarda not only directs but is the exclusive audience for an inverted production, the success of which demands that it remain publicly silent and visually unavailable to a disapproving outside audience in the town. Bernarda's situation thus recalls the predicament of the Director of *El público*.

Bernarda's decision to close off her house is motivated by essentially the same consideration as the Director's decision, a lack of capital that forces her to retreat to an isolated space. There is simply not enough money (or *finanza*) for her to continue to risk her moral standing by appearing in public before a town that she resentfully regards as a hostile audience. As the director of a scriptless private scenario, Bernarda understands her task in terms of visual dominance—"Mi vigilancia lo puede todo" ("My vigilance can do anything," 2:1051)—despite repeated warnings that her eyes are betraying her. Since the failure of the type of vigilance Bernarda undertakes is expressed in the town destructively in brutal public condemnations—leveled by Bernarda herself in her role as the town's condemnatory mouthpiece—any negative consequences for Bernarda ultimately portend a confrontation with herself, a self-condemnation authored in a loathsome public discourse organized and authorized around her own person. Bernarda's will to create an absolutely private space, however, actually hastens the collapse of the distinction so important to her between inside and outside spaces. Allowing the house to become exposed to criticism, therefore, means self-exposure, under conditions fully analogous to photography, where unmediated images emerge instantaneously as if the space between medium and referent did not exist.

The inherent vulnerability of Bernarda's private medium is alluded to from the outset as the Criada (Servant) complains about the physical effects of the mourning bells that have penetrated the house's thick walls: "Ya tengo el doble de esas campanas metido entre las sienes" ("I already have the tolling of those bells deep within my temples," 2:973).

Their largely unmediated effects mark but the first instance of a subsequent pattern of involuntary or spontaneous intrusions into the space of the house communicated through indexes whose effects herald Bernarda's failure to maintain her enclosed space. With the exception of Angustias, the death of Bernarda's husband leaves everyone, and especially Bernarda, insecure and economically vulnerable. The prospects of reduced economic circumstances may also offer an explanation for Bernarda's severe treatment of La Poncia, whose earlier, more intimate, role in the house is now abruptly curtailed: "Me sirves y te pago. ¡Nada más!" ("You serve me and I pay you. Nothing more!"; 2:991). Bernarda's disparagement of the poor ("Los pobres son como los animales; parece como si estuvieran hechos de otras sustancias" ["The poor are like the animals; it seems as if they were made from other things," 2:979]) is a further reflection of her insecurity in a space that is ordained as private but that she must continue to share with those whom she considers outsiders. In a manner paralleling that of her mistress, La Poncia's response to Bernarda's rebuffs is to retreat into a more conventional servant's role and to refrain from offering further unsolicited advice. By the time events reach a critical point, La Poncia has become little more than a bystander.

La Poncia's many unheeded admonitions are unmistakably communicated, however, to the spectator, who quickly becomes privy to a much different understanding. If La Poncia's warnings and the steadily more bitter and jealous exchanges among the daughters about Angustias's pending marriage are not enough, explicit declarations by the lucidly demented Maria Josefa summarize clearly what is happening to the house and to Bernarda's daughters: "Pepe el Romano es un gigante. Todas lo queréis. Pero él os va a devorar porque vosotras son granos de trigo. No granos de trigo. ¡Ranas sin lengua!" ("Pepe el Romano is a giant. All of you want him. But he is going to devour you because you are grains of wheat. Not grains of wheat. Frogs without a tongue!" 2:1058). As in earlier plays, the audience occupies a privileged position in the house, where very nearly everything points to the untenableness of Bernar-

da's intentions. In a scene also filled with "cuadros con paisajes invero-
símiles de ninfas o reyes de leyenda" ("pictures with unreal landscapes
of nymphs or legendary kings," 2:973), it becomes very nearly impossible for the spectator to fail to recognize the inappropriateness and insufficiency of Bernarda's response to such powerful developments.

The overabundant evidence of the deterioration of Bernarda's position makes it clear that a destructive, fragmenting point of view is progressively assuming control of the scene. Bernarda's ability to direct her
household is steadily undermined by the discourse on Pepe el Romano
that erupts from the very space designated to embody her authority. Bernarda's pretensions to control are thus discredited almost from the outset, since the spectator clearly understands that something more powerful ("una cosa muy grande") is making its uninvited presence felt in her
private scene. The spectator emerges as an authoritative observer as a
consequence of understanding Pepe el Romano, and not Bernarda, as the
play's "true" protagonist. Although he is never visually present on stage,
Pepe's prominence is communicated through his disruptive effects on
the daughters, as the "author" of a "dialog" that spoils the house's silence. From the outset, Pepe enjoys an unusually favorable position. His
interest in marrying an unattractive, nearly forty-year-old spinster unsuitable for childbearing leaves little room to doubt Magdalena's contention
that he comes to the house "por el dinero" ("for the money," 2:997), Angustias's apparently considerable inheritance/dowry. More than simply to
grab the lion's share of assets that still accrue to the estate, Pepe eventually takes from Bernarda something that she values much more highly, her
moral authority. The scandal provoked by Adela's suicide, however, also
prevents Pepe from profiting from this lucrative arrangement. Instead
of fathering the child that Angustias will be unable to bear, which as La
Poncia envisions will leave him free to use the money as he pleases and
thus to marry the much younger Adela, Pepe instead becomes the agent
of something far more destructive and fragmenting. If Pepe does indeed
come "por el dinero," he not only leaves penniless but comports himself,
like Bernarda, in a remarkably inept fashion that fully undermines any

such intention. By becoming enmeshed in the very sexual desire that enhances his authority in the house, Pepe also falls victim to something un-
foreseen that originally seemed to center in himself. Angustias's admis-
sion that when she attempts to focus on Pepe intently his image "se me
borra" ("erases me," 2:1047) suggests that a significant shortcoming of
the house's occupants is their inadequacy as containing mediums. The
demented Maria Josefa's contention that Pepe has degraded the daughters into tongueless frogs (2:1058), croaking mouthpieces of a force over
which they have no control, thus rings true. By the time Bernarda acknowledges, late in act 2, that Martirio's stealing of Pepe's photograph
signifies something more serious than a joke, it is clear that Pepe's most
significant penetration of the house is as a "photographic" trace upon a
sensitive yet destructible medium. Mocking the type of authority that Bernarda commands in the community, Pepe also manifests a dual presence,
inside and outside the house. In distinct contrast to the unchanging silence that Bernarda covets, Pepe is progressively redefined and imagina-
tively aggrandized by the daughters, especially Adela.

Traditionally considered by most critics of the play as a freedom-
loving rebel, Adela demonstrates essentially the same weakness of imagination as Bernarda in the face of the challenge of the force summoned
in the name of Pepe. Adela progresses through what initially appears to
be a steady intensification of her resistance to her mother in an apparently valiant quest for personal autonomy. In act 3, she gives an explicit
indication of what she has been imagining when she associates Pepe's
sexual authority with the stallion in the adjoining stable, the creature
whose sexual intentions are unmistakably communicated by the thun-
derous effects of his hooves against the walls of the house—that is, by
indexical means. Adela simultaneously reveals, however, that she also
remains dominated by the idea of the house, that she does not possess
the strength of imagination necessary to envision a fundamentally different mode of existence, even with Pepe. Discounting La Poncia's advice to bide her time, Adela declares instead late in act 3 her resolve to
become Pepe's mistress: "Me pondré la corona de espinas que tienen las

que son queridas de algún hombre casado" ("I'll put on the crown of thorns of those who are the lovers of some married man," 2:1062). She is willing, therefore, to exchange one house where she is kept for another: "yo me iré a una casita sola donde él me verá cuando quiera, cuando le venga en gana" ("I will go to a little house alone where he will see me when he wants, when he has the desire," 2:1062). Desire is not liberating for Adela but rather affords her the dubious capacity to proclaim her fragmentation: "en mí no manda nadie más que Pepe" ("in me no one except Pepe rules," 2:1063).

The play's climactic moment is ordered around another index, Bernarda's shotgun blast intended for Pepe—a spectacularly ill-considered act that destroys the coveted public silence of the house—and that instead triggers Adela's suicide. So desperate to be seen that at one point she had even begged the chickens to notice her (2:995), Adela takes the word of a jealous and untrustworthy sister that Pepe has been killed and thus rushes immediately to put an end to herself. Not high tragedy, however, but another *broma* "brings down the house," a stage trick worthy of the *El público's* Prestidigitador, adept at removing items from the stage, whom Bernarda parodies at this moment as she waves her loud-sounding "wand" at Pepe, only to make Adela disappear. Adela's suicide is also the consequence of her own narrow understanding of a scene in her imagination intended for only one person. In "death," Pepe attains his most destructive form. Bernarda's acquiescence in Martirio's "joke," ironically, authorizes one form of Pepe to suppress another. Pepe's absence destroys Adela, the human medium in which he attained his fullest presence, along with destroying the idea of the house in which Bernarda had placed her hopes. That deluded understanding, nevertheless, is the exclusive means by which the spectator has been able to obtain an enhanced perspective. The status and significance of the house resides in the fact that it is a closed space, and the spectator's perspective rises and falls along with the space of the house. At its most essential level, the play has thus been a temporal-spatial embellishment upon the words of the *advertencia*, which apprise the spectator of the intention to bring to the stage a photographic documentary. Exactly in manner of the *advertencia*'s relationship to the play—as an "outside text" not part of the representation—the real authority in Bernarda Alba's house is neither Bernarda nor Pepe but a hidden force that collapses mimetic space as it leaves its destructive "photographic" trace on everyone in the house, including the spectator.

Clearly the best-informed and most competent medium in the house is the audience, whose near omniscience throughout the representation fully conflates its position with the house itself. Like La Poncia, who worries about how a scandal will affect her own standing in the community, the spectator depends for authoritative perspective on the house's continued stability as an enclosed and publicly silent space. The scandal that comes to the house, which forever destroys the silence that no amount of insistence by Bernarda will be able to reimpose, means that the theater audience's own authoritativeness as a repository of privileged information is also decisively overturned. As the scandal in Bernarda's house becomes known, the importance of the house as the privileged container of the scene disappears along with the audience's role as its best-informed party. Bernarda's loss of standing, evidence of which is her vociferous attempt to reimpose her interpretation upon events, is paralleled in the audience's equal incapacity to stabilize the fragmented scenario over which it has visually presided. At the play's conclusion, that authority, which never centered in Bernarda but became closely identified with the spectator's powers of vision, fully belongs to the "cosa muy grande" which succeeds in exposing Bernarda's private scene to the outside public. As a second audience, of townspeople, emerges to encounter the scene at Bernarda's house, the theater audience as well must confront the ruinous effects of a force that has diminished everyone. Upon the scandal's becoming public, the spectator's knowledge is no longer privileged or unique, and thus the audience is forced to become—like Bernarda, who screams in public—merely one of a growing crowd of critics and commentators.

As the townspeople, whose values and outlook had also been identified with Bernarda's, begin to be made aware of the details of what has happened, they also participate in the fragmentation of the house and the subjective hubris that carried Bernarda to ruin. The scandal now makes it more difficult for the community to sustain the way of life epitomized in Bernarda (recall the ominous scandals, Paca la Roseta and the girl who kills her child, that had already shaken the village). A second representation injurious as well to the *pueblo* (the theme and content of which are also "la casa de Bernarda Alba") thus begins in the imaginations of the townspeople. This final moment, which announces the entrance upon the scene of the second audience, again recalls the conclusion of El *público* in which the Director's last act before expiring is to welcome the entry of another audience to a scene of relentless destruction and fragmentation. As in El *público*, the most significant dimension of this production has been the progressive revelation of the authority of a hidden force that has conflated and collapsed the space of the stage in a manner that also exposes the insufficiency of conventional mimeticism in relation to a superior indexical-"photographic" medium. What most critics consider to be Lorca's most realistic play demonstrates fundamental affinities with the experimental agenda, as well as responds to the need to "[revelar] el perfil de una fuerza oculta cuando ya el público no tuviera más remedio que atender, lleno de espíritu y subyugado por la acción" ("reveal the profile of a hidden force when the public can do nothing except pay full attention, full of spirit and overwhelmed by the action").

As with the Director, the struggle here has been to manage a force that, in the manner of Pepe el Romano's marriage arrangement, exacts impossible terms from all those called upon to billet its debilitating and fragmenting effects. Amelia's complaint of "esta crítica que no nos deja vivir" ("this criticism that does not let us live," 2:993), Martirio's dirge that "veo que todo es una terrible repetición" ("I see that everything is a terrible repetition," 2:993), and Magdalena's lament that "ni siquiera nuestros ojos nos pertenecen" ("not even our eyes belong to us," 2:1020) refer to their own predicaments but also to the accumulating effects of a tormenting force that disrupts their sense of belonging to a stable scene.

Just as Bernarda fails to maintain the autonomy of her house "levanta-da por mi padre para que ni las hierbas se enteren de mi desolación" ("built by my father so that not even the grasses will know of my deso-lation," 2:1029), so too her dramatic father, who must likewise attempt to maintain autonomy in a "house" of the imagination, has understood that, whatever else it may become, theater is also a continuing response to the recognition of its own inherent vulnerability and fragmentation by hostile forces.

As it manifests itself in this play, the most powerful demonstration of authority is to discredit a mimetic understanding of a play that seems to be Lorca's most realistic and socially sensitive undertaking. Parallel-ing that of his principal character, Lorca's social awareness expresses it-self not in terms appropriate to social realism but in the particular, and peculiar, terms of what goes on in one specific house, a theater dedicat-ed to obliging its audience to acknowledge the human, subjective price of exercising authority over a "pequeño rincón de realidad" ("small cor-ner of reality," 2:1069). More than condemning the tyrannical will of Bernarda Alba, Lorca exposes the tormenting paradox of subjectivity: it can exist only in the context of an audience. More than to direct the scene of her authority, Bernarda wishes to free herself altogether of the burden of having to satisfy the demands of her public. There is, howev-er, no such space. The "telón rápido" with which the play concludes is thus both a final curtain and a final allusion to the shutter movement of a camera that has documented the trace of the presence of a destructive force upon insufficient and ultimately fragmented mediums.

Conclusion

The conditions established for critical inquiry into one of the most productive periods of Spanish literary history are predicated on an extreme generational model that is very much a product of the radical positions that so adversely influenced European political and cultural life during the 1930s. In the ensuing authoritarianism of the Franco dictatorship, the ultranationalism and cultural isolationism inherent in such an immoderate literary paradigm became the unquestioned norm during the consequent harsh conservatism of the Cold War years, ensuring that Spanish literature was cast adrift from other European writing for more than half a century. I have believed it necessary to confront the issue of the persistence of the influence of the literary generation in the Spanish critical consciousness in an attempt to provide a more affirmative basis from which to study early contemporary Spanish literature. I make no apology that I have chosen to study canonical writers for the most part instead of using this study as an occasion to resurrect neglected talents. All early contemporary Spanish writing has been made marginal because the conditions under which it has been organized and studied have presented a distorted picture of its substantial contributions. In presenting a reorganized framework under the rubric of an international literary movement that lasts much longer than a generation, I have provided a vehicle by which early contemporary Spanish writing can claim a more prominent role in a trans-European movement. Spanish modernism is not peripheral to European modernism. It is not necessary to lump it together with an overly specialized idea of "Hispanic modernism" or a modernism "at the margins."

Spanish modernism is integral to the modernist movement in general, and the history of Spanish participation in modernism needs to be studied not for its exceptions but for its original and sustained contributions to mainstream European literary culture. While Spain's connection to the larger Hispanic world is certainly not to be overlooked, nevertheless it can stand along with the modernist literature produced elsewhere in Europe as an equal partner.

For many Hispanists whose major research interests lie in twentieth-century Spanish literature, the literary generation approach to early contemporary writing in Spain remains a convenient and useful designation, a seemingly innocuous vehicle to group together successive waves of literary talent. Yet it is the convenience of generational groupings, along with the critical inertia that has been a by-product of such deeply ingrained patterns, that continues to make the task of critical reorientation seem unduly complicated. In fact, it has been easier for a number of prominent critics (Debicki, Morris, Silver) to advocate a return to traditional categories and the critical assumptions of half a century ago than to embrace a universal period concept that is in consonance with the type of literary historiography that has long been the model in other areas of the profession. Debicki's advocacy of the traditional view of the generation of "1927," very nearly identical to that of Dámaso Alonso's 1948 pronouncement, and Silver's idiosyncratic endorsement of "romanticism" to describe phenomena in Spanish literary history a full century after romanticism's prominence elsewhere in Europe, are only the more obvious manifestations of a much larger critical reluctance to embrace appropriate critical models. Indeed, outside the immediate circle of specialists in contemporary Spanish literature the attitudes are, if anything, even more conventional and ingrained, the direct consequence of the pervasiveness of such traditional groupings in the Hispanic critical consciousness. For undergraduate courses especially, it often remains more "convenient" to adopt generational tenets in connection with such offerings than to present a comprehensive model to account for the same phenomena in the wider context of European modernism.

Equally important, however, even as the period concept for early contemporary Spain has begun to find its initial advocates, is the necessity to present a fully developed concept of modernism that does not . fall into another unfortunate isolationism inherent in the idea of a Spanish participation in a marginal "Hispanic modernism." This is, indeed, a shortcoming in theses propounded along these lines by Mainer/Gracia, Cardwell, Geist/Monleón, and Bretz. Additionally, any concept of modernism, Hispanic or otherwise, that does not make room for the inclusion of the historical avant-garde is also lacking. In a Spanish context this is in part also a consequence of the adherence for so long to the generational models that have made it exceedingly difficult for Spanish criticism to acknowledge that avant-garde groups are an integral part of modernism. In all but a handful of studies, the advocates of positions adopted in relation to Spanish participation in the historical avant-garde go out of their way to emphasize that Spanish associations with such groups are minimal, imitative, and very short-lived (Harris). With the possible exception of Gómez de la Serna, no canonical Spanish author is fully identified as belonging to "la vanguardia." Although there is a great practical overlap with the emergence of "high" modernist European avant-garde groups and the poets of "1927," the ultimate aims of these groups, in the opinions of many Spanish critics, are diametrically opposed. If the waves of European "-isms" that come into prominence in the 1920s and '30s are to be considered "revolutionary" and/or antagonistic to the institutional definitions of art and the mechanisms of artistic production, their Spanish counterparts have been consistently portrayed as conservative, tradition-minded, and nationalistic. Even though many scholars of early contemporary Spanish literature are not satisfied with current approaches, such attitudes continue to remain deeply ingrained among many professional Hispanists.

As a challenge to this state of affairs, I have proposed a simple yet workable aesthetic/ideological approach to early contemporary Peninsular literature in order to make a case for substantial and sustained Spanish participation in modernism. I consider that perhaps the most significant theme of all the literature that may be called modernist is the bringing forth of new subjective models qualitatively different from the dominant "autonomous thinking subject" that achieves full hegemony by the mid-to-late nineteenth century in realism-naturalism. The subjective model of realism is premised upon the capacity of free-thinking individuals to fashion spaces for themselves in which to function freely. The aesthetic of realism is mimesis, the understanding that representation is the sustaining principle from which all other elements emerge. The realist aesthetic, however, is inseparable from the institutional premises that place the greatest value on personal autonomy and freedom to make informed choices. The institutional crises of the European liberal democracies, especially after World War I, in which parliamentary and republican forms of representative government are progressively repudiated in favor of alternatives at extreme ends of the political spectrum, are accompanied by new models for the constitution of human subjectivity. In political terms, the modernist "new man" is much more willing to advocate or embrace "direct action," that is, force or violence for the implementation of political goals that progressively reject liberal democracy and representative forms of government premised in the "rule of law." The new political doctrines and accompanying beliefs bring with them much different attitudes toward the predominant middle-class culture, and this has strong aesthetic resonances throughout the early decades of the century. Although the type of force invoked is often quite different among a multivalent milieu of modernist writers, the appeal to force is central, whether as an expression of an aggressive personal will or as a disinterested psychological or historical model.

As modernism develops, there is a progressive resistance to mimesis in favor of more direct or unmediated modes of expression that in some manner posit a notion of "presence" as an aesthetic ideal. I have identified three rather distinct aesthetic practices that approximate "presence" to varying degrees, beginning with a variety of meta-fictional techniques that most often find expression in the novel as an "aesthetics of interruption" (Eysteinsson). The more intense manifestations of this tendency are typically found in poetry, which I have called a hieroglyphic mode, in which conventional language is redirected to designate a new set of unconventional meanings. The aim is to reorder mimetic representation toward bringing forth "primary apparitions," or as Jorge Guillén has succinctly expressed it, the creation of a "realidad no [. . .] reduplicada en copias sino recreada de manera libérrima" ("reality not [. . .] duplicated in copies but created in the freest manner").[1] As a practical achievement, modernist hieroglyphics suggests the outer limits of what can be achieved in the name of "presence." Nevertheless, the supposition that an unmediated form of presence no longer burdened by conventional language can actually be achieved—for example, the automatic writing techniques of the surrealists whose goal is direct contact with the unmediated core of being—undergirds the literary and ideological premises of many of the most radical literary experimenters. Although full presence in literary expression is never a practical possibility, the ideal is a guiding principle in all literature that may be designated as modernist.

The ideological and aesthetic dimensions of modernist expression coalesce around the formation of new subjective models during modernism. Spanish literature is favorably positioned in this regard because of a long history of dialectical resistance to the evolution of the dominant European subject position of modernity. Autonomous subjectivity has always been portrayed in negative terms in Spanish literature throughout the modern period. This, in turn, has fostered throughout the modern period a tradition of resistance to such a model, in which autonomous subjectivity is invariably suspect and quite often portrayed as "monstrous." The political extremism inherent in the "monster subject" had long been recognized for the danger that it posed for social, cultural, and political life. During modernism, this is manifested in the invariably flawed positions of a variety of "new modernist men," protagonists that exalt the aggressive and often violent activity of the human will. The prominence of the "monster subject" in modernism is ultimately the alienated response to the perceived insufficiencies of the

---

1. Guillén, *Argumento*, 20.

predominant cultural model of autonomous subjectivity. The appeal to aggressiveness, force, and violence is a direct reflection of the dissatisfaction among many Europeans disenchanted with the political failures of liberal governments that bring much of the Western world to war and economic disaster. In such a context, Spanish modernist writers explore the implications of the monster subject, which I have outlined in chapters 3 and 4. The Spanish modernist novel is not, as Ortega would have it, an occasion to play literary games. Rather, the novel responds to the awareness that there is a new context for what the Spanish tradition had identified in monstrous terms, and it is the role of the Spanish modernist novel to continue that dialogue. The underlying theme of all the novels discussed is a search for a means to respond to the negative possibilities inherent in the modernist version of monstrous subjectivity. There is an implicit dialogue among Spanish novelists to encounter the means to move beyond the labyrinthine, solipsistic impasse that the new modernist man creates for himself.

If the novel keeps fresh the Spanish dialectic with Europe, poetry and theater move in more expansive directions to exemplify the more fully developed subjective positions in modernism. Although the poetry of Jorge Guillén and Vicente Aleixandre has been variously treated, when viewed from the vantage point of the new subjective constructions during modernism, it is quite evident that their poetry exemplifies a much more extreme version of the monstrous characterization of autonomous subjectivity that had been the hallmark of Spanish attitudes throughout the modern period. Here, however, there is a much more forceful and willful intellectual aggressiveness in the subjective postures of these poets, which has hitherto not been encountered in Spanish literature. There is an intellectual violence suggested in this poetry; existential presence is achieved at the expense of the raw materials of empirical reality that are transformed into the means for the affirmation of a much different state of consciousness. Such attitudes fully reflect the historical moment in which such positions seem justified and even self-evident. Yet they align themselves with attitudes prevalent in other areas of European cultural and political life that glorify aggressiveness and force. Ultimately, these are proto-fascistic positions that herald the violence that is visited upon Europe and the world only a few years later. The sympathy of this poetry to rightist attitudes is unmistakable.

The alternative to such a model is a mode of "structural" subjectivity that had a much more positive role in the Spanish tradition in premodern Christian attitudes that aligned themselves against the idea of secular autonomous subjectivity. The structural subject during modernism is a position that acknowledges that a confluence of forces exist beyond the independent will or consciousness, and they take predominantly two forms. The first is the psychoanalytic subject that understands the primacy of unconscious forces in the constitution of human subjectivity, while the other is a political position that advances the idea that the constitution of political units is a historical process whose ultimate goal is socialist revolution that will ensure the victory of the laboring masses over their present bourgeois masters. Both attitudes are portrayed at least to some degree in the poetry of Luis Cernuda and Rafael Alberti. Cernuda's experience of daimonic power is in keeping with the growing tendency in some modernist quarters to ascribe agency to irrational forces, albeit more typically the unconscious, as is the case with the surrealists. While Alberti does not seem to be a doctrinaire Marxist, there can be little doubt that his poetry is deeply influenced by his desire to move beyond the alienated solipsism that characterizes the poetry of Guillén and Aleixandre. Indeed, Cernuda's and Alberti's life experiences move them beyond such postures. While unable to experience the type of existential presence triumphantly proclaimed by their colleagues, these poets adopt a public posture that understands that their humanity depends upon their relationship with a historical milieu to which they are inextricably linked, reluctantly in the case of Cernuda and in comradely fashion for Alberti. The Spanish response to and critique of the autonomous thinking subject during modernism is fully in consonance with developments elsewhere in Europe.

In the case of the theater of Federico García Lorca, however, there are few equivalents in other parts of Europe to the tragic vision portrayed therein. Lorca's theater chronicles the fragmenting effects of an unrelenting creative-destructive force that partakes of both the alienated solipsism of the poetic visions of Guillén and Aleixandre and the destructive public consequences of such a tragic vision. It is most significant that in El público the stage director becomes tragically aware of two distinct yet simultaneously functioning theaters, the public spectacle of the "teatro al aire libre" and the private theater "bajo la arena," whose competing demands he struggles tragically to reconcile. Such attempts to mediate the private visions and the public demands of theater tragically express themselves in destructive, fragmenting consequences. Comparable in the bleakness of his vision perhaps only to Kafka, the theater of García Lorca ultimately portrays the untenableness of the conflicting subjective positions that inform his tragic vision. Perhaps nowhere in the modernist canon does the failure and futility of modernist subjective models express itself with greater intensity or tragedy.

Although modernism has been invoked by many as a phenomenon that emerges from the experiences typically encountered in the modern metropolis, the fact remains that many of the most sublime expressions of "high modernism" develop in the most unlikely places. Arguably the greatest modernist of them all, James Joyce, found himself as a young man in much the same predicament as the writers identified with the generation of "1898." Like them, he had given up on politics quite early, and he saw his mission as a writer, in part, to be to challenge the spiritual malaise of his homeland, to become a great fabbro, to express the "uncreated conscience of my race," which was as much a symptom of a budding postcolonial mentality as was Spain's equally underdeveloped national conscience in the aftermath of having lost its remaining colonies in the ignominious war with the United States. Joyce and Eliot and Pound and Woolf also pay homage to a larger-than-life literary tradition in much the same way as Unamuno and Azorín and Ortega call upon Don Quijote and "intrahistoria" to set a new course for Spanish writing. Spain's backwardness in economics and politics at this time is arguably no more so than Ireland's. The same objections to Spain's full participation in modernism, especially because the name may not seem to apply to a seemingly "un-modern" country, certainly extend to Joyce and many of his modernist colleagues all across Europe. There are, however, no objections to Joyce's being called a modernist.

The critical attitudes that have persisted in Spanish criticism that modernism, like every other literary movement from the Renaissance onward, is a pale reflection, a second-rate imitation of writing styles best studied elsewhere, serve no constructive purpose. In fact, they reinforce the same "colonial" attitudes that the modernists themselves, Spanish modernists certainly included, were resisting. Spanish unwillingness to embrace entrenched European ideologies at the turn of the twentieth century is not unusual or remarkable. Indeed, this is the fundamental Spanish response to Europe throughout the entire modern period. The novelty during modernism, of course, is that it is Europe that is behind the times. Modernists in other parts of Europe are catching up, so to speak, to the dominant Spanish discourse regarding the most important European cultural construction of its modern history—the nightmare from which the tortured souls of its greatest writers are trying to awake—the seemingly untenable consequences of the ideology that has engendered the autonomous thinking subject.

The modernist debate over anything and everything having to do with the paradigm shift away from this dominant model is prefigured and developed in Spanish positions well before the critique emerges in other parts of Europe. Joyce's *non serviam* around 1914 to bourgeois culture and Catholicism, his mission to become an independent artificer, had already taken place in Spain. The inadequacy of Spanish critical positions in relation to the more universal literary model long the norm in other literary disciplines is, of course, exacerbated by the Spanish Civil War and its consequences. The generational approach to contemporary writing emerges to a great degree in response to that debacle. The rest, as the saying goes, is history, a literary history that has done a great injustice to its early contemporary national tradition. The legacy of postwar criticism has been to compound the infelicities of these unfortunate and ungenerous attitudes with the institutional inertia of the generational model in order to atomize early contemporary Spanish literary history to the point of unrecognizableness. This study has been undertaken as a challenge to such entrenched attitudes. I offer it in the spirit of an intellectual challenge to Hispanists who disagree with the positions taken in this study to justify their continued allegiance to what I have called an inherently extremist literary historical model that has no place in enlightened discourse. The discourse of literary modernism is a superior paradigm that, for whatever reason, Spanish critics can no longer afford to ignore, at the risk of making themselves irrelevant to the larger profession that has embraced this model for over fifty years. At the dawn of the twenty-first century, in which the Spanish nation has resoundingly accepted its role as an integral partner in the European community, it is time that students of early-twentieth-century Spanish literature take the necessary steps to embrace a new literary paradigm for one of the greatest moments of Spanish literary history.

Works Cited

Aguirre, J. M. "Primeras poesías de Luis Cernuda." In Luis Cernuda, ed. Derek Harris. Madrid: Taurus, 1977. 215–27.

Alberti, Leon Battista. On Painting, trans. John R. Spenser. New Haven: Yale University Press, 1966.

Alberti, Rafael. Poesía (1924–1967). Madrid: Aguilar, 1972.

———. El poeta en la calle. Madrid: Aguilar, 1978.

Aleixandre, Vicente. Obras completas. Madrid: Aguilar, 1968.

Alonso, Dámaso. "Una generación poética (1920–36)." In Obras completas. Vol. 4. Madrid: Gredos, 1975. 653–76.

———. "Federico García Lorca y la expresión de lo español." In Obras completas. Vol. 4. Madrid: Gredos, 1975. 755–66.

Anderson, Andrew A. "The Strategy of García Lorca's Dramatic Composition, 1930–36." Romance Quarterly 33 (1986): 211–30.

Azorín. "La generación del 1898." In Clásicos y modernos. Vol. 12 of Obras completas. Madrid: Caro Raggio, 1919. 233–55.

Balakian, Ana, ed. The Symbolist Movement in the Literature of European Languages. Budapest: Akademiai Kiadó, 1982.

Baroja, Pío. El árbol de la ciencia, ed. Pío Caro Baroja. Madrid: Caro Raggio / Cátedra, 1985.

Barthes, Roland. Image, Music, Text, trans. Stephen Heath. New York: Hill and Wang, 1977.

Blanco Aguinaga, Carlos. Juventud del 98. 2nd ed. Barcelona: Editorial Crítico, 1978.

Bonet, Manuel. Diccionario de las vanguardias en España. Madrid: Alianza Editorial, 1995.

Bradbury, Malcolm, and James McFarlane. "The Name and Nature of Modernism." In Modernism, ed. Malcolm Bradbury and James McFarlane. Hammondsworth, UK: Penguin, 1985. 19–55.

Bretz, Mary Lee. Encounters across Borders: The Changing Visions of Spanish Modernism. Lewisburg, Pa.: Bucknell University Press, 2001.

Bürger, Peter. Theory of the Avant-Garde, trans. Michael Shaw. Minneapolis: University of Minnesota Press, 1984.

———. *The Decline of Modernism*, trans. Nicholas Walker. Cambridge: Polity Press, 1992.

Burke, Edmund. *A Philosophical Enquiry into the Origin of Our Ideas of the Sublime and the Beautiful*, ed. James T. Boulton. South Bend, Ind.: Notre Dame University Press, 1968.

Butt, John. "The 'Generation of 98': A Critical Fallacy?" *Forum for Modern Language Studies* 16 (1980): 136–53.

Calderón de la Barca, Pedro. *La vida es sueño*, ed. A. E. Sloman. Manchester: University of Manchester Press, 1961.

Cano, José Luis. *La poesía de la generación del 27*. Madrid: Guadarrama, 1973.

Capote Benot, José María. *El surrealismo en la poesía de Luis Cernuda*. Sevilla: Universidad de Sevilla, 1976.

Cardwell, Richard. "Los componentes del fin de siglo." In *En el 98 (Los nuevos escritores)*, ed. José-Carlos Mainer and Jordi Gracia. Madrid: Visor, 1997. 172–75.

Carlston, Erin G. *Thinking Fascism: Sapphic Modernism and Fascist Modernity*. Stanford: Stanford University Press, 1998.

Cernuda, Luis. *Estudios sobre la poesía española contemporánea*. Madrid: Guadarrama, 1957.

———. *La realidad y el deseo*, ed. Miguel J. Flys. Madrid: Castalia, 1982.

———. *Prosa completa*, ed. Derek Harris and Luis Maristany. Madrid: Barral, 1975.

Chacel, Rosa. *Estación. Ida y vuelta*, ed. Shirley Mangini. Madrid: Cátedra: 1989.

"Contra el 98 (Manifiesto de Valladolid)." In *En el 98 (Los nuevos escritores)*, ed. Jose-Carlos Mainer and Jordi Gracia. Madrid: Visor, 1997. 177–78.

Debicki, Andrew P. *Spanish Poetry of the Twentieth Century: Modernity and Beyond*. Lexington: University Press of Kentucky, 1994.

Delgado, Agustín. *La poética de Luis Cernuda*. Madrid: Editora Nacional, 1975.

Delgado, Luisa Elena. *La imagen elusiva: lenguaje y representación en la narrativa de Galdós*. Amsterdam: Rodopi, 1999.

De Man, Paul. *Blindness and Insight: Essays in the Rhetoric of Contemporary Criticism*. New York: Oxford University Press, 1977.

Diego, Gerardo. *Poesía española: Antología*. Madrid: Signo, 1931.

Donougho, Martin. "Postmodern Jameson." In *Postmodernism-Jameson-Critique*, ed. Douglas Kellner. Washington, D.C.: Maisonneuve Press, 1989. 75–95.

Drucker, Johanna. *Theorizing Modernism: Visual Art and the Critical Tradition*. New York: Columbia University Press, 1994.

Eagleton, Terry. *Criticism and Ideology: A Study in Marxist Literary Theory*. London: Verso, 1978.

Eco, Umberto. *A Theory of Semiotics*. Bloomington: University of Indiana Press, 1979.

Eliot, T. S. "*Ulysses*, Order, and Myth." *Dial* 75 (1923): 480–83.

Eysteinsson, Astradur. *The Concept of Modernism*. Ithaca, N.Y.: Cornell University Press, 1990.

Feijoo y Montenegro, Fray Benito Jerónimo. *Obras escogidas. Biblioteca de autores españoles*. Vols. 56 and 142. Madrid: Atlas, 1952 and 1961.

Fenollosa, Ernest. *The Chinese Written Character as a Medium for Poetry*, ed. Ezra Pound. San Francisco: City Lights, 1936.

Ferguson, Francis. "A Commentary on Susanne Guerlac's 'Longinus and the Subject of the Sublime.'" *New Literary History* 16 (1985): 291–97.

Fernández-Morera, D. "The Term 'Modernism' in Literary History." In *Proceedings of the Xth Congress of the International Comparative Literature Association*. New York: Garland, 1985. 271–79.

Foucault, Michel. *The Order of Things*. New York: Vintage, 1970.

Fox, E. Inman. "Hacia una nueva historia literaria para España." In *Dai Modernismi alla Avanguardie*. Palermo: Flaccovio Editorie, 1990. 7–17.

Frank, Joseph. *The Widening Gyre: Crisis and Mastery in Modern Literature*. New Brunswick: Rutgers University Press, 1963.

García Lorca, Federico. *Obras completas*, ed. Arturo del Hoyo. 3 vols. Madrid: Aguilar, 1986.

Gaos, Vicente. *Antología del grupo poético del 1927*. Madrid: Anaya, 1965.

Geist, Anthony L., and José B. Monleón. *Modernism and Its Margins: Reinscribing Cultural Modernity for Spain and Latin America*. New York: Garland, 1999.

Gigante, Denise. "The Monster in the Rainbow: Keats and the Science of Life." *PMLA* 117 (2002): 433–48.

Gómez de la Serna, Ramón. *El novelista*. Madrid: Espasa-Calpe, 1973.

———. *Una teoría personal del arte. Antología de textos y éstetica y teoría del arte*. Madrid: Taurus, 1988.

Gónzalez, Angel. *El grupo poético de 1927*. Madrid: Taurus, 1979.

Goya, Francisco de. *The Complete Etchings of Goya*. New York: Crown Publishers, 1943.

Greenfield, Sumner. *La generación de 1898 ante España*. 2nd ed. Rev. and ed. by Luis González-del-Valle. Boulder, Colo.: Society of Spanish and Spanish-American Studies, 1997.

Guillén, Jorge. *Cántico*. 2nd ed. Madrid: Cruz y Raya, 1936.

———. *El argumento de la obra*. Barcelona: Sinera, 1969.

Gullón, Ricardo. *Direcciones del modernismo*. Madrid: Alianza Editorial, 1990.

———. "La generación poética de 1925." *Insula* No. 117 (1955): 3, 12.

———. "La invención del 98." In *La invención del 98 y otros ensayos*. Madrid: Gredos, 1969. 7–19.

Habermas, Jürgen. *The Philosophical Discourse of Modernity*, trans. F. Lawrence. Cambridge: MIT Press, 1987.

Hamilton, George Heard. *19th and 20th Century Art*. New York: Prentice-Hall and Harry N. Abrams, 1970.

Harris, Derek. *Luis Cernuda: A Study of the Poetry*. London: Tamesis, 1973.

———, ed. *Perfil del aire*. London: Tamesis, 1971.

————, ed. *The Spanish Avant-Garde*. Manchester: Manchester University Press, 1995.

Hartman, Geoffrey. *Saving the Text: Literature, Derrida, Philosophy*. Baltimore: Johns Hopkins University Press, 1981.

Hewitt, Andrew. *Political Inversions: Homosexuality, Fascism, and the Modernist Imaginary*. Stanford: Stanford University Press, 1996.

Jameson, Fredric. *Fables of Aggression: Wyndham Lewis, the Modernist as Fascist*. Berkeley: University of California Press, 1979.

————. *Postmodernism, or, the Cultural Logic of Late Capitalism*. Durham: Duke University Press, 1991.

Johnson, Roberta. *Gender and Nation in the Spanish Modernist Novel*. Nashville: Vanderbilt University Press, 2003.

Julius, Anthony. *T. S. Eliot: Anti-Semitism and Literary Form*. Cambridge: Cambridge University Press, 1995.

Kant, Immanuel. *Critique of Judgment*, trans. J. H. Bernard. London: Macmillan, 1914.

————. *Observations on the Feeling of the Beautiful and Sublime*, trans. John T. Goldthwait. Berkeley: University of California Press, 1960.

Kermode, Frank. *The Sense of an Ending: Studies in the Theory of Fiction*. London: Oxford University Press, 1966.

Kirkpatrick, Susan. *Mujer, modernismo y vanguardia en España (1898–1931)*. Madrid: Cátedra, 2003.

Kolocotroni, Vassiliki, Jane Goldman, and Olga Taxidou, eds. *Modernism: An Anthology of Sources and Documents*. Chicago: University of Chicago Press, 1998.

Krauss, Rosalind. "The Photographic Conditions of Surrealism." In *The Originality of the Avant-Garde and Other Modernist Myths*. Cambridge, Mass.: MIT Press, 1986. 87–118.

Laín Entralgo, Pedro. *España como problema*. Madrid: Seminario de Problemas Hispanoamericanos, 1947.

————. *España como problema*. Vol. 2. Madrid: Aguilar, 1956.

————. *La generación del noventa y ocho*. Madrid: Diana, 1945.

————. *Las generaciones en la historia*. Madrid: Instituto de Estudios Políticos, 1945.

Lamos, Colleen. *Deviant Modernism: Sexual and Textual Errancy in T. S. Eliot, James Joyce, and Marcel Proust*. Cambridge: Cambridge University Press, 1998.

Lessing, G. E. *Laocoön: An Essay on the Limits of Painting and Poetry*, trans. Edward Allen McCormick. Baltimore: Johns Hopkins University Press, 1984.

Levenson, Michael, ed. *The Cambridge Companion to Modernism*. Cambridge: Cambridge University Press, 1999.

Levin, Harry. "What Was Modernism?" In *Refractions: Essays in Comparative Literature*. New York: Oxford University Press, 1966. 271–95.

Lovejoy, Arthur O. "On the Discrimination of Romanticisms." *PMLA* 39 (1924): 229–53.

Lukács, Georg. "The Ideology of Modernism." In *The Meaning of Contemporary Realism*, trans. John and Necke Mander. London: Merlin, 1962.

Mainer, José-Carlos. *La edad de plata*. Madrid: Cátedra, 1981.

Mainer, José-Carlos, and Jordi Gracia. *En el 98 (Los nuevos escritores)*. Madrid: Visor, 1997.

Mangini, Shirley. "Women and Spanish Modernism: The Case of Rosa Chacel." *Anales de la literatura española contempoánea* 12 (1987): 17–28.

Martínez Nadal, Rafael. *El público: amor, teatro y caballos en la obra de Federico García Lorca*. Oxford: Dolphin Book, 1970.

Mayhew, Jonathan. "Poetry, Politics and Power." *Journal of Spanish Cultural Studies* 3 (2002): 237–48.

Menand, Louis. *Discovering Modernism: T. S. Eliot and His Context*. New York: Oxford University Press, 1987.

Miller, J. Hillis. *Fiction and Repetition*. Cambridge: Harvard University Press, 1982.

Mitchell, W. J. T. *Iconology: Image, Text, Ideology*. Chicago: University of Chicago Press, 1986.

Morris, C. Brian. *Son of Andalusia: The Lyrical Landscapes of Federico García Lorca*. Nashville, Tenn.: Vanderbilt University Press, 1997.

———. "The 'Austere Abode': Lorca's *La casa de Bernarda Alba*." *Anales de la literatura española contemporánea* 11 (1986): 129–41.

Morrison, Paul A. *The Poetics of Fascism: Ezra Pound, T. S. Eliot, Paul de Man*. New York: Oxford University Press, 1996.

Murphy, Richard. *Theorizing the Avant-Garde*. Cambridge: Cambridge University Press, 1998.

Nantell, Judith. *Rafael Alberti's Poetry of the Thirties: The Poet's Public Voice*. Athens: University of Georgia Press, 1986.

Ortega y Gasset, José. *El tema de nuestro tiempo*. Vol. 3 of *Obras completas*. Madrid: Revista de Occidente, 1955.

———. *Ensayos sobre la generación del 98*. Madrid: Revista de Occidente, 1981.

———. *En torno a Galileo*. *Obras completas*. Vol. 5. Madrid: Revista de Occidente, 1951.

———. *La deshumanización del arte y otros ensayos estéticos*. Madrid: Revosta de Occidente, 1970.

Parker, A. A. "The Spanish Drama of the Golden Age: A Method of Analysis and Interpretation." *The Great Playwrights*, vol. 1, ed. Eric Bentley. New York: Doubleday, 1970. 679–707.

Parr, James. "A Modest Proposal: That We Use Alternatives to Borrowing (Renaissance, Baroque, Golden Age) and Leveling (Early Modern) in Periodization." *Hispania* 84 (2001): 406–16.

Paz, Octavio. "La palabra edificante." *Papeles de Son Armadans* 36 (1964): 41–82.

Paulson, Ronald. "Goya and the Spanish Revolution." In *Representations of Revolution (1789–1820)*. New Haven: Yale University Press, 1983. 286–387.

Pearsall, Priscilla. "Azorín's Myth of the Generation of 1898: Toward an Esthetic of Modernism." *Revista Canadiense de Estudios Hispánicos* 11 (1986): 179–84.

Peirce, Charles Sanders. "The Icon, Index, and Symbol." *Collected Works*, ed. Charles Hartshorne and Paul Weiss. 8 vols. Cambridge: Harvard University Press, 1931–58. Vol. 2.

Perloff, Marjorie. *21st Century Modernism: The "New" Poetics*. Malden, Mass.: Blackwell, 2002.

Petersen, Julius. "Las generaciones literarias." In *Filosofía de la ciencia literaria*, ed. Emil Ermatinger, trans. Carlos Silva. Mexico City: Fondo de Cultura Económica, 1946. 137–93. Original German title: "Die literarischen Generationen." In *Philsophie der Literaturwissenchaft*. Berlin: Junker and Dünnhaupt, 1930. 130–87.

Reichenburger, Arnold G. "The Uniqueness of the Comedia." *Hispanic Review* 27 (1959): 303–16.

Reiss, Timothy J. *The Discourse of Modernism*. Ithaca: Cornell University Press, 1982.

Ribbans, Geoffrey. "Some Subversive Thoughts on Modernismo and the Generation of 98." *West Virginia Philological Papers* 39 (1994): 1–17.

Ricks, Christopher. *T. S. Eliot and Prejudice*. London: Faber and Faber, 1988.

Rozas, Juan Manuel. *El 27 como generación*. Santander: Isla de los Ratones, 1978.

Rozas, Juan Manuel, and Gregorio Torres Nebrera. *El grupo poético del 27*. 2 vols. Madrid: Cioncel, 1980.

Ryan, Judith. *The Vanishing Subject: Early Psychology and Literary Modernism*. Chicago: University of Chicago Press, 1991.

Salinas, Pedro. "El concepto de 'generación literaria' aplicado a la del 98." In *Literatura Española. Siglo XX*. Mexico City: Séneca, 1941. 43–58.

———. "Luis Cernuda, poeta." In *Literatura española. Siglo XX*. Mexico City: Séneca, 1941. 316–33.

Santiáñez-Tió, Nil. "Temporalidad y discurso histírico. Propuesta de una renovación metodológica de la historia literaria española moderna." *Hispanic Review* 65 (1997): 267–90.

Sass, Louis Arnorsson. *Madness and Modernism: Insanity in the Light of Modern Art*. New York: Basic Books, 1992.

Scott, Nina M. "Sight and Insight in *La casa de Bernarda Alba*." *Revista de estudios hispánicos* 10 (1976): 297–308.

Sheppard, Richard. "The Problematics of European Modernism." In *Theorizing Modernism: Essays in Critical Theory*, ed. Steve Giles. New York: Routledge, 1993. 1–52.

Sherry, Vincent. *Ezra Pound, Wyndham Lewis, and Radical Modernism*. Oxford: Oxford University Press, 1993.

Silver, Philip. "Et in Arcadia Ego": A Study of the Poetry of Luis Cernuda. London: Tamesis, 1965.

———. *Ruin and Restitution: Reinterpreting Romanticism in Spain*. Nashville: Vanderbilt University Press, 1997.

Soria Olmedo, Andrés, ed. *Correspondencia (1923–1951). Pedro Salinas / Jorge Guillén.* Barcelona: Tusquets, 1992.

———. "Ramón Gómez de la Serna's Oxymoronic Historiography of the Spanish Avant-Garde." In *The Spanish Avant-Garde,* ed. Derek Harris. Manchester: Manchester University Press, 1995. 15–26.

Soufas, C. Christopher, and Teresa S. Soufas. "*La vida es sueño* and Post-Modern Sensibilities: Towards a New 'Method of Analysis and Interpretation.'" In *Studies in Honor of Bruce W. Wardropper,* ed. Dian Fox, Harry Sieber, and Robert ter Horst. Newark, Del.: Juan de la Cuesta, 1989. 291–304.

Soufas, C. Christopher. *Audience and Authority in the Modernist Theater of Federico García Lorca.* Tuscaloosa: University of Alabama Press, 1996.

———. "Cernuda and Daimonic Power." *Hispania* 66 (1983): 167–75.

———. *Conflict of Light and Wind: The Spanish "Generation of 1927" and the Ideology of Poetic Form.* Middletown, Conn.: Wesleyan University Press, 1990.

———. "The Sublime, the Beautiful, and the Imagination in Zorrilla's *Don Juan Tenorio.*" *MLN* 110 (1995): 302–19.

———. "'Esto sí que es leer': Learning to Read Goya's *Los Caprichos.*" *Word and Image* 2 (1986): 311–30.

Unamuno, Miguel de. *Niebla,* ed. Mario J. Valdés. Madrid: Cátedra, 1985.

Valender, James. "Cuatro cartas de Luis Cernuda a Juan Guerrero (1928–1929)." *Cuadernos Hispanoamericanos,* no. 315 (1976): 53.

Valle-Inclán, Ramón María. *Tirano Banderas.* Madrid: Espasa-Calpe, 1972.

Wellek, René. "The Concept of 'Romanticism' in Literary History." *Comparative Literature* 1 (1949): 1–23; 147–62.

———. "What Is Symbolism?" In *The Symbolist Movement in the Literature of the European Languages,* ed. Ana Balakian. Budapest: Akademiai Kiadó, 1982. 17–28.

Wentzlaff-Eggebert, Harald, and Doris Wansch, eds. *Las vanguardias literarias en España. Bibliografía y antología crítica.* Frankfurt: Verveurt, 1999.

Wimsatt, William. *The Verbal Icon.* Lexington: University Press of Kentucky, 1954.

Wohl, Robert. *The Generation of 1914.* Cambridge: Harvard University Press, 1979.

Young, Alan. *Dada and After: Extremist Modernism and English Literature.* Manchester: Manchester University Press, 1981.

Selected Bibliography

Albright, Daniel. *Quantum Poetics: Yeats, Pound, Eliot, and the Science of Modernism*. New York: Cambridge University Press, 1997.

Alldritt, Keith. *Modernism in the Second World War: The Later Poetry of Ezra Pound, T. S. Eliot, Basil Bunting, and Hugh McDiarmid*. New York: Peter Lang, 1989.

Armstrong, Tim. *Modernism, Technology, and the Body: A Cultural Study*. New York: Cambridge University Press, 1998.

Auslander, Philip. *From Acting to Performance: Essays in Modernism and Postmodernism*. London: Routeledge, 1997.

Berg, Christian, and Geert Lernout. *The Turn of the Century: Modernism and Modernity in Lierature and the Arts*. New York: Walter de Gruyter, 1995.

Besserman, Lawrence, ed. *The Challenge of Periodization: Old Paradigms and New Perspectives*. New York: Garland, 1996.

Booth, Allyson. *Postcards from the Trenches: Negotiating the Space between Modernism and the First World War*. New York: Oxford, 1996.

Brown, Dennis. *Intertextual Dynamics within the Literary Group—Joyce, Lewis, Pound, and Eliot: The Men of 1914*. New York: St. Martin's Press, 1990.

———. *The Modernist Self in Twentieth-Century English Literature: A Study in Self Fragmentation*. New York: St. Martin's Press, 1989.

Bush, Ronald, ed. *T. S. Eliot: The Modernist in History*. New York: Cambridge University Press, 1991.

Collier, Peter, and Judith Davies, eds. *Modernism and the European Unconscious*. Cambridge: Polity, 1990.

Compagnon, Antoine. *Five Paradoxes of Modernity*. Trans. Franklin Philio. New York: Columbia University Press, 1994.

Connolly, Cyril. *100 Key Books of the Modern Movement from England, France, and America*. London: Allison and Busby, 1986.

DiBattista, Maria, and Lucy McDiarmin. *High and Low Moderns: Literature and Culture, 1889–1939*. New York: Oxford University Press, 1996.

Downing, David B., and Susan Bazargan. *Image and Ideology in Modern/Postmodern Discourse*. Albany: State University of New York Press, 1991.

Federic, Madeleine, and Jacques Allard, eds. *Modernite/postmodernite du ro-*

man contemporain. Brussels: Centre d'etudes canadiennes de l'universite libre de Bruxelles, 1987.

Fisher, Andreas, Martin Heusser, and Thomas Hermann. *Aspects of Modernism*. Tubingen: G. Narr, 1997.

Fokkema, Douwe Wessel. *Modernist Conjectures: A Mainstream in European Literature, 1910–40*. New York: St. Martin's Press, 1988.

Gravier, David. *The Aesthetics of Disturbance: Anti-Art in Avant-Grade Drama*. Ann Arbor: University of Michigan Press, 1995.

Halpern, Richard. *Shakespeare among the Moderns*. New York: Cornell University Press, 1997.

Harrison, Charles. *Modernism*. New York: Cambridge University Press, 1997.

Jackson, Tony E. *The Subject of Modernism: Narrative Alternations in the Fiction of Eliot, Conrad, Woolf, and Joyce*. Ann Arbor: University of Michigan Press, 1994.

Jrade, Cathy Login. *Modernism, Modernity, and the Development of Spanish American Literature*. Austin: University of Texas Press, 1988.

Karl, Frederick Robert. *Modern and Modernism: The Sovereignty of the Artist, 1885– 1925*. New York: Atheneum, 1985.

Kindelan, Nancy Anne. *Shadows of Realism: Dramaturgy and the Theories and Practices of Modernism*. Westport, Conn.: Greenwood Press, 1996.

Lentricchia, Frank. *Modernist Quartet*. New York: Cambridge University Press, 1994.

McGann, Jerome J. *Black Modernism: The Visible Language of Modernism*. Princeton: Princeton University Press, 1993.

Nicolls, Peter. *Modernisms: A Literary Guide*. Berkeley: University of California Press, 1995.

North, Michael. *The Dialect of Modernism: Race, Language, and Twentieth-Century Literature*. New York: Oxford University Press, 1994.

Pecora, Vincent P. *Self and Form in Modern Narrative*. Baltimore: Johns Hopkins University Press, 1989.

Pike, David L. *Passage through Hell: Modernist Descents, Medieval Underworlds*. Ithaca: Cornell University Press, 1997.

Schwarz, Daniel R. *Reconfiguring Modernism: Explorations in the Relationships between Modern Art and Modern Literature*. New York: St. Martin's Press, 1997.

Scott, Bonnie Kime, ed. *The Gender of Modernism: A Critical Anthology*. Bloomington: Indiana University Press, 1990.

Segal, Harold B. *Pinocchio's Progeny: Puppets, Marionettes, Automatons, and Robots in Modernist and Avant-Garde Drama*. Baltimore: Johns Hopkins University Press, 1995.

Smith, Bernard. *Modernism's History: A Study in Twentieth-Century Art and Ideas*. New Haven: Yale University Press, 1998.

Stein, Kevin. *Private Worlds, Worldly Acts: Public and Private History in Contemporary American Poetry*. Athens: Ohio University Press, 1996.

Stevenson, Randall. *Modernist Fiction: An Introduction*. Lexington: University Press of Kentucky, 1992.

Tratner, Michael. *Modernism and Mass Politics: Joyce, Woolf, Eliot, Yeats*. Stanford: Stanford University Press, 1995.

Weir, David. *Anarchy and Culture: The Aesthetic Politics of Modernism*. Amherst: University of Massachusetts Press, 1997.

———. *Decadence and the Making of Modernism*. Amherst: University of Massachusetts Press, 1995.

Weston, Richard. *Modernism*. London: Phaidon, 1996.

Williams, Raymond. *The Politics of Modernism: Against the New Conformists*. Edited and introduced by Tony Pinkney. New York: Verso, 1989.

Index

4274   INDEX

90; narration as, 124–27; power of, 147, 241; private, 166; tragic, 251. *See also* seeing
visual realm, 12, 64–66, 100–101, 133–34, 173, 187
vocabulary. *See* words
voices, 32, 35–36, 202–4, 212
vorticists, 9

wars, 249. *See also* World War I; World War II
weakness. *See* impotence
weathervane, symbolism of, 57, 216–17, 219–21, 224
Wellek, René, 7, 43
whiteness, 144
will, 95–97; consciousness and, 133, 135, 137, 141, 145, 161, 206, 250; contest of, 158; creative, 137, 208, 211; failure of, 146, 193; force of, 14, 59, 130, 154–58, 162–63, 226; generational, 30–33, 35; human, 207, 209, 247–48; independent, 250; intellect and, 77, 84, 128, 130–33, 156–58; of leaders, 27, 28; new, 29; of poets, 147, 155–56, 171, 173; subjective, 190; triumph of, 129–30
Wimsatt, William, 55
Wohl, Robert, 3
woman, 162; new, 14, 116. *See also* form, female; writers/writing, women

Woolf, Virginia, 251
words, 12, 64–66, 101, 106, 134, 158, 215; images and, 73, 135, 138, 146, 149–57, 159; spoken, 59, 63; terrible, 181; written, 73
world: conceptions of, 31, 72–73, 83, 185; new, 62, 63–64, 106, 166–67. *See also* geographies
World War I, aftermath of, 37, 52, 66, 247, 252–53
World War II, aftermath of, 8–9, 19, 68
writers/writing: automatic, 43, 66–67, 235, 248; characters and, 108; Chinese, 65–66; European, 2, 81, 167; experimental, 44, 52, 86, 108–10, 212, 233; modernist, 54, 60, 68, 96, 247; novels, 110–14, 116, 121–22, 124; Spanish, 55, 72, 82; styles of, 40, 63, 252; Western, 14, 66; women, 47–48, 85. *See also* canonical writers

Yeats, William Butler, 4, 128, 206
Yo soy un tonto . . . (I Am One Fool . . ., Alberti), 202
youth, 29–30, 32–33, 115, 120–21, 145–46, 169–80, 184–86, 201–4. *See also* Joven

Zorrilla, José, 79

The Subject in Question: Early Contemporary Spanish Literature and Modernism was designed and typeset in Quadraat by Kachergis Book Design of Pittsboro, North Carolina. It was printed on 60-pound Natures Natural and bound by Thomson-Shore of Dexter, Michigan.